Best Short Hikes
in California's
Southern Sierra

Best Short Hikes in California's Southern Sierra

A Guide to Day Hikes Near Campgrounds

. . . .

BY KAREN AND TERRY WHITEHILL

THE
MOUNTAINEERS

First edition: first printing 1991, second printing 1992,
third printing 1994, fourth printing 1997

Published by The Mountaineers
1001 S.W. Klickitat Way, Suite 201, Seattle, Washington 98134

Published simultaneously in Great Britain by Cordee, 3a DeMontfort Street, Leicester, England LE1 7HD
Manufactured in the United States of America

Edited by Dana Fos
Maps by Carla Majernik
All photographs by the authors
Cover design by Elizabeth Watson
Book design and layout by Barbara Bash
Cover photo: Bishop Pass
Frontispiece: A rock-lined trail climbs toward Mist Falls.

Library of Congress Cataloging in Publication Data

Whitehill, Karen, 1957-
    Best short hikes in California's southern Sierra : a guide to day hikes near campgrounds / by Karen and Terry Whitehill.
        p.   cm.
    Includes bibliographical references (p. 233) and index.
    ISBN 0-89886-282-5
    1. Hiking — Sierra Nevada Mountains (Calif. and Nev.) — Guide-books.
2. Sierra Nevada Mountains (Calif. and Nev.) — Description and travel — Guide-books.   I. Whitehill, Terry, 1954-
II. Mountaineers (Society)   III. Title.
GV199.42.S55W49   1990
917.94'4 — dc20   90-27756
                                                                              CIP

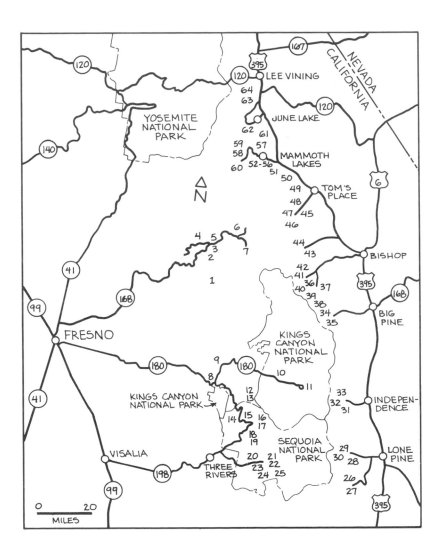

· · · · · · · ·
Contents

MAP LEGEND

—— PAVED ROAD	⬳ U.S. ROAD	▲ CAMPGROUND
— — — GRAVEL ROAD	◯ STATE ROAD	▲ MOUNTAIN PEAK
– – – – TRAIL	▭ FOREST SERVICE OR PARK ROAD	■ POINT OF INTEREST OR BUILDING
··········· OTHER TRAILS	◯ TOWN	)(MOUNTAIN PASS
ᗡᐯᗡᐯ RIVER / STREAM	℗ PARKING	–·– WILDERNESS OR PARK BOUNDARY

The famed Mount Whitney Trail tempts hikers of all ages and abilities.

INTRODUCTION

· · · · · · · · · · ·

The Southern Sierra Nevada

Thousands upon thousands of eager prospectors thronged to California's Sierra Nevada during the gold and silver rushes of the nineteenth century. They came in search of fantastic fortunes—streams running with gold nuggets, hillsides pulsing with thick veins of silver. But the mountains bestowed their favors haphazardly. Some who made the long Sierra journey found the realization of all of their dreams of wealth and glory. Others found only hardship and poverty.

Today, millions of people still make the pilgrimage to the Sierra Nevada, fleeing the summer heat of the inland urban centers and the crowds and pollution of the coastal megacities. But these people are seeking a less palpable commodity than the prospectors of old. Yesterday's dreams of gold and silver have faded.

Yet these twentieth-century "prospectors" are searching for something just as precious as silver ore or gold nuggets. They seek the timeless beauty and the unspoiled serenity of a majestic chain of mountains. And they do not go away with "empty pockets." They turn for home renewed and strengthened, steeped in the incredible riches of the untamed Sierra Nevada.

This book, *Best Short Hikes in California's Southern Sierra,* is dedicated to helping modern-day prospectors "stake their claims" to the treasures of the High Sierra. This book isn't for long-haul backpackers, skilled cross-country ramblers, or mountain climbers—other volumes already address their needs. No, this book is for first-time visitors to the Sierra, for average hikers, for families, for anglers, for older walkers.

This book is for anyone who has a day and a desire: a day to spend exploring these matchless mountains, a desire to touch the treasures of the Sierra with their eyes and then leave those treasures unspent and unspoiled, awaiting all who will come after.

The focus of this volume is on day hikes, although many of the outings described here will probably appeal to weekend backpackers as well. Hikes range from short trips of less than 5 miles to all-day treks of 15 miles or more. Some hikes lead to alpine lakes, others climb to lofty passes, and still others end on mountaintops.

Admittedly, a few of the book's 64 hikes may be too difficult for all but the most energetic outdoors enthusiast. Other hikes may seem too tame for visitors who seek a demanding physical challenge. Fortunately, with so many trips to choose from, anyone who studies this volume carefully should find a wide assortment of treks to fit his or her personal criteria.

This book is designed as a companion volume to *Best Short Hikes in California's Northern Sierra* (The Mountaineers, Seattle). It covers the area of the High Sierra south of Yosemite National Park, extending to the Mineral King district of Sequoia National Park (on the west side of the mountains) and to the trailheads accessed via the town of Lone Pine on Highway 395 (on the east side of the Sierra crest).

Because so many Sierra Nevada visitors come to the mountains to camp as well as to hike, a secondary focus of this volume is on public campgrounds. A listing of family campgrounds accompanies each grouping of hikes in the book. Beginning with the Huntington Lake area on the west side of the mountains (chapter 1), the 64 hikes and their corresponding campgrounds are arranged in geographic clusters. From Huntington Lake, the hike groupings (and chapters) move in a counterclockwise direction down the west side of the Sierra and then up the eastern flank of the mountains, along Highway 395.

Perhaps one of the most amazing things about the incredibly rugged section of the Sierra Nevada this book explores is that not a single auto road carries vehicle traffic from one side of the mountains to the other anywhere along its length. To the north, the Tioga Pass Road (Highway 120) takes travelers across the Sierra Nevada crest at an elevation of 9,945 feet. To the south, lowly Walker Pass (elevation 5,250 feet) spans the mountains, carrying travelers on Highway 178. Between the two thoroughfares, a vast, unpaved wilderness awaits only those who come on foot or horseback.

HOW TO USE THIS BOOK

The 64 hike descriptions that follow are grouped by area, national park boundary, or ranger district boundary, and each group of hikes is accompanied by a listing of nearby campgrounds. Preliminary data for each chapter includes Forest Service office locations and mailing addresses, background information on the national parks or wilderness areas accessed by the hikes, and special recommendations on hiking, camping, and safety concerns specific to the region.

Information blocks. Initial information for each hike begins with the hike distance, given in miles rounded to the nearest tenth. All distances are specified as either one-way, loop, or round-trip mileage. Each hike is also rated for difficulty, utilizing the terms *easy, moderate,* and *strenuous.* Owing to an almost limitless array of variables, these ratings are highly

A good map is one of the Ten Essentials that every hiker should carry.

subjective. Be sure to examine each hike's mileage and elevation gain to form your own opinion.

The starting point and high point for each hike are listed in feet. If a hike's total elevation gain is significantly greater than the difference between its starting point and high point (owing to ups and downs along the way), a figure for the total climb is provided.

Also included in each hike's preliminary data is the United States Geological Survey (USGS) quadrangle map or maps that show the trek. These maps are an excellent resource for curious hikers who wish to familiarize themselves with their surroundings. USGS maps also provide necessary data for those who might want to deviate from this book's described routes or try a bit of cross-country rambling.

Quadrangle maps can be purchased at Forest Service offices or ordered by mail from the USGS. Write to Distribution Branch, USGS, Box 25286, Federal Center, Denver, CO 80225. Please remember that it's important to identify the state and use the exact map name when ordering USGS maps.

If you're hiking in several scattered areas, the cost of quadrangle maps will add up quickly. Check the map department of your local library. You may be able to save some money with a photocopy or two.

Forest Service maps provide another option. These inexpensive maps, which cover larger areas with less detail than the USGS maps, are especially valuable for campground information. Individual area maps for Kings Canyon and Sequoia national parks may be purchased at visitor centers within the parks as well.

If a very simple area map with accompanying text will satisfy your curiosity about your surroundings, just use the individual hike maps provided in this volume, and stay on recommended trails.

Trip descriptions. Speaking of accompanying text, the 64 hike descriptions that follow are designed with several purposes in mind.

First, the text for each hike will help you decide if it's the trek for you. What do you want in a day hike? Is it a mountain vista you desire? Is a lake with good fishing or swimming at the top of your wish list? Do you avoid steep inclines at all costs? Read through the text to discover each hike's highlights, trials, and temptations. Then, decide which trip is right for you.

Second, the goal of each hike description in this book is to guide you effortlessly to the trailhead, lead you smoothly through the journey's twists and turns and junctions (signed and unsigned alike), and deposit you happily (and without unwanted detours) at your goal. Along the way, a running commentary on the surrounding scenery will entertain, inform, and enhance your Sierra experience even more.

When to go. Because weather conditions in the Sierra Nevada vary greatly from one year to the next, this book avoids predicting when certain hikes will be open for snow-free exploration. Please be aware that the Sierra's winter snowpack will dictate your summer hiking schedule.

In a heavy snow year (Rejoice, you thirsty reservoirs!), many of the high-elevation hikes listed in this volume won't be free of snow until mid-August. In fact, some of the higher trails described here might never escape the grasp of winter. In a light snow year (more brown lawns in Los Angeles), even the loftiest trails could be open by July 1.

Use the starting point and high point listed for each hike as you attempt to follow the receding snow line upward. Whatever you do, don't rush it. Steeply sloped snowfields are extremely treacherous. Never attempt to negotiate a snow-covered section of the trail if you are inexperienced, unequipped, or hiking alone.

The best way to find out if a particular trail is snow free is to ask at the local Forest Service office. Trail rangers can provide you with the latest information on trail conditions and offer recommendations on alternate routes, if necessary. If the snow is lingering on your chosen trail, play it safe and choose a lower-elevation goal instead.

Campground listings. Because many outdoor lovers like to combine their hiking trips with camping excursions, each of this book's six chapters includes a listing of convenient campgrounds. Driving directions for campgrounds are combined with information on fees, reservations, and facilities. Number of sites and open dates are given as well.

Please be aware that campground arrangements are often subject to change. A campground that's on a first-come, first-served setup this year may be reservation-only next season. And a campground that was thriving last August could be closed completely next July, owing to a Forest Service budget whim, an urgent need for renovation, or even a winter avalanche.

Unpredictable or not, camping in the Sierra Nevada is an inexpensive and rewarding alternative to staying in hotels or inns. Best of all for hikers, campgrounds usually offer the most convenient access to the often isolated Sierra trailheads.

Some Sierra campgrounds are extremely primitive, with rustic outhouses and no drinking water (these campgrounds are nearly always free). Other Sierra campgrounds are virtually "tent cities," complete with grocery stores and laundromats. These developed campgrounds often require advance reservations.

To obtain more specific camping information for your own Sierra trip, please refer to the chapter introduction and campground listing for the area you plan to visit. If you'll be staying at a campground that requires reservations, you'll probably be contacting either Ticketron or the Forest Service. You can visit Ticketron outlets in person or write to Ticketron Reservations, PO Box 2715, San Francisco, CA 94126. To obtain reservations through the Forest Service for Forest Service campgrounds, call 1-800-280-2267 (CAMP).

If you don't have a favorite campground or a prior reservation, always stop at the local Forest Service office on your way into the mountains. You can pick up a free listing of area campgrounds at the office, and if you're unfamiliar with the sites available, you can probably coax a campground recommendation from the person behind the desk.

If you'd like even more input on where to camp, consider purchasing a California campground guide. One source we've found extremely helpful throughout our exploration of the Sierra is *California Camping, the Complete Guide to California's Recreation Areas* (see "Further Reading"). This book lists more than 1,500 campgrounds, with details on facilities, fees, locations, and nearby recreation opportunities. First published in 1987, the book contains some information that is already outdated; however, it's still one of the most extensive sources of campground data you can find.

Another camping option you might want to explore is the practice of free camping on Forest Service land. This is completely legal and acceptable, providing the land is Forest Service property and is not posted as a restricted recreation area with "no camping" signs. Drawbacks to free camping include lack of facilities (drinking water and toilets), limited security, and potential harm to the environment.

If you do decide to camp on Forest Service land, please be a responsible and courteous guest. Drive only on established roadways, and carry out all trash. If you must build a fire, do so only in an existing firepit (and not if fire restrictions are in effect). Dispose of human waste by digging a 6- to 8-inch hole at least 50 yards away from any water source.

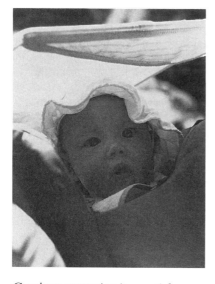

Good sun protection is essential even if you're riding in a backpack.

HIKING AND SAFETY

Just as the prospectors of the nineteenth century soon learned to venture into the Sierra armed with caution and respect, today's foot travelers must also respect the mountains they explore. Please make sure your journey is a safe one by taking necessary precautions and using common sense.

Solitude. If you must enter the mountains alone, always notify someone of your intended route and destination. Leave a note on your tent when you leave the campground, or share a morning chat with the campground host. Sign the hikers register at the trailhead (if there is one), or check in with a trail ranger before you go.

Twisted ankles, sudden stomach woes, unexpected changes in the weather—any of these can leave a solitary hiker stranded and in trouble. If someone else knows about your plans, you'll have needed backup when you get into a jam.

Supplies. Always carry the "Ten Essentials" on your Sierra outings, no matter how brief the distance or how tame the destination. Make sure your rucksack holds the following: a map, extra clothing, matches, a knife, a compass, a flashlight, some form of fire starter (for igniting wet wood), a first aid kit, sunglasses, and an emergency food supply. And don't forget one more essential item for summer hiking in the Sierra Nevada: strong sunscreen.

Water. The first rule for judging the potability of the water in the mountains is, Don't believe your eyes. You'll see Sierra streams that literally sparkle, they're so clear; lakes that look like polished stones; waterfalls that run with icy, tempting rivulets, just begging to be tasted. Don't do it.

Giardia is everywhere in the Sierra Nevada. Heavy cattle grazing on Forest Service land and irresponsible human visitors in national parks and forests compound the problem every summer. You might drink safely from Sierra streams nine times out of ten, but if the tenth time leaves you writhing with the symptoms of giardiasis (severe diarrhea and stomach cramps), your gamble wasn't worth it.

Play it safe and drink only treated water on your visit. Day hikers should be able to carry all the fluids they'll need for one-day outings. Backpackers will probably want to utilize a water filter or a chemical treatment system. Otherwise, untreated water must be boiled at least 5 minutes to make it safe to drink.

Weather. Just as you can't predict the potability of a sparkling Sierra stream, neither can you predict the longevity of a clear Sierra sky. Mountain weather can change in minutes, and Sierra Nevada storms are notoriously destructive. Many of the hikes described in this volume attain elevations of 9,000 feet and higher. Snow and hail often whiten the Sierra crest in August, and lightning strikes are an ongoing summer threat. Please don't ever take a sunny Sierra day for granted.

Day hikers should always carry extra clothing on the trail (we recommend a sweater or light windbreaker). Even more important, all Sierra hikers must know when to call it quits. Don't press on to the crest of your pass if thunderheads are building. Don't continue for the summit of your peak if you see lightning flash. Stay alive to greet the mountains on another day. Head for lower ground when the sky turns black.

Routefinding. The majority of the trails described in this volume's 64 hikes are well defined and easy to follow. However, some trails cut across bare slabs of granite or get such little use that they're partially overrun by vegetation. If you're familiar with some simple Sierra "signposts," you'll keep to your intended route more easily.

Ducks are an invaluable aid to Sierra Nevada routefinding. Usually consisting of a few flat stones piled one atop another, ducks often mark the passage of a trail across barren expanses of unyielding granite. If your trail disappears when you hit solid stone, look for irregularly spaced piles of rocks to lead you onward.

Cairns are less common on Sierra trails. These larger heaps of stones are often waist-high or higher. Cairns sometimes decorate ridgetops or mark mountain summits, but perhaps their greatest usefulness is found when they identify recommended fording spots on rambunctious Sierra streams.

Blazes are yet another trademark of Sierra trails. These shallow cuts made in the trunks of trees, usually at eye level or above, are especially helpful when the trail is obscured by snow or overeager ground cover.

Another method of trail marking involves outlining a route with a border of stones or logs. Again, this routefinding aid is very useful when a trail crosses barren granite or when the path is somewhat overgrown.

As mentioned earlier, a good map is a must for every Sierra hiker. Refer to your map whenever you have a question. Always be alert to your surroundings. And please don't venture off the trail unless you're an experienced scrambler, equipped with a compass.

SIERRA VEGETATION

One of the most wondrous things about the southern Sierra Nevada is the presence of majestic groves of giant sequoias. Until you've lingered at the feet of one of these magnificent forest creatures, gazing skyward along its massive red-hued trunk, you haven't fully experienced the magic of the Sierra. The giant sequoia speaks of timelessness, of strength, and of the incredible diversity of nature.

With the sequoias, an amazing variety of firs and pines and cedars awaits. The sugar pine boasts the longest pine cone in the world. The sequoia claims the largest trunk. The incense cedar wears its bark like a shaggy coat. The Jeffrey pine must have one of the world's most tantalizing odors.

Immerse yourself in the amazing variety of trees and bushes and wildflowers the Sierra has to offer. The more you know about Sierra vegetation, the more you'll be able to appreciate what you see. We've noted trailside trees, bushes, and wildflowers with each hike description in this volume, but specialized guidebooks will enhance your identification efforts even more. Please refer to "Further Reading" for suggestions.

Even if you're not ready to begin toting several extra books with you on the trail, you can make use of the free handouts provided in most Forest Service offices. These well-written, informative flyers on Sierra trees and wildflowers make a good addition to any hiker's knapsack.

SIERRA ANIMALS

Of course, you'll see many life-forms that aren't rooted to the ground during your time in the Sierra, ranging in size from tiny lodgepole chipmunks to graceful mule deer. Again, Forest Service flyers can help you differentiate between a Douglas squirrel and a golden-mantled ground squirrel or identify a Clark's nutcracker or a Steller's jay. If you're visiting the Sierra Nevada with young children, Forest Service

An inquisitive ground squirrel searches for a handout.

offices stock an assortment of wonderful coloring books about Sierra plants and animals as well.

It's easy to stay in harmony with Sierra Nevada vegetation. Don't pick the flowers, don't trample the meadows, and don't let a sugar pine cone hit you in the head. But what about keeping the peace with Sierra animals? Here's some advice to ensure good relations between you and your native hosts.

Bears. The big *B* is every Sierra visitor's first concern. Will you see one while you're hiking? Probably not. Most bear encounters occur in campgrounds or at backpackers' campsites, not on the trail. Still, it's wise to keep an eye on the assorted footprints in the dust when you're out hiking. If you do spot a bear print, stay alert and pick up your conversation level by several decibels.

If you're staying at campgrounds while visiting the mountains, please be responsible with your groceries. Scavenging bears have become an increasingly serious problem in the Sierra over recent years, resulting in the trapping and destroying of far too many animals. The sad truth is, careless people compound the problem. Don't blame the bears for choosing a goody-laden cooler over a dried-up thimbleberry bush. Blame the irresponsible people who contribute to the bears' delinquency.

Some people will do anything to avoid mosquito bites.

If your campsite has a bear box, use it. Otherwise, conceal all food stuff in your vehicle whenever you're not cooking or eating. Place your cooler in the trunk of your car or cover it with a blanket. Bears know what coolers look like. They know what treasures coolers hold. And they'll do everything in their power to get at them.

Never leave groceries on your picnic table, and please don't take food into your tent at night. Dispose of all garbage promptly, too— your discards may just be a bear's buffet. And if by chance you should forget all these instructions one fateful evening and you wake up to find a bear consuming your last chocolate bar, remember the one all-important rule of bear relations: possession is proof of ownership. Wish your guest *bon appetit* and never, never argue.

Bugs. Unlike the more elusive (and much larger) bears, you'll meet Sierra bugs just about everywhere—on the trails, in the campgrounds, and probably in your sleeping bag. Mosquitoes are major pests in June and July, when the ground is damp from receding snows. Arm yourself with repellent, if you can stand slopping chemicals on your skin.

Otherwise, cover up with light cotton clothing, and use a bandana to protect your head and neck. Hats, long socks, hooded sweatshirts—the more you detest mosquitoes, the hotter you'll probably be.

Ticks are a more worrisome (if less annoying) Sierra pest, especially with the recent flurry of Lyme disease infections. Keep to the High Sierra and your tick encounters should be infrequent—ticks are rare above 6,000 feet. Still, you'll want to keep an eye out for the little beasties whenever you're in the mountains.

Do a "tick check" at the end of every Sierra hiking day. Comb or brush your hair thoroughly, and visually examine every inch of skin. Check your clothes and bedding, too. Ticks often survey their surroundings for a while before digging in. If you do find a tick that has already embedded itself in your skin, remove it promptly and completely.

Tweezers may work if the tick isn't in too deep. If you can't get the tick out easily, if the area around the bite is inflamed or sore, or if redness or swelling appears later on, please consult a doctor immediately. Lyme disease is not a Sierra souvenir you'll want to bring home with you.

Snakes. Another concern of Sierra hikers is the threat of rattlesnakes. Like ticks, rattlesnakes are seldom seen at higher elevations. If you're hiking below 7,000 feet, you can lessen your chances of an unhappy encounter with a rattlesnake by staying out of brush and rocks, keeping on the trail, and always watching where you put your feet.

Pack animals. If you do much hiking in the Sierra, you'll surely meet some of the sturdy beasts that carry food, equipment, and saddle-sore tourists into the backcountry on any given summer day. Pack animals are a common fixture on many of the trails that this book covers. If you dislike the scent and sight of a path frequented by mules and horses, you may want to avoid treks where an abundance of pack animals is noted in the hike description.

If you follow some simple rules for peaceful coexistence with the humble pack animals, you shouldn't have any problems sharing your way with these four-footed Sierra transport vehicles. First of all, remember that pack animals always have the right-of-way. If you're approached or overtaken by a string of heavy-laden mules or horses, it's your responsibility to give way.

For your own safety, please leave the trail on the uphill side, and avoid loud noises or flamboyant gestures while the animals pass. Inexperienced riders usually have their hands full enough on the rough Sierra trails, and a startled horse or mule is dangerous to everyone in the vicinity.

A REMINDER

The fortune-seeking prospectors of the nineteenth century couldn't deplete the wealth of the Sierra Nevada. Nor could the burly loggers vanquish the sequoias, firs, and pines. The aspiring developers of the twentieth century couldn't tame the spirit of the wilderness, and the millions of travelers who come to the Sierra today can't trample down the soaring peaks.

But this delicate wilderness is wounded each time a monkeyflower is ground into a meadow carpet beneath a straying hiker's heel, each time a stand of trees is reduced to ashes by a carelessly discarded match, each time a bear must be destroyed because of a lazy camper that fed its taste for thievery, and each time a trout dies gasping in a polluted stream.

The Sierra Nevada hold riches beyond your wildest dreams—glorious vistas, ice-encrusted peaks, serene alpine lakes, and gigantic trees. But the mountains' wealth is neither limitless nor eternal. Please walk reverently and softly while you're here. Touch the treasure joyfully, and then leave it as you found it, as a legacy for those who will come after you.

A NOTE ABOUT SAFETY

Safety is an important concern in all outdoor activities. No guide book can alert you to every hazard or anticipate the limitations of every reader. Therefore, the descriptions of roads, trails, routes, and natural features in this book are not representations that a particular place or excursion will be safe for your party. When you follow any of the routes described in this book, you assume responsibility for your own safety. Under normal conditions, such excursions require the usual attention to traffic, road and trail conditions, weather, terrain, the capabilities of your party, and other factors. Keeping informed on current conditions and exercising common sense are the keys to a safe, enjoyable outing.

The Mountaineers

CHAPTER ONE
. . . .
Huntington Lake

Blessed with easy access, ample facilities, and an abundance of recreation opportunities, the area around Huntington and Shaver lakes attracts a multitude of visitors during the summer months. Although the region is particularly popular with recreation seekers from the Fresno metropolitan area, visitors from Los Angeles and points beyond aren't uncommon either.

Huntington and Shaver lakes boast several developed campgrounds as well as limited indoor lodgings. Shopping opportunities are abundant at Shaver Lake, but they're a bit less varied at Huntington Lake. Fishermen and boaters will love both areas (Huntington Lake is open to nonmotorized craft only).

If you venture deeper into the wilderness by traveling the winding route across Kaiser Pass, you'll lose some of the development and a few of the people but none of the scenic beauty characteristic of the area. Trails here explore four different wildernesses—the Dinkey Wilderness, the Kaiser Wilderness, the Ansel Adams Wilderness, and the John Muir Wilderness.

The 22,700-acre Kaiser Wilderness is named for rugged Kaiser Ridge (see Hike 4, Kaiser Peak), which acts as a geologic dividing line for the area. Located just north of Huntington Lake, the Kaiser Wilderness boasts dense forests, alpine slopes, and dozens of attractive lakes. Overnight visitors can obtain permits from Pineridge Ranger District, Sierra National Forest, PO Box 300, Shaver Lake, CA 93664.

The trek to Doris Lake and Tule Lake (Hike 6) crosses into the Ansel Adams Wilderness, a vast area of more than 200,000 acres that encompasses the former Minarets Wilderness. The Ansel Adams Wilderness holds the headwaters of the Middle Fork and the North Fork of the San Joaquin River. Again, permits are required for overnight visitors and may be obtained from the Pineridge Ranger District office at the address above.

The third wilderness area approached via Kaiser Pass Road is the John Muir Wilderness, weighing in at a whopping 584,000 acres and possessing the highest point in the Sierra Nevada, the 14,496-foot summit of Mount Whitney. Hike 7, to Crater Lake, probes the John Muir Wilderness. Overnight visitors can request permits at the Pineridge

Ranger District office at Shaver Lake.

In addition, seasonal Forest Service offices are open from Memorial Day to Labor Day at the Highway 168 – Kaiser Pass Road junction on the east end of Huntington Lake and on Kaiser Pass Road east of the Kaiser Pass summit.

Yet another wilderness awaits those who sample this volume's Hike 1, Dinkey Lakes. The diminutive Dinkey Lakes Wilderness is adjacent to the John Muir Wilderness, separated only by the Ershim–Dusy Off-Highway Vehicle Route (an extremely popular haunt for four-wheel-drive vehicle users). The wilderness is named for the delightful Dinkey lakes, which, according to popular lore, honor a lonely trapper's faithful dog, Dinkey.

Overnight wilderness users can seek permits at either the Pineridge Ranger District office at Shaver Lake or from Kings River Ranger District, 34849 Maxon Road, Sanger, CA 93657.

CAMPGROUNDS

Dinkey Creek Campground *(Hike 1, Dinkey Lakes)* Dinkey Creek Campground boasts more than 100 sites for tents or motorhomes, strung out along pretty Dinkey Creek. With flush toilets, piped water, fireplaces, picnic tables, and a nearby grocery store, the campground is less than rustic. The campground's rising popularity has contributed to the recent establishment of a reservation system for campsites. (Please check with the Forest Service for additional information.)

To find Dinkey Creek Campground, drive Highway 168 to the south end of Shaver Lake, and turn east onto Dinkey Creek Road. Follow this main paved road to the campground entrance at road's end (about 14 miles).

Dinkey Creek Campground is open May to October. Reservations accepted. Moderate fee.

Deer Creek Campground *(Hike 2, Indian Pools; Hike 3, Rancheria Falls; Hike 4, Kaiser Peak)* This popular campground on Huntington Lake has 29 shaded sites (14 for motorhomes) with piped water, picnic tables, and fireplaces. Convenient lake access and flush toilets contribute to the weekend crowds. Make reservations through Ticketron to be assured of a weekend spot.

To find Deer Creek Campground, drive Highway 168 to Huntington Lake, and turn left onto Huntington Lake Road at the junction with Kaiser Pass Road. Continue 0.9 mile along the lakeshore to a sign for Deer Creek Campground.

Not only is this campground delightfully close to trailheads in the Huntington Lake area, but it's also on the way to an interesting geologic formation known as Mushroom Rock. A massive wind-carved

Mushroom Rock is a facinating roadside destination.

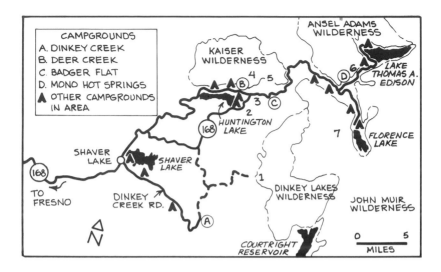

pinnacle of stone that looks like it should be gracing some hungry giant's tossed green salad, Mushroom Rock commands a lofty view of Shaver Lake and the San Joaquin Valley.

Reach Mushroom Rock Vista by driving Huntington Lake Road for 6.2 miles beyond the lake's lodge and the post office. Go right on the unpaved Road 8S32 (signed for Mushroom Rock Vista) and continue 4.4 miles uphill, staying with the vista signs along the main dirt road. You'll veer left before a final 0.3 mile leads to a parking area 300 yards from the vista point.

Deer Creek Campground is open June to October. Reservations accepted. Moderate fee.

Badger Flat Campground *(Hike 5, Twin Lakes)* Rustic Badger Flat Campground is a super spot for the bargain-seeking camper, and it offers great access to the trailhead for Twin Lakes. The campground is roomy and pleasant, blessed by the passage of fish-rich Rancheria Creek. Add a wildflower meadow that boasts a colorful constellation of shooting stars and this lofty campground is hard to beat.

To find Badger Flat Campground, drive Highway 168 to the shore of Huntington Lake, and turn right onto the Kaiser Pass Road (signed for Mono Hot Springs and Florence Lake). Continue 5.0 miles from the junction, and turn right at a sign for the campground. There are approximately 15 campsites for tents or motorhomes in this free campground, but you will have to haul in your own drinking water.

Shaded sites offer picnic tables, fireplaces, and non-flush toilets. Be careful with your foodstuff here (and at all campgrounds in the area), as bears are occasional visitors.

Badger Flat Campground is open June to October. No reservations. No fee.

Mono Hot Springs Campground *(Hike 6, Doris Lake and Tule Lake; Hike 7, Crater Lake)*   Although it's a long drive in off Highway 168 to Mono Hot Springs Campground, this pleasant spot on the South Fork of the San Joaquin River attracts many campers, swimmers, and anglers. Come early in the day if you're hoping for a weekend site.

Mono Hot Springs Campground's 31 tentspots boast piped water, picnic tables, fireplaces, and non-flush toilets. Stretched out along the rushing San Joaquin River, the campground is a short walk away from Mono Hot Springs Resort (with a spa and grocery store), and it's just a short stroll to the trailhead for Hike 6.

To find the campground, drive Highway 168 to the shore of Huntington Lake, and turn right onto Kaiser Pass Road (signed for Mono Hot Springs and Florence Lake). Continue 5.7 miles on good, two-lane road, and then endure 11.2 miles of roughly paved, one-lane road (not recommended for motorhomes).

Arrive at another junction signed for Mono Hot Springs and Florence Lake. Turn left here for Mono Hot Springs, drive 1.7 miles to another Hot Springs sign, and go left once more. It's 0.2 mile to the campground from here (18.8 total from Highway 168).

Mono Hot Springs Campground is open June to September. Reservations accepted. Moderate fee.

• •

1 DINKEY LAKES

Distance: 7.0 miles (loop)
Difficulty: Moderate
Starting point: 8,590 feet
High point: 9,380 feet
Map: USGS Dogtooth Peak 7.5'

The trailhead for Dinkey Lakes is hard to find and difficult to get to, but this delightful hike would be worth a drive that was twice as aggravating. Simply put, the Dinkey Lakes loop is a Sierra masterpiece, especially in July when the wildflowers are at their best.

To reach the trailhead, turn off Highway 168 at the south end of Shaver Lake, and drive the paved Dinkey Creek Road 9.1 miles. Turn left onto a rough, unpaved road signed for the Dinkey Lakes trailhead. Continue 6.0 miles to another junction signed for the trailhead, and go right.

Stay on this main, unpaved route 4.7 miles (shunning branches to the left and right), and watch for yet another Dinkey Lakes trailhead sign, marking a spur road to the right. A second sign says, "Road not suited for passenger cars," and it's probably right; however, a skillful driver can make it.

A final 2.2 miles of slow, bouncy driving leads to the trailhead parking area. You'll want to keep to the left through a cleared-out gathering point for four-wheel-drive vehicles as you near your goal.

Begin the hike with a short, steep descent to the columbine-decked banks of Dinkey Creek. Cross the pretty waterway, and climb gently for a time. You'll regain the creek's company at 0.3 mile. Enjoy level walking through lodgepole pines, savoring the abundance of blossom-covered Labrador tea on the forest floor.

Recross Dinkey Creek, and reach a sign for the Dinkey Wilderness at 0.5 mile. Continue gently uphill with the water. Watch for the blooms of mountain pennyroyal, meadow penstemon, sticky cinquefoil, and golden brodiaea as you walk to a junction at 1.3 miles. Go right for Mystery Lake, and recross Dinkey Creek soon after.

It's a steady climb to the shore of midsize Mystery Lake at the 1.6-mile point. Go left with the trail along the meadowy lakeshore, stealing views out across the water. Leave Mystery Lake at 2.0 miles, and cross the outlet creek descending from Swede Lake.

A gradual ascent leads into a full-scale assault of the hillside. The trail climbs steeply, slicing up a tree-sprinkled slope in a score of switchbacks. Arrive at Swede Lake, gasping, after about 0.3 mile. What a lovely spot to catch your breath!

With a shoreline ruled by Labrador tea, lodgepole pines, and mountain hemlocks, Swede Lake paints a serene Sierra picture. After you've rested your lungs and legs, push on to cross an outlet creek choked with shooting star and tiger lily. Continue along the shore, and resume climbing at 2.7 miles.

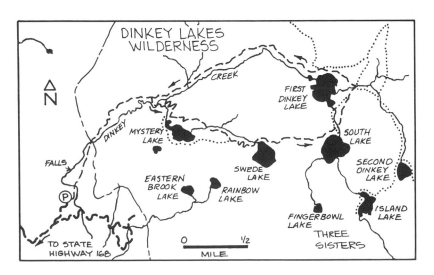

The Dinkey Lakes Wilderness owes its name to a lonely trapper's dog.

A mercifully brief uphill melts into a downhill ride to South Lake at the 3.2-mile point. This large lake boasts a score of campspots, good fishing, and a handsome granite backdrop to tempt those who wish to linger.

Cross South Lake's outlet creek, and then descend beside it, with views of Dinkey Lake ahead. You'll arrive on First Dinkey Lake's meadowy shore shortly after. Go right with the trail along the lake-shore, and come to an unsigned junction at 3.7 miles. Keep left toward Dinkey Lake.

Draw in close to the lake as you continue, and savor what must be one of the most beautiful meadow scenes in the entire Sierra Nevada. If you time your hike for the height of the wildflower season, you'll be treated to Lemmon's paintbrush, bistort, primrose monkeyflower, meadow penstemon, and shooting star—to name just a few of Dinkey Lake's meadow treasures.

With the meadow in the foreground, the view out toward 10,612-foot Three Sisters Peak above Dinkey Lake's calm surface is a Sierra scene you'll never forget. Drink your fill of Dinkey Lake's calm beauty, and then press on to another junction at 4.1 miles. Keep left along the shore, and begin a gradual descent beside Dinkey Creek soon after.

You'll regain your entry route at 5.7 miles as you go right at a signed junction for Willow Meadow. A final 1.3 miles leads to the trailhead parking lot. With any luck, the memory of this loop's matchless scenery will keep you humming throughout your pothole-peppered drive back toward civilization.

2 INDIAN POOLS

Distance: 1.4 miles round trip
Difficulty: Easy
Starting point: 7,050 feet
High point: 7,120 feet
Map: USGS Huntington Lake 7.5'

The walk to Indian Pools is overrun with wildflowers.

The hike to Indian Pools along cascade-filled Big Creek is an ideal outing for families with little hikers. It's short and level, and it has scores of opportunities for picnicking and supervised splashing. Small

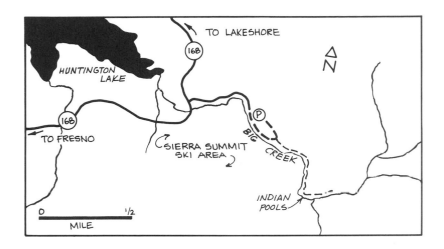

children should be able to do most of the walk themselves. However, the trail is a bit rough in spots, so short-legged walkers may need a boost now and then.

To find the trailhead for Indian Pools, drive Highway 168 toward Huntington Lake, and leave the highway before its junction with Kaiser Pass Road, turning into the signed Sierra Summit Ski Area. Proceed 0.5 mile through the ski area parking lot, following the course of Big Creek as you go. Look for signs for Indian Pools parking at the far end of the lot.

Set out on foot, following trail signs along a private road past several mobile homes. You'll spy an official trailhead sign at 0.1 mile and gain a level trail through a forest of lodgepole pines and white firs. If you're walking early in the season, your way will be brightened by the blossoms of larkspur, golden brodiaea, and bistort.

Find the first of many pools along Big Creek at 0.4 mile. More pools await ahead, so continue gently uphill beside the water. Scattered rocky sections will slow you just enough to allow you to delight in the abundance of azaleas in bloom along the waterway.

The end of the official creekside trail comes at 0.7 mile, and the largest pool is here—clear and cold, overhung with incense cedars and Jeffrey pines and lined with sweet-smelling azaleas and mountain heather. This is a pretty spot, especially when it's not overrun with the usual weekend hordes.

Unpack your lunch and unleash your toes, or, if you're hankering for a bit more privacy, continue upstream in search of smaller and quieter pools.

3 RANCHERIA FALLS

Distance: 1.6 miles round trip
Difficulty: Easy
Starting point: 7,600 feet
High point: 7,800 feet
Maps: USGS Huntington Lake 7.5' and USGS Kaiser Peak 7.5'

Like the trek to Indian Pools (Hike 2), the Rancheria Falls walk is an ideal family outing. It's short and easy, with a climb that youngsters can handle without difficulty. One note of caution: small children should be closely supervised along the way. The trail traverses steep hillsides at times, and the rocky area around Rancheria Falls warrants care. Perhaps the one drawback of this hike is its popularity. Please avoid weekends if at all possible, as the compact area around the falls just can't absorb big crowds.

To reach the trailhead for this walk, drive Highway 168 toward Huntington Lake, and turn off at the sign for Rancheria Falls, 0.5 mile from the junction with Kaiser Pass Road. Leave the pavement and follow the gravel road 1.2 miles, staying with signs for Rancheria Falls. There's limited trailhead parking here.

Begin your hike with a gentle climb on a dusty trail. Your way will be decorated with broadleaf lupine, pearly everlasting, and gayophytum in July. The incline eases at 0.2 mile, and white and red firs cast their shadows on the trail. A gentle climb intensifies at 0.6 mile, but any

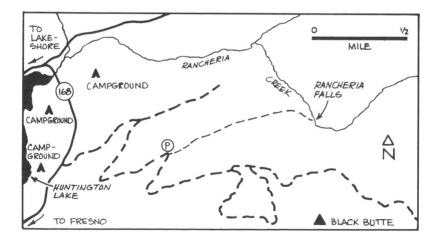

complainers in your group will soon be silenced by the murmur of the falls.

Catch your first look at the 150-foot-high Rancheria Falls at 0.7 mile, and descend briefly to reach the water. This lively waterfall is a joy to behold, especially on a hot summer afternoon. The froth-flecked water fans out across a wide granite wall as though it were a glistening wedding veil, tossing icy spray like handfuls of white rice in the faces of its visitors.

A score of large boulders piled at the base of the waterfall provide sun-warmed perches for toe dipping and sandwich chewing. Space is limited and footing is tricky, however, so keep a tight rein on children.

. . . .

4   KAISER PEAK

Distance: 10.6 miles round trip
Difficulty: Strenuous
Starting point: 7,150 feet
High point: 10,320 feet
Map: USGS Kaiser Peak 7.5'

This hike to the summit of Kaiser Peak stands out from all the other outings in the Huntington Lake area. Its rewards are bountiful, but its cost is great. There's no getting around it—this is one tough hike. Start early on a cloudless day, carry plenty of water and a windbreaker, and you should agree that this is a fantastic trek.

To find the Kaiser Peak trailhead, drive Highway 168 to Huntington Lake, and turn left onto Huntington Lake Road at the junction with Kaiser Pass Road. Continue to a sign for Kinnikinnick Campground, and go right. Follow signs for the stables about 0.6 mile to reach the edge of the D & F Pack Station. You'll spot a hikers parking area when you arrive.

Walk through the pack station yard to find a trailhead sign calling out the Kaiser Loop Trail, and start into an uphill climb that will be with you for a long, long time. You'll pass a sign marking the boundary of the Kaiser Wilderness soon after.

Ascend steadily on a trail blessed by the welcome shade of white and red firs. The climb is unrelenting, but the tiny white blossoms of gayophytum will do their best to cheer you when you begin to grumble. Come in beside a small creek at 0.6 mile, and pass an unmarked trail to the right shortly after (it goes to Potter Pass).

The summit of Kaiser Peak offers a feast for all the senses.

You'll see the tracks of many horses and an occasional mule deer as you continue uphill at a steady pace, climbing in long switchbacks through open areas of pinemat manzanita and chinquapin. Enjoy a wide panorama of Huntington Lake after 1.5 miles. The shade grows more scarce as you traverse a boulder-strewn hillside.

A rocky outcropping yields a fine view of Huntington Lake at 1.9 miles. Watch for another viewpoint ruled by a lone Jeffrey pine at the 2.2-mile point. Pause for a breather here, and gaze down at the tiny white sails of countless sailboats, slicing through the surface of the lake like a score of shark fins.

Trace a winding trail uphill through a red fir forest as you push onward to the massive rock outcropping known as College Rock at 3.0 miles. It's a bit of a scramble to the top of the rock, but you'll have views of distant eastern peaks in addition to Huntington Lake and the western plains from this lofty perch.

Resume climbing to reach a flower-flooded marshy area at 3.5 miles. The trail levels off at last, as you wade through a knee-deep jumble of shooting star, Indian paintbrush, Sierra wallflower, and single-stem groundsel. Enjoy it while it lasts, as the ascent returns with a vengeance much too soon.

Negotiate a gruesomely steep pitch as the trail follows a streambed

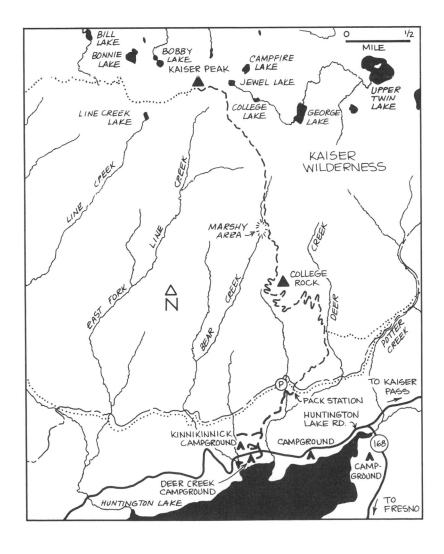

up to a lofty saddle at 4.3 miles. From here, you'll get your first look at Kaiser Peak ahead. Savor a snatch of level walking with far-ranging vistas to the west as you continue. Don't let the distant scenery distract you from the loveliness at your feet, however. Alpine buckwheat and pussypaws weave a gorgeous high-elevation carpet.

Steal a peek at distant Mount Ritter to the north just before you descend to cross a small gully, and look for Lake Thomas Edison to the right at the bottom of the dip. Now a truly punishing section of the climb begins. Endure 0.3 mile of steep, steep uphill before a brief level stretch at the 4.8-mile point convinces you that you might make it after all.

The final assault on Kaiser Peak's elusive summit leads to a small (but oh, so beautiful) sign for Kaiser Peak at 5.3 miles. Follow a rocky trail up to the mound beyond to reach the high point of your climb. This is it—and what a spot it is! Rest your trembling legs, and savor a 360-degree panorama unmatched anywhere in this section of the Sierra.

On a clear day, the view to the north will reach to the Minarets and Mount Ritter. You'll see Mammoth Pool Reservoir to the northwest, Huntington Lake to the south, Mount Goddard to the southeast, and Mount Humphreys to the east. A host of smaller peaks completes the breathtaking vista.

If all this Sierra scenery has infused your muscles with new energy, you can exchange the simple 5.3-mile backtrack to your car for a 9- to 10-mile detour onward along the ridge, following the continuation of the Kaiser Peak Loop Trail back to your starting point. However, this route involves not only more miles but also a bit more up and down, so please don't try it unless you're certain of your strength.

. . . .

5   TWIN LAKES

Distance: 7.2 miles round trip
Difficulty: Moderate
Starting point: 8,200 feet
High point: 8,980 feet
Total climb: 1,350 feet
Maps: USGS Kaiser Peak 7.5' and USGS Mount Givens 7.5'

This hike into the lovely Twin Lakes basin offers both a tantalizing lakeside destination and an extra dose of wonderful Sierra scenery, provided by the trek over 8,980-foot Potter Pass. The hike's ascents are challenging but never brutal, and the surroundings offer ample re-

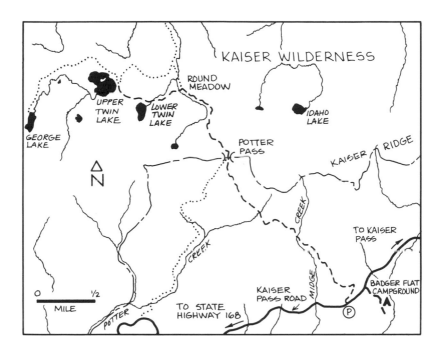

wards for all your puffing. Unfortunately, the treasures of this trail are no secret, so you'll want to avoid weekends if you don't like crowds.

To reach the Twin Lakes trailhead, drive Highway 168 to the shore of Huntington Lake, and turn right onto the Kaiser Pass Road (signed for Mono Hot Springs and Florence Lake). Continue 4.8 miles from the junction, and look for a road sign for riding and hiking trail 24E03. There's trailhead parking on the south side of the road. Cross carefully to gain the signed Twin Lakes–Potter Pass trail on the north side of the pavement.

Begin climbing immediately, ascending a lodgepole-covered hillside in a score of switchbacks. You'll be glad for the shade of scattered Jeffrey pines, Sierra junipers, and red firs as you labor uphill for the first 0.4 mile.

Enjoy easier going for a short time, and then resume climbing to cross a stream at 1.0 mile. A flower-filled meadow beckons here, alive with shooting star, bistort, Sierra wallflower, and Macloskey's violet.

Climb gently to a saddle, and then savor more-level walking through a red fir forest. You'll catch a wonderful view out toward Huntington Lake at 1.6 miles as you cross an open hillside decorated with broadleaf lupine, mule ears, and bright purple larkspur.

The ascent continues to the crest of Potter Pass at 2.1 miles. If you're hiking on a clear day, you'll surely want to linger, as the vista from the pass is magnificent, extending north to the Minarets and 13,157-foot Mount Ritter. The view is even more spectacular from a small knoll near the pass (on the left as you approach the saddle). This spot also offers a chance for some solitude on a busy hiking day.

Enter the Kaiser Wilderness as you begin descending on a rocky trail, hewn through an avalanche of wildflowers. Your downhill tumble will ease at 2.5 miles, as you continue gently down through a flower-flooded basin. Reach a junction at 2.8 miles, and go left for Twin Lakes, climbing moderately with fine views north toward the Minarets.

You'll reach the shore of granite-backed Lower Twin Lake at 3.3 miles, but don't break out your picnic yet, as Upper Twin Lake is the real treasure of this trek. Continue with the level trail to find this rocky gem at the 3.6-mile point.

Kaiser Peak rules the scene above the lake, and a large rock island dominates the water, luring hearty swimmers to its shores. Backed by granite slopes, Upper Twin Lake is truly lovely, and you'll surely want to linger and enjoy. Be sure to check out the lake's remarkable outlet stream while you're here. It dives underground as it exits the lake and then reappears a little farther down.

If you want to make a longer day of it, an additional 2.5-mile round trip will take you steeply uphill to attractive (and much lonelier) Lake George.

• •

6 DORIS LAKE AND TULE LAKE

Distance: 4.0 miles round trip
Difficulty: Easy
Starting point: 6,550 feet
High point: 6,920 feet
Map: USGS Mount Givens 7.5'

This easy family hike probably isn't worth the arduous drive to the trailhead unless you're visiting Mono Hot Springs Resort, fishing on the South Fork of the San Joaquin River, or camping at Mono Hot Springs Campground. With the drive behind you, though, this is a very pleasant walk, and families with young children can shorten it even further by hiking only to Doris Lake (1.8 miles round trip).

To find the trailhead, please refer to the driving directions for Mono Hot Springs Campground, but continue on through Mono Hot Springs Resort. The spur road to the trailhead turns off just beyond the spa and just before the second entrance to the campground.

A rocky shoreline cradles little Doris Lake.

This road is extremely rough. It's best to leave your vehicle in the settlement's day-use parking area or on the roadside near the spur road. The hike mileage begins here.

Set out walking on the dusty secondary road, and enjoy the blossoms of meadow penstemon, meadow goldenrod, cinquefoil, yampah, and wild rose. You'll spot the official Tule Lake–Doris Lake trailhead at 0.4 mile.

Abandon the roadway, and climb to a junction and a sign for the Ansel Adams Wilderness soon after. Go left for Doris and Tule lakes, and continue ascending through a landscape of manzanita, sage, and rock. Arrive at a second junction at 0.7 mile, and veer right for Doris Lake.

Note: If you're doing the entire hike and would prefer to end your trek with a refreshing swim, you can reverse the route and visit Tule Lake first (go left here) before dipping into lovely Doris Lake.

Climb steeply from the junction, and then follow a creekbed up more gently to gain a flat basin ruled by Jeffrey pines and Sierra junipers. Arrive at enchanting Doris Lake at 0.9 mile.

Backed by a canvas of distant mountains, this sparkling gem is definitely a swimmers' paradise. Its unique shoreline boasts steep rock embankments with sheer drops into the water, sure to tempt adventurous leapers on a summer afternoon. Please use caution as you enjoy the lake, however, and never dive without making certain of water depth.

If you can tear yourself away from the beauty of Doris Lake, backtrack to the junction signed for Tule Lake to continue your trek. Turn right, taking the trail signed for Tule Lake, and climb a rocky route lined with sage and manzanita. The terrain levels off at the 1.4-mile point, and you'll descend to pass a pothole lake at 1.6 miles.

Enjoy easy walking to a junction at 1.8 miles, and angle left for Hell Meadow. Follow the snaking, undulating trail to reach a rose-scented

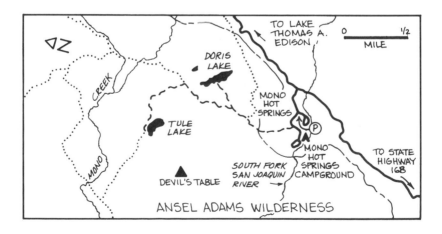

meadow that marks the 2.1-mile point. You'll continue on beside a vast tule marsh before arriving at the aptly named Tule Lake at 2.3 miles.

Although not particularly scenic, this petite lake with a tule-lined shore does have good fishing opportunities. Scramblers can add a detour to the top of the nearby Devil's Table, a lava formation still dusted with volcanic ash. Devil's Table yields an excellent view of the surrounding area; however, there is no good trail to its summit.

You'll have a 1.7-mile backtrack to your starting point from Tule Lake.

7 CRATER LAKE

Distance: 8.0 miles round trip
Difficulty: Strenuous
Starting point: 7,350 feet
High point: 9,380 feet
Maps: USGS Dogtooth Peak 7.5',
 USGS Mount Givens 7.5', and
 USGS Florence Lake 7.5'

The trek to Crater Lake explores the John Muir Wilderness.

As with the hike to Doris Lake and Tule Lake (Hike 6), the major drawback of this trek to Crater Lake is the drive to the trailhead. As of 1990, there was no open campground at Florence Lake; however, there are camping opportunities at Mono Hot Springs Resort (see Mono Hot Springs Campground) and in the surrounding area (Bolsillo and Ward Lake campgrounds).

The trail to Crater Lake is extremely popular with backpackers, so try to avoid a weekend visit, if possible. One word of advice: this trek begins with a vicious uphill grind across a sun-baked slope, so be sure to get an early start to beat the heat.

To find the Crater Lake trailhead, drive Highway 168 to the shore of Huntington Lake, and turn right onto Kaiser Pass Road (signed for Mono Hot Springs and Florence Lake). Continue 5.7 miles on good, two-lane road, and then endure 11.2 miles of roughly paved, one-lane road (not recommended for motorhomes).

Serene Crater Lake is a delightful hiking destination.

Arrive at another junction signed for Mono Hot Springs and Florence Lake. Stay right here for Florence Lake, and drive 6.1 miles to a large day-use parking area (just beyond the overnight trailhead parking). Restrooms are available here.

The Crater Lake trailhead is at the far end of the day-use parking lot. It's signed for Dutch and Crater lakes. Start ascending on a rocky trail lined with Sierra junipers and manzanita. You'll enter the John Muir Wilderness right away. Come to a creek at 0.3 mile, and begin to climb beside it.

Savor the shade of white firs, Jeffrey pines, and Sierra junipers. Unfortunately, the trees are much too scarce on this sun-exposed hillside. You'll be perspiring freely as you endure a tough uphill grind marked by rocky terrain and lousy footing. Watch for ducks to guide you in spots where the trail grows faint.

It's a steady, unrelenting up through a thin covering of trees for 1.5 miles, but then the climb mellows mercifully. Continue upward, winding through a lodgepole pine forest, and regain open granite terrain at the 1.8-mile point. Again, you'll need to watch for ducks to help you find the way. Look for pretty stonecrop, mountain pride penstemon, and meadow penstemon, and lift your eyes for stunning views of distant mountains as you climb.

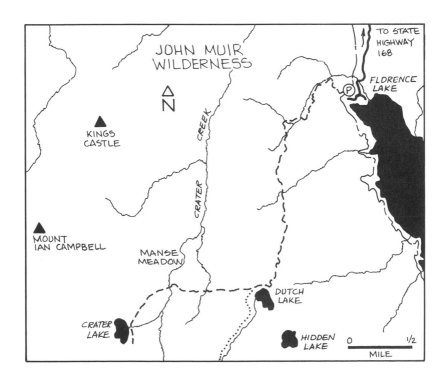

The grade intensifies at 2.2 miles (and so do the mosquitoes, if you're hiking in July). Ascend through trees to reach Dutch Lake and the crest of this section of your climb at 2.6 miles. Large but shallow, Dutch Lake is ringed by trees and a host of tule weeds. If the bugs are buzzing, you probably won't want to linger.

Go right with the trail around the shore, and arrive at a trail junction at 2.8 miles. Keep right here for Crater Lake. You'll enjoy level walking through trees and cross a flower-filled stream at 3.4 miles. From here, the climb to Crater Lake resumes.

Ascend gently at first, delighting in a ground cover of cheery Brewer's lupine, and then begin working harder as the grade intensifies across a rocky hillside. You'll have a fine view of surrounding peaks from the ridgeline just before Crater Lake. Arrive at the lakeshore at 4.0 miles.

Suddenly, you'll know the arduous climb was worth it. This is a breathtakingly beautiful Sierra lake, set into a granite amphitheater dominated by a single, lofty peak. The scene is almost reverent, with the lone rock spire reminiscent of a stout cathedral tower.

Fishing and camping opportunities abound at Crater Lake, and you won't find a prettier spot for a picnic anywhere in the area. Peel off your shoes, lean back, and listen to the hymns hummed by Crater Lake.

CHAPTER TWO
• • • • • • • • • •
Kings Canyon National Park/ Sequoia National Forest

The rich wilderness area known as Kings Canyon National Park was set aside by the United States government in 1940. The creation of this national park also involved the absorption of General Grant National Park, which was established in 1890.

It's difficult to speak about Kings Canyon National Park without referring to Sequoia National Park in the same breath. The two share such close association, both geographically and administratively, that most visitors think of the 864,000-acre package as a single, if diverse, entity.

And visitors are one thing Kings Canyon and Sequoia national parks certainly don't lack—the parks' combined total in 1989 topped two million people. Although this is an exceedingly popular area in the summer months, opportunities for solitude still outnumber those to be found in tourist-tortured Yosemite National Park. Avoid weekend visits if you can, and you'll have even more breathing room.

Even with 12 campgrounds offering approximately 1,500 campsites, Kings Canyon and Sequoia national parks are often full to overflowing by Saturday afternoons. It is possible to find sites without reservations, but it's risky business. Please refer to our individual campground descriptions for recommendations.

Visitor centers in both national parks provide a wealth of excellent information for those who take the time to investigate. Maps, brochures, campground listings, and hiking advice are all readily available. Visitor-center personnel will also let you know about ranger-led hikes and fireside talks. Also look for schedules of activities in the parks' newspaper, *The Sequoia Bark.*

Visitors entering the parks via Highway 180 from Fresno can stop at the Grant Grove Visitor Center, while those coming from Visalia on Highway 198 can stop at either the Ash Mountain Visitor Center (just past the park entrance) or the Lodgepole Visitor Center (at Lodgepole Campground).

And what is it that draws more than two million people a year to

Kings Canyon and Sequoia national parks? You'll find a further discussion of Sequoia National Park in the next chapter, but here's a three-word description of Kings Canyon National Park: trees and rivers.

Kings Canyon boasts some of the finest representatives of the mighty giant sequoia to be found anywhere. A network of well-maintained, self-guiding trails leads to scores of impressive forest giants as well as to the remnants of logging operations that once threatened their existence. Families will find many opportunities for both recreation and education.

The namesake of the park is the canyon of the Kings River, and the south and middle forks of this waterway cut an awesome swath through the wilderness. Kings Canyon measures 7,891 feet from its highest point, at the summit of Spanish Mountain (10,051 feet), to water level at the confluence of the south and middle forks of the Kings River. The Junction View overlook (see the information on Sentinel Campground) is a must for any traveler to the Cedar Grove area of the park.

There are a few things park visitors need to remember. A moderate entry fee is required of all vehicles. Because of the relatively low elevation and heavy vegetation, mosquitoes are a problem here, especially in June and July. Be sure to arm yourself with repellent for your stay. Because the heat can be intense in late summer, try to plan your hikes for early in the day.

The crowds of people that come to Kings Canyon and Sequoia national parks contribute to increasing animal delinquency. You'll have to guard your foodstuff closely in the campgrounds. Ground squirrels will carry away anything that's edible. Bears are less-frequent campground visitors, but caution dictates concealing all food in your vehicle when not preparing meals or eating. As with all trips into the wilder-

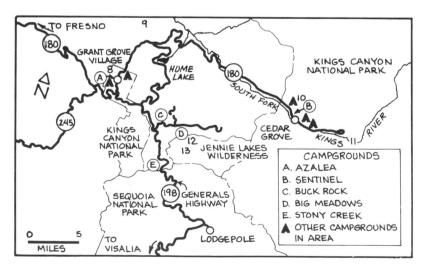

ness, good sense and good manners will help ensure an enjoyable visit and an enduring legacy.

Three hikes in this chapter (hikes 9, 12, and 13) are located in the Sequoia National Forest, adjacent to Kings Canyon National Park. The treks to Weaver and Jennie Ellis lakes (hikes 12 and 13) probe part of the Jennie Lakes Wilderness, a recently designated wilderness area that encompasses 10,500 acres within the Hume Lake Ranger District.

For Forest Service information, campground listings, campfire permits, and such, contact the Hume Lake Ranger District office on Highway 180 east of Fresno. The address is 35860 E. Kings Canyon Road, Dunlap, CA 93621.

CAMPGROUNDS

Azalea Campground *(Hike 8, North Grove Loop; Hike 9, Boole Tree)* This huge campground near the Big Stump Entrance Station to Kings Canyon National Park is a delightfully convenient base for hikers and sightseers alike. With more than 100 sites for tents or motorhomes, Azalea Campground can absorb a lot of visitors. Even so, it's best to come early to claim a spot.

To find Azalea Campground, drive Highway 180 from Fresno, and enter Kings Canyon National Park at the Big Stump Entrance Station. Continue 1.6 miles, go left for Kings Canyon Cedar Grove, and drive 1.4 miles to the Grant Grove Visitor Center. (Be sure to explore the visitor center for maps and information.)

From the visitor center, proceed 0.3 mile to a signed turnoff for Azalea Campground and the Grant Tree. Turn left here, and then turn into the campground to seek your site. An easy footpath from Azalea Campground leads to the General Grant Tree and the start of Hike 8, North Grove Loop.

Sites offer fireplaces, picnic tables, piped water, and flush toilets. Beware of marauding ground squirrels here—the campground's popularity has combined with campers' carelessness to create a bold gang of thieves.

Azalea Campground is open all year. No reservations. Moderate fee.

Sentinel Campground *(Hike 10, Hotel Creek; Hike 11, Mist Falls)* Tucked into the deep recesses of Kings Canyon National Park, Sentinel Campground requires a long but very scenic drive from the Big Stump Entrance Station. However, the surrounding landscape and the nearby trailheads combine to make Sentinel Campground an ideal spot to pound in your stakes and stay awhile.

To reach Sentinel Campground, drive Highway 180 from Fresno, and enter Kings Canyon National Park at the Big Stump Entrance Station. Continue 1.6 miles, go left for Kings Canyon Cedar Grove, and

Buck Rock Lookout is an amazing feat of engineering.

drive 1.4 miles to the Grant Grove Visitor Center. (Be sure to explore the visitor center for maps and information.)

From the visitor center, proceed 29.2 miles on an often winding but exquisitely beautiful route, and then turn left for Cedar Village. Go left again 0.1 mile later to find Sentinel Campground. Be sure to pause along the way to enjoy Junction View, a wonderful vista point above the confluence of the south and middle forks of the Kings River. (The signed viewpoint is 10.8 miles from the Grant Grove Visitor Center.)

Busy Sentinel Campground has approximately 83 sites for tents or motorhomes, scattered along a shaded shore of the South Fork of the Kings River. The campground offers fireplaces, picnic tables, piped water, and flush toilets.

Sentinel Campground is open April to October. No reservations. Moderate fee.

Buck Rock Campground *(Hike 12, Weaver Lake; Hike 13, Jennie Ellis Lake)* Besides its easy access to the trailhead for Jennie Ellis and Weaver lakes, rustic Buck Rock Campground has another plus to its credit: it's on the way to Buck Rock Lookout. This is an attraction any visitor to the area definitely won't want to miss.

To find Buck Rock Campground, drive Highway 180 from Fresno, and enter Kings Canyon National Park at the Big Stump Entrance Station. (You'll exit the park and enter Sequoia National Forest farther on, and no national park entry fee is required.) Continue for 1.6 miles, and go right for Sequoia and Giant Grove.

Proceed 7.0 miles, and turn left for Big Meadows. Drive the paved road toward Big Meadows for 2.9 miles, and go left once more for Buck Rock Campground, abandoning the pavement to travel a gravel road 0.4 mile to the camping area.

This primitive campground has a handful of shaded sites scattered along the road. There is no drinking water, but picnic tables, fireplaces, and non-flush toilets are available. If you're visiting during the height of mosquito season (July and early August), be sure to bring repellent —the bugs can be nasty here.

While at Buck Rock Campground, visit the impressive Buck Rock Lookout. It's only a couple of miles from the campground and well worth the trip. Continue on the unpaved road, and park at the pulloff to the left when the way branches. Walk the very rough, left branch of the road, and reach the unstaffed lookout soon after.

Lack of funding forced the closure of Buck Rock Lookout in 1989. Even if you can't climb the stairway to the top, the spectacle of the little lookout atop its massive pillar of stone is sure to amaze and delight all comers.

Buck Rock Campground is open June to October. No reservations. No fee.

Big Meadows Campground *(Hike 12, Weaver Lake; Hike 13, Jennie Ellis Lake)* Although a bit less secluded than Buck Rock Campground, Big Meadows Campground has a more-pleasant situation along the banks of Big Meadows Creek. More than 20 sites for tents or motorhomes attract scores of forest lovers and anglers. You'll have to bring your own drinking water, but the campground does offer picnic tables, fireplaces, and non-flush toilets.

To reach Big Meadows Campground, drive Highway 180 from Fresno, and enter Kings Canyon National Park at the Big Stump Entrance Station. (You'll exit the park and enter Sequoia National Forest farther on, and no national park entry fee is required.) Continue for 1.6 miles, and go right for Sequoia and Giant Grove.

Proceed 7.0 miles, and turn left for Big Meadows. Drive the paved road toward Big Meadows for 2.9 miles, and continue straight for Big Meadows at the junction. Another 1.2 miles will take you to the sprawling campground on Big Meadows Creek.

Big Meadows Campground is open June to October. No reservations. No fee.

Stony Creek Campground *(Hike 12, Weaver Lake; Hike 13, Jennie Ellis Lake; Hike 14, Muir Grove; Hike 15, Little Baldy)* This Forest Service campground is an excellent option for the site-seeking visitor to the Kings Canyon and Sequoia national parks area. Located right on the Generals Highway, Stony Creek Campground is tucked into a parcel of Forest Service land between the national park campgrounds of Azalea and Dorst (see the next chapter for Dorst Campground).

To find Stony Creek Campground, drive Highway 180 from Fresno, and enter Kings Canyon National Park at the Big Stump Entrance Station. (You'll exit the park and enter Sequoia National Forest farther on, and no national park entry fee is required.) Continue for 1.6 miles, and go right for Sequoia and Giant Grove.

Proceed 12.2 miles (passing the turnoff for Big Meadows) to the signed campground entrance. This pleasantly shaded campground sits on the banks of Stony Creek and comes equipped with a friendly campground host and a legendary (and often troublesome) campground bear. "Old Stony" makes properly stowing foodstuff a must while staying here.

Currently, Stony Creek Campground offers some reserved sites through the Forest Service's 280-CAMP number and some on a first-come, first-served basis. Fireplaces, picnic tables, drinking water, and flush toilets are standard equipment at the approximately 50 sites for tents or motorhomes. A more primitive camping area just across the road boasts additional campsites. Even so, you'll need to come early if you hope to find a vacant spot for the weekend.

Stony Creek Campground is open June to October. Reservations accepted. Moderate fee.

8 NORTH GROVE LOOP

Distance: 1.8 miles (loop)
Difficulty: Easy
Starting point: 6,320 feet
High point: 6,400 feet
Total climb: 400 feet
Maps: USGS Hume 7.5' and
USGS General Grant Grove 7.5'

The diminutive sequoia cone gives birth to one of the largest trees on earth.

Few visitors to the Grant Grove of Kings Canyon National Park neglect a stop at the famous General Grant Tree. The hordes of people pausing in awe at the roots of this old warrior may suffocate your "wilderness experience." Combine a visit to the Grant Tree with this easy loop walk through the usually quiet North Grove to mingle some serenity with your sightseeing.

This is an ideal hike for families, as the distance is short and the grades are mellow. A picnic lunch at either end of the jaunt will make

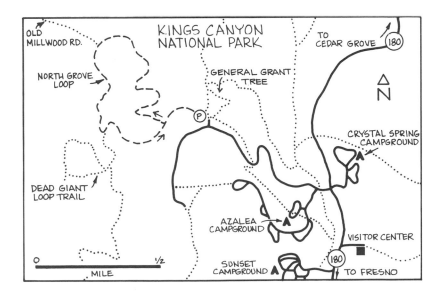

Giant sequois (left) and incense cedars (right) grow side by side on the North Grove Loop.

an afternoon of it. If you're staying at the nearby Azalea Campground, you won't even need to climb in the car. Just take the connecting trail from the campground.

To find the General Grant Tree and the start of this hike, follow driving directions provided for Azalea Campground. After turning off Highway 180 for Azalea Campground and the Grant Tree, continue 0.8 mile to reach a large parking area beside the much-visited grove. (If you want to park closest to where the actual North Grove loop begins, drive to the far end of the parking area that's signed for recreational-vehicle and bus parking.)

Proclaimed "the nation's Christmas tree" in 1926, the mighty General Grant Tree doesn't appear to have faded much in popularity since then. It's easy to see why when you linger beneath this masterpiece of nature. You'll certainly get a feel for the sheer size of the giant sequoias while standing here.

Walk the 0.5-mile, self-guided, loop trail past the Grant Tree, the Robert E. Lee Tree, and the awesome Fallen Monarch. Then, abandon the zooish parking area with its tour buses, restrooms, and overflowing garbage cans to start your North Grove hike.

Look for a sign for the North Grove Loop at the far end of the recreational-vehicle parking area, and begin with a gentle descent on an asphalt roadway.

Angle right after 0.1 mile at a sign for the North Grove Loop Trail, and continue downhill on an old logging road, hiking in the shade of sugar and ponderosa pines, white firs, and incense cedars. Keep an eye out for scattered giant sequoias along the way. They look particularly majestic among the smaller trees.

If you can tear your gaze from the lofty branches overhead, scan the forest floor for an abundance of wildflowers. A wonderful outburst of Sierra rein orchids can be found in a grassy nook to the right of the trail at the 0.4-mile point. Pass an interesting "twin" sequoia on the left side of the trail at 0.7 mile, and continue downhill through a varied forest that's delightful in its quietness.

Reach the bottom of the hill and the old Millwood fire road at 0.9 mile. This nearly obliterated roadway leads to the site of Millwood, a busy lumber town in the 1890s. From the mill at Millwood, vanquished giant sequoias were floated down a flume to Sanger, on the valley floor near Fresno.

Look for a fire-scarred sequoia on the left side of the trail, and start uphill with the loop route, passing a handful of living sequoias along the way. The presence of sugar pines in this forest makes for an amusing study in contrasts: sugar pine cones are often more than a foot in length, while the tiny giant sequoia cones, fallen from their towering hosts, nestle comfortably in a child's palm.

The route levels out at 1.2 miles, and you'll regain the paved road at 1.3 miles. Go left here (or go right if you want to lengthen your hike by taking in the Dead Giant Loop Trail), and climb uphill with the asphalt. Pass the turnoff you took on your way in at the 1.7-mile point (on the left), and continue straight to reach the parking area at 1.8 miles.

· ·

9 BOOLE TREE

Distance: 2.0 miles round trip
Difficulty: Easy
Starting point: 6,260 feet
High point: 6,750 feet
Map: USGS Hume 7.5'

A journey to the base of the gigantic Boole Tree is markedly different than a visit to the much-publicized General Grant Tree of Hike 8. Since the Boole Tree is outside the boundaries of Kings Canyon National Park, you won't have the Grant Grove crowds to deal with. You can revel in the solitude and splendor of the Sequoia National Forest

The massive Boole Tree overwhelms all who come to see it.

even as you absorb the awesome spectacle of a record-breaking giant sequoia.

Named for Frank Boole, the general manager of the Sanger Lumber Company, the Boole Tree was discovered (and spared the loggers' sawblades) in 1903. The tree is 269 feet high, and it holds claim to being the largest sequoia in a national forest.

To reach the trailhead for the Boole Tree, drive Highway 180 from Fresno, and enter Kings Canyon National Park at the Big Stump Entrance Station. If you're not camping or hiking within national park boundaries, the park entry fee will be waived. Continue 1.6 miles, and go left for Kings Canyon Cedar Grove. Then drive 5.8 miles (exiting the park along the way) to reach an easy-to-miss turnoff signed for the Boole Tree.

Go left onto the unpaved Road 13S55, and follow signs for the Boole Tree Trail, keeping to the main route for 2.7 miles to arrive at the trailhead parking area. Your trail, marked by a sign for the Boole Tree, takes off from the right.

Begin climbing on a dusty footpath lined by fragrant mountain misery. Watch for golden brodiaea and mariposa lily, too. It's a steady uphill pull as you traverse a hillside covered with manzanita and bracken ferns. You'll see occasional young sequoias sprinkled in among incense cedars, white firs, and canyon live oaks.

Puff through a series of switchbacks at 0.6 mile, and continue up a stair-stepped trail to reach the crest of the ascent at 0.8 mile. You'll get your first look at the battered top of the Boole Tree from here. Scramble up to the top of a burned sequoia stump on the left side of the trail for a fine view out to the canyon of the Middle Fork of the Kings River while you catch your breath.

A brief descent leads to an informational plaque and an excellent photo opportunity for the Boole Tree at 0.9 mile. Continue your descent to reach the base of the behemoth at 1.0 mile.

What an amazing spectacle! Savor the silence of the spot as you

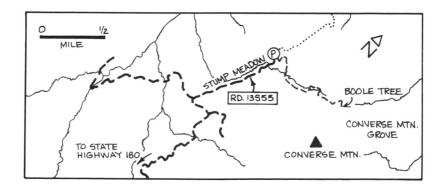

gaze heavenward along a seemingly unending tree trunk. Then pace a reverent circle around the giant's feet and marvel at this masterpiece of nature before retracing your steps back to the parking area.

• •

10 HOTEL CREEK

Distance: 5.2 miles round trip
Difficulty: Moderate
Starting point: 4,660 feet
High point: 6,150 feet
Map: USGS Cedar Grove 7.5'

If you want to try out the Hotel Creek Trail, remember one important detail: leave an early wake-up call! This challenging hike becomes a monster when the sun is high. You'll bake all the way up the canyon wall. Get an early start and you'll be treated to lonely, scenic walking and an enchanting overlook of Kings Canyon and surrounding peaks. Probably the best thing about this hike is that it's quiet— and quietness is a scarce commodity in this busy corner of Kings Canyon National Park.

Despite the manageable distance, this isn't a great hike for children. (Check out Hike 11, Mist Falls, if you have a family in tow.) This trail climbs steeply in an abundance of exposed switchbacks. Carry lots of water and a snack.

If you're especially energetic, you can turn this hike into an approximately 8-mile loop by continuing up to the junction with the Lewis Creek Trail and then descending toward Cedar Grove Village via that route. Dramatic mountain vistas await those who take on the entire loop, and views extend to the Monarch Divide on a hazeless day. Consult an area map for details.

To find the trailhead for Hotel Creek, drive Highway 180 from Fresno, and enter Kings Canyon National Park at the Big Stump Entrance Station. Continue 1.6 miles, and go left for Kings Canyon Cedar Grove. Then drive 30.6 miles on a beautiful but tortuously twisting road. Veer left for Cedar Grove Village, and keep to the right past the little settlement, following signs toward the pack station. (Detour to the left if you want to pause at the ranger station first.)

Begin at the signed Hotel Creek Trail, keeping to the right with the Hotel Creek route as you begin. (The trail to the left is the loop hookup from Lewis Creek.) Climb on a sandy footpath, enjoying the shade of incense cedars and ponderosa pines. The haunting aroma of

A thirsty hiker celebrates the high point of the Hotel Creek climb.

mountain misery blossoms is everywhere.

Look for a footpath veering off toward Hotel Creek at 0.3 mile, but continue climbing with the main trail. If you're hiking early in the day, you may spot a mule deer coming downhill for a drink. Deer tracks are often more numerous than footprints on this path.

The switchbacks kick in with enthusiasm at 0.4 mile, and you'll lose most of your shade as you climb between sun-loving patches of chinquapin, manzanita, and canyon live oaks. *Manzanita* means "little apple" in Spanish. Pretty pinkish white flowers decorate manzanita branches in the spring. Watch for the plant's small, round berries in August.

Sneak improving views down toward Cedar Grove Village as you continue to ascend. The grade eases slightly at 1.1 miles, and another use trail exits toward Hotel Creek shortly afterward. With a mile of hot hill behind you, this detour is much more tempting than the first.

Continue upward through scattered regal ponderosa pines, and marvel at the multitude of lightning-seared trees still standing on the

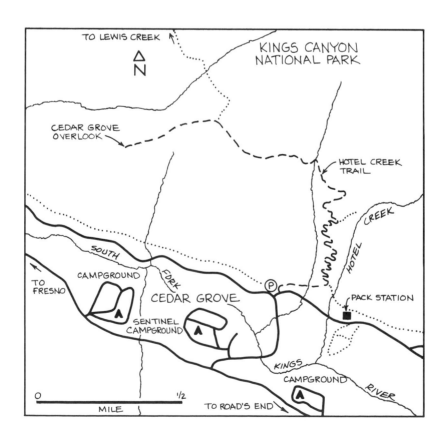

heights. At the 1.7-mile point, a too-brief downhill leads into yet more climbing. You'll be panting hard by the time you reach the crest of your ascent at 2.1 miles. With any luck, a refreshing breeze will greet you on the ridgetop.

Arrive at a junction with a trail signed for the "Overlook," and abandon the route toward Lewis Creek to go left toward your goal. (Continue straight if you're doing the loop.) Descend along the ridgeline with views of the opposite canyon wall.

The delightfully easy trail levels off for a time, and then a gentle climb ends at the overlook at the 2.6-mile point in your trek. There's no sign to identify the spot, but the trail comes to a crashing halt atop a little rocky knoll.

Settle down on a comfortable boulder, and savor the bird's-eye vista of the canyon floor. You'll see Sheep Creek Campground just below, and you'll hear the roar of the South Fork of the Kings River filtering up on the breeze. Gaze across the canyon toward Sentinel Ridge. Up the canyon, the backcountry of Kings Canyon National Park beckons those with backpacks and strong legs.

• •

11 MIST FALLS

Distance: 8.6 miles (loop)
Difficulty: Moderate
Starting point: 5,030 feet
High point: 5,680 feet
Map: USGS The Sphinx 7.5'

Despite its somewhat daunting length, this hike to Mist Falls is a pleasant family outing. The trail is excellent, the ascent is not too steep, and the waterfall provides a lovely picnic destination. One piece of advice: start early in the day to beat the heat, as the hike's low elevation can make for toasty trekking.

Ideally, you'll be staying at one of the Cedar Grove campgrounds when you try this hike—the long ride in on Highway 180 doesn't combine well with an 8.6-mile day hike. To find the trailhead, drive Highway 180 from Fresno, and enter Kings Canyon National Park at the Big Stump Entrance Station. Continue 1.6 miles and go left for Kings Canyon Cedar Grove. Then drive 35.9 miles on a scenic, paved, but very winding route to reach a welcome sign for Road's End.

Turn right into the paved parking area, and make use of the piped water, toilets, and staffed information booth before you start. Look for the trailhead sign for Bubbs Creek and Mist Falls at the far end of the parking area (near the information booth), and set out on a level trail beneath a canopy of black oaks, incense cedars, and ponderosa pines.

Cross a stream on a wooden footbridge, and walk gently uphill. Views of the impressive canyon walls will attract your eyes, even as the murmur of the South Fork of the Kings River floods your ears. At midday, the sun is punishing throughout this section, so you'll be thankful for a thickening of the trees at 1.5 miles.

Bracken ferns cover the ground beneath an umbrella of green branches as you continue. Look for massive boulders among the vegetation, castoffs from the sheer canyon walls. Reach a junction at 1.9 miles, and go left for Mist Falls.

Start uphill more noticeably as you get a peek at Bubbs Creek joining the South Fork of the Kings River, to the right. Continue up beside the South Fork, ascending through a proliferation of ferns and thimble-

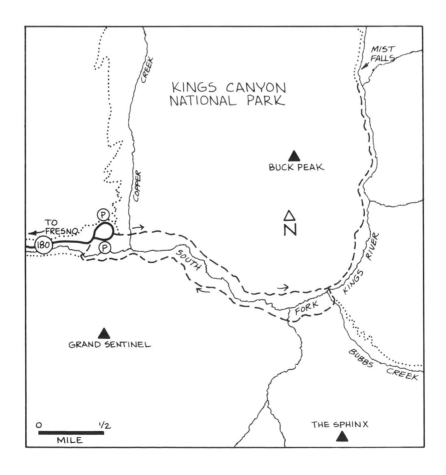

The sugar pine produces the longest pine cone in the world.

berries. The riverbed is overhung with willow and alder.

Draw in beside the prancing water at 2.7 miles. The river is a beautiful shade of aqua, decorated with a mane of frothy white. Your climb intensifies at 3.0 miles, and you'll be treated to fine views of the cliffs on both sides of the canyon. Reach a small waterfall at 3.1 miles. The steady up continues.

Exchange trees and shadows for manzanita and hot granite as you climb in shadeless switchbacks. Spectacular views of the opposite (south) canyon wall will reward you for your efforts. Pause often to breathe deeply of this lovely scene.

Arrive at a sign for Mist Falls at 3.9 miles. Veer right onto a short use trail to reach the water's edge. You'll be greeted by a lovely waterfall, fanning out across a wide wall of granite.

Picnic spots abound beside the water. Choose a place just below the falls, and you'll consume your sandwich with the caress of Mist Falls moistening your lips. If you have children along, please be sure to keep an eye on them. This waterfall's opportunities for rock hopping are tempting and plentiful—but dangerous.

When you've finished savoring the sweetness of Mist Falls, backtrack 2.0 miles to the junction beside Bubbs Creek (at the 5.9-mile point). You can add a scant 0.8 mile to your day and enjoy a return route along the opposite bank of the South Fork of the Kings River by going left at the junction.

Cross the South Fork on a footbridge, and continue to a second junction at 6.1 miles. Go right here for Road's End. This side of the river has fewer people, more trees to offer shade, and a hefty dose of pleasant scenery. It's well worth the extra distance.

Enjoy gradual downhill walking to a trail junction and another bridge at 8.4 miles. Go right here to recross the South Fork. Then swing upstream toward the parking area to gain your starting point at 8.6 miles.

- -

12 WEAVER LAKE

Distance: 4.2 miles round trip
Difficulty: Moderate
Starting point: 7,900 feet
High point: 8,700 feet
Map: USGS Muir Grove 7.5'

The pleasant jaunt to Weaver Lake is a perfect family outing. The trail is good, the inclines aren't too tough, and the destination will please every member of your party. Carry a fishing pole if you're in the mood, and don't forget a picnic lunch for Weaver Lake's lovely shoreline.

To find the trailhead for Weaver Lake, drive Highway 180 from Fresno, and enter Kings Canyon National Park at the Big Stump Entrance Station. (You'll exit the park and enter Sequoia National Forest farther on, and no national park entry fee is required.) Continue for 1.6 miles, and go right for Sequoia and Giant Grove.

Proceed 7.0 miles, and turn left for Big Meadows. Drive the paved road for 2.9 miles, and continue straight for Big Meadows at the junction. Note your odometer mileage here. Another 1.2 miles will take you to the sprawling campground on Big Meadows Creek. Pass the campground, and stay right for Horse Corral Meadow.

Cross Big Meadows Creek, and turn right onto an unpaved road 2.6 miles from the Buck Rock–Big Meadows junction. Keep left when the road branches. The way is rough but passable. Reach the road's end and the (as yet unsigned) trailhead 1.4 miles from the paved route. This recently established trailhead shortens the trek to Weaver and Jennie Ellis lakes a full 1.5 miles in each direction, making the bumpy drive well worth it.

You'll start hiking on a trail that skirts along the lower edge of a large tree plantation and then cross pretty Fox Creek soon after. Look for tiger lily and bistort on the banks of the little waterway. Begin climb-

The shoreline of Weaver Lake is a treat for photographers and picnickers alike.

ing through a shady red fir forest, and pass flower-filled Fox Meadow as you go.

A signed trail coming in from the old trailhead joins you at 0.2 mile. Continue to the left, being sure to note the junction so that you don't miss it on your way back. Hike steadily uphill beneath a red fir ceiling, enjoying occasional outbursts of nude buckwheat and mariposa lily.

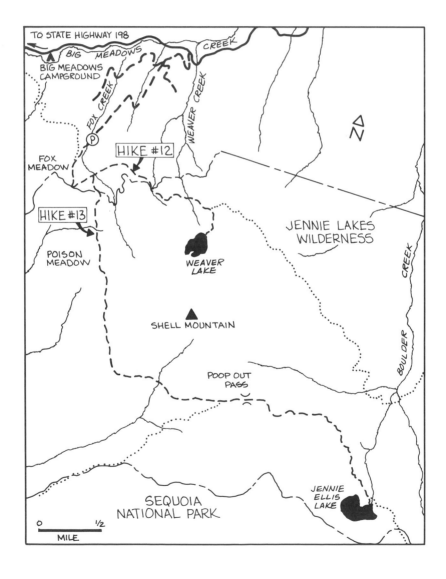

Arrive at a second junction signed for Weaver and Jennie Ellis lakes at 0.7 mile. Continue to the left for Weaver Lake. Cross a small creek and climb again, negotiating a gentle incline across a hillside carpeted with pinemat manzanita. Pass an entry sign for the Jennie Lakes Wilderness at 0.8 mile.

Granite, trees, and more granite surround you as you walk onward, enjoying open vistas of the mountainous country to the north. The grade eases atop a fir-covered hill at 1.0 mile. Wind on in welcome shade, and reach a lush ravine flooded with ranger buttons, lupine, and Labrador tea at the 1.3-mile point.

Climb away from the wildflowers, working your way across a boulder-sprinkled hillside not long afterward. More fine vistas await you here. The route levels out at 1.6 miles. Then you'll cross a seasonal stream, Weaver Creek, descending from Weaver Lake. Gentle uphill walking follows.

Hike onward through red firs and western white and lodgepole pines to arrive at an unsigned trail junction with 1.9 miles behind you. Keep to the right, and climb gently to reach the shore of Weaver Lake at 2.1 miles.

Although it's fairly shallow, Weaver Lake is very attractive, set off by the stark, granite slope that rises up behind it. A grass-edged shoreline tempts picnickers and anglers alike. This lake is popular with backpackers as well, so you'll probably spot a few tents on the far side of the water.

· ·

13 JENNIE ELLIS LAKE

Distance: 10.4 miles round trip
Difficulty: Strenuous
Starting point: 7,900 feet
High point: 9,180 feet
Total climb: 1,700 feet
Map: USGS Muir Grove 7.5'

This challenging hike to Jennie Ellis Lake is definitely not for the timid. It's long and difficult, and the trail crosses some rugged rocky sections that make for slow and strenuous hiking. In fact, this is one Sierra day hike where boots should be listed as standard equipment —the trail is just too tough for tennis shoes.

With those warnings out of the way, the positives of the trek to Jennie Ellis Lake are myriad. The scenery is lovely. The route explores

A fisherman tests the icy depths of Jennie Ellis Lake.

the recently formed Jennie Lakes Wilderness. And the trail is much less crowded than routes in the nearby Kings Canyon and Sequoia national parks environs.

To find the trailhead for Jennie Ellis Lake, please refer to the driving directions for Hike 12, Weaver Lake. Follow the directions for Hike 12 up to the signed trail junction at the 0.7-mile point. Then abandon the Weaver Lake route to veer right for Jennie Ellis Lake.

Ascend to enter the Jennie Lakes Wilderness soon after. The grade mellows slightly as you continue. Cross a small creek at 1.2 miles, and enjoy the cheery company of Labrador tea, shooting star, arrowleaf groundsel, and California corn lily. You'll climb to the edge of Poison Meadow at 1.4 miles and then enjoy more level walking for a time.

Gain a haze-dulled vista to the west at 1.9 miles. The hillside opens up as you traverse a landscape of pinemat manzanita and rock. Watch for views of peaks to both the south and the east as you begin to turn toward Poop Out Pass at 2.4 miles. If the day is clear, you should spot Sequoia National Park's Alta Peak in the distance.

Descend gently for a time, and then resume climbing at 2.7 miles. The grade intensifies soon after, as you traverse a rocky trail along the hillside. Pass a side trail descending toward Generals Highway at 3.3 miles, and continue straight. Breathe easier as the incline eases once again.

Reach the rather uninspiring Poop Out Pass at 3.7 miles. Trees obscure the vista here. Too bad there's no excuse to linger, as the route ahead is nothing less than nasty. Begin an excruciatingly steep descent on an awful trail. It's extremely rough going as you circumvent a massive slide area. Mercifully, things level out after 0.5 mile.

You'll be treated to views of the mountains to the north as you continue across a rocky hillside and then begin the climb toward Jennie Ellis Lake at 4.9 miles. Ascend through a forest of red firs and lodgepole and western white pines as you endure a moderate grade for 0.3 mile.

Keep an eye out for Jennie Ellis Lake's outlet stream, its banks awash in dense Labrador tea. Leave the main trail to veer right along the little waterway, striking out toward Jennie Ellis Lake. You'll reach the lake at 5.2 miles.

Suddenly, the past few hours of rock hopping and sweating won't seem so cruel. This lovely lake is tucked into a pocket of stone 9,012 feet above sea level, backed by a solemn semicircle of glowing white granite. A forested shoreline faces the windswept rocky side, offering shaded picnic places and placid perches for restless anglers. Jennie Ellis Lake's water is deep and clear and cold, tempting to boot-weary toes but daunting to all but the bravest of swimmers.

CHAPTER THREE
· · · · · · · · · · · · ·
Sequoia National Park

Please refer to the introductory section of chapter 2 for general information on Kings Canyon and Sequoia national parks. Sequoia National Park marked its hundredth anniversary amid great fanfare in September 1990. The park's creation preceded its famous cousin, Yosemite National Park, by but a week. The area encompassed by Sequoia National Park increased significantly in 1926, when more of the High Sierra was included. The matchless Mineral King region was added to the park in 1978.

Those entering the park via Highway 198 and the Ash Mountain Entrance Station can anticipate a twisting, one-hour drive to the Giant Forest area. The Giant Forest grove boasts four of the five largest sequoias in the world, and the forest here possesses a serene beauty that visitors will long remember. Hale Tharp was the first white man to walk beneath the behemoths of the Giant Forest. The adventurous cattle-man and an Indian guide explored the area in 1856.

Cattle grazing, logging, and mining threatened the lands encompassed by Sequoia National Park, but the area's establishment as America's second national park in 1890 helped ensure its preservation. Today, the major threat to the park drifts upward from the populated valley floor to the west. Air pollution endangers the forest by making trees more susceptible to disease and death.

The Mineral King area of Sequoia National Park has its own unique history. A mining rush in the 1870s brought bevies of prospectors to the valley in search of silver ore. The White Chief Mine was established in 1873. Torturous winters, devastating avalanches, and disappointing yields contributed to the bust of the mining boom less than 10 years later.

Fortunately for Mineral King, the United States government gained interest in the area, even as the miners lost it. Mineral King was made part of the Sierra Forest Preserve in 1893. All wasn't smooth sailing from there, however, as the area nearly fell victim to development by the ski industry in the 1960s and 1970s. Opponents stalled the process with lawsuits, and Congress declared the area a part of Sequoia National Park in 1978.

A day hiker shares the White Chief Canyon trek with a lone Sierra juniper.

A climbing, twisting, narrow road brings visitors to Mineral King, and it's the punishing drive in that helps preserve this priceless corner of the wilderness from being trampled by admirers. All but one of the Mineral King hikes described here begin at an altitude of at least 7,500 feet. If you have the time to spare, you may want to allow yourself a day to adapt to your surroundings before you take on one of the tougher treks.

Bears do frequent the campgrounds here, so be sure to store food properly. And munching marmots have been known to wreak havoc on the hoses of parked cars (you might see some backpackers' vehicles at the trailheads enmeshed in chicken wire). Sunscreen is an absolute necessity at these high elevations, too. Please be sure to carry the "Ten Essentials" (see the introduction) on all outings in this rugged, isolated area.

Use caution and respect when entering this incredibly beautiful corner of the Sierra. Then simply savor it. You'll never forget the time you spend here.

CAMPGROUNDS

Dorst Campground *(Hike 14, Muir Grove; Hike 15, Little Baldy)* The recently refurbished Dorst Campground is an excellent accommodation option for the Giant Forest area of Sequoia National Park. It's not quite so conveniently located as Lodgepole Campground, but what it lacks in convenience it more than makes up for in modernity. If you like camping in style, you'll like Dorst Campground.

To reach Dorst Campground, enter Sequoia National Park via Highway 180 from Fresno or Highway 198 from Visalia and Three Rivers. Both routes are long, twisting, and tough on radiators. You'll find Dorst Campground 16.7 miles from the Big Stump Entrance Station (Fresno route) or 12.0 miles northwest of Giant Forest Village (Visalia route) on the Generals Highway.

With more than 200 sites for tents or motorhomes, Dorst Campground has picnic tables, fireplaces, piped water, and flush toilets. The campground is situated on pretty Dorst Creek, but you'll probably be hard pressed to find the little waterway amid all the asphalt.

Upon its reopening, Dorst's 218 remodeled campsites were on a first-come, first-served basis. Some sites may be available through Ticketron by now. Please check with the National Park Service for information. Reserved or not, Dorst's sites will be hard to get, so come early for a spot.

Dorst Campground is open June to September. No reservations. Moderate fee.

Lodgepole Campground *(Hike 15, Little Baldy; Hike 16, Tokopah Falls; Hike 17, Heather Lake; Hike 18, Big Trees Hike; Hike 19, Crescent Meadow)* The first rule for sprawling Lodgepole Campground is to make reservations. Unclaimed sites are distributed on a first-come, first-served basis, but without reservations your chances of claiming a site are slim to none. Contact Ticketron for details. The second rule for Lodgepole Campground is an outgrowth of the first: expect a zoo. This campground is a bustling testimony to the popularity of Sequoia National Park.

Situated on the Marble Fork of the Kaweah River (fishing and swimming opportunities abound), Lodgepole Campground has a market, showers, and a laundromat to accommodate its hundreds of daily residents. Its 258 sites for tents or motorhomes offer picnic tables, fireplaces, piped water, and flush toilets. Bears are frequent visitors to this grocery-laden corner of the wilderness. Each campsite has a bear box, and patrolling rangers will make sure you use yours.

To reach Lodgepole Campground, enter Sequoia National Park via Highway 180 from Fresno or Highway 198 from Visalia and Three Rivers. Both approach routes are long and arduous. You'll find Lodgepole Campground 4.3 miles northeast of Giant Forest Village on the Generals Highway.

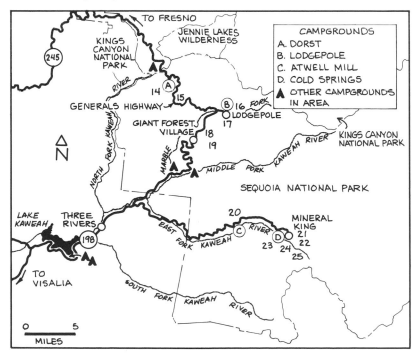

Lodgepole Campground is open all year. Reservations accepted. Moderate fee.

Atwell Mill Campground *(Hike 20, Atwell Grove and Paradise Peak; Hike 21, Lower Monarch Lake; Hike 22, Crystal Lakes; Hike 23, Mosquito Lakes; Hike 24, Eagle Lake; Hike 25, White Chief Canyon)* The first question you'll ask as you drive through the lovely Atwell Mill Campground is, Why doesn't this campground have more people? The gruesome drive up the Mineral King Road is one obvious reason. The other reason is the presence of Cold Springs Campground, 4.3 miles closer to the Mineral King trailheads. Since most visitors to the area come to hike, the majority choose to stay at Cold Springs Campground, opting for proximity to the trails.

Still, Atwell Mill Campground is a charmer. It's situated in the Atwell Grove of giant sequoias, and handsome trees and mighty stumps lend the spot its personality. The campground is seldom crowded, and its 23 quiet tentspots are near the banks of Atwell Creek. One Mineral King hike, Atwell Grove and Paradise Peak (Hike 20), starts just across the road from the camping area. The campground offers drinking water, fireplaces, picnic tables, and non-flush toilets.

To reach Atwell Mill Campground, drive Highway 198 northeast from Visalia, and turn off at Hammond (3.6 miles beyond Three Rivers) at a sign for Mineral King. The narrow, winding Mineral King Road climbs and twists its way into the mountains in a manner totally inappropriate for oversize vehicles. You'll enter Sequoia National Park along the way (an entry fee is required) and arrive at the campground after 19.4 tortuous miles.

Atwell Mill Campground is open May to September. No reservations. Moderate fee.

Cold Springs Campground *(Hike 20, Atwell Grove and Paradise Peak; Hike 21, Lower Monarch Lake; Hike 22, Crystal Lakes; Hike 23, Mosquito Lakes; Hike 24, Eagle Lake; Hike 25, White Chief Canyon)* Cold Springs Campground owns a pleasant spot on the East Fork of the Kaweah River. It's shaded and peaceful. Even so, this isn't a campground to choose if you're simply planning to sit around the campfire. The punishing drive to Cold Springs Campground is worth it only for the wealth of hiking opportunities to be found in the Mineral King section of Sequoia National Park.

To find the campground, please refer to driving directions for Atwell Mill Campground. Continue past Atwell Mill Campground another 4.3 miles, arriving at Cold Springs Campground after 23.7 miles of the unforgettable Mineral King Road.

With its proximity to the Mineral King trailheads and ranger station, Cold Springs Campground is usually a hub of activity. Its 37 tentsites are often full, so try to arrive early in the day to claim a spot.

Cold Springs Campground offers drinking water, non-flush toilets, picnic tables, and fireplaces. Bears have been a serious problem here in recent summers, so be sure to use the bear box provided at your campsite. Cold Springs Campground is open May to September. No reservations. Moderate fee.

• •

14 MUIR GROVE

Distance: 5.0 miles round trip
Difficulty: Moderate
Starting point: 6,750 feet
High point: 6,850 feet
Total climb: 450 feet
Map: USGS Muir Grove 7.5'

The hike from Dorst Campground to the Muir Grove of giant sequoias is a "don't-miss" trek for anyone staying in a Dorst campsite. The hike offers mellow walking, pleasant vistas, and a chance to visit a serene and lovely grove of majestic sequoias, as yet untouched by asphalt and tour buses.

Unfortunately, the renovation of Dorst Campground and the required relocation of the Muir Grove trailhead were still in progress as this book was being written. As a result, early portions of this hike description must remain a little vague. Check with a park ranger or with the Dorst Campground host for the latest information on the trail.

To reach the trailhead for Muir Grove, please refer to this chapter's driving directions for Dorst Campground. Enter the campground and follow signs for the amphitheater to gain a day-hiker parking area beside the trailhead. (If you're camping at Dorst, you'll be able to walk to the trailhead from your campsite.)

Set out on the signed Muir Grove trail, and skirt along the hillside above Dorst Campground's 200-plus busy sites. Hike through a shady white fir forest where sunlight-seeking ferns push their fronds toward the sky. A gently undulating trail leads to a seasonal stream crossing at 0.9 mile. Watch for crimson columbine, cow parsnip, and angelica along the banks.

Begin to climb more steadily, enjoying the company of thick firs and pines. An occasional sugar pine cone will amaze you with its size. Bend down to heft one of these monstrous cones, and you'll be thankful you weren't underneath it when it fell.

Ascend in a handful of long, well-graded switchbacks, and gain the summit of a little knoll at 1.3 miles. You'll get your first peek at the tantalizing Muir Grove from here—look for the stately forms of the Muir sequoias atop a distant hill. To the right of the trail, a granite-covered knob peppered with stout Jeffrey pines makes an excellent vista point.

Continue on a level trail as you begin the long detour around the tree-filled ravine that separates you from the sequoia grove. Wild spearmint, spreading dogbane, Indian paintbrush, and nude buckwheat are just a few of the flowers you'll find along the trail. More-open areas boast scrub oaks and bushy manzanita.

At 2.0 miles, cross a creek overhung with Pacific dogwoods and lush with moisture-loving ferns. Then start out along the hillside toward the sequoia grove. Shaded, easy walking follows, and you'll come face to face with the first of the Muir Grove giants at 2.5 miles. What a sight!

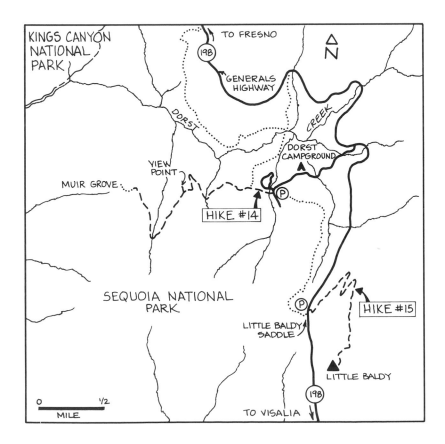

The Muir Grove rules an unspoiled hilltop in Sequoia National Park.

Even if you've seen sequoias a dozen times before, you'll marvel at the grandeur of these trees. And something about their setting here, hidden away on a forested hilltop, miles from parking lots and vending machines, makes the Muir sequoias seem even more magnificent. Wander and wonder and worship, and then retrace your steps toward your starting point.

15 LITTLE BALDY

Distance: 4.0 miles round trip
Difficulty: Moderate
Starting point: 7,340 feet
High point: 8,040 feet
Maps: USGS Giant Forest 7.5' and USGS Muir Grove 7.5'

If you've had enough of sequoia watching for a while, this jaunt to the top of Little Baldy is a wonderful Sequoia National Park hiking option, especially on a hazeless day. The trek is easy enough for families with children, although you'll want to keep close tabs on your little ones when you reach the exposed summit. Carry drinking water, a

Two day hikers survey the vista from the summit of Little Baldy.

windbreaker, and binoculars, and please don't attempt this hike when thunderclouds are present.

To find the Little Baldy trailhead, enter Sequoia National Park via Highway 180 from Fresno or Highway 198 from Visalia and Three Rivers. Both approach routes have seen more curves than a retired Dodgers catcher. Reach the signed Little Baldy Trail 6.7 miles beyond Lodgepole Campground (via Visalia) or 1.6 miles beyond Dorst Campground (via Fresno), and park in the roadside pulloff at the 7,335-foot Little Baldy Saddle.

Set out on a shaded trail, which climbs gently beneath thick white firs. The forest floor boasts a host of ferns and a multitude of wildflowers. Watch for tall, red pinedrops hiding in the shadows. The steady incline eases briefly at 0.2 mile, but the ascent soon kicks in again.

Continue up the hill to gain a view of Big Baldy at the 0.4-mile point. You'll see this barren, granite dome off to the left, glowing above a dark-green foreground of unending trees. The murmur of the almost constant traffic on the Generals Highway will keep pace with you as you press on.

Ascend the hill in increasingly rocky switchbacks and lose the cooling shade as the trees begin to thin. Scattered Jeffrey pines sweeten the air with the aroma of their butterscotch-scented trunks. Top a rise at 1.3 miles, and begin a gentle descent through thick red firs. A brief climb at 1.5 miles yields a dramatic view of distant mountains.

Continue on as a jagged line of peaks unfolds on the horizon. You'll be gazing at the heights of Sequoia National Park as you begin to climb more steeply. With any luck, the scenery will take your mind off your legs.

Start into the final uphill push toward Little Baldy's summit at 1.8 miles. Your pain will end atop this treeless granite dome, 2.0 miles from the trailhead and 8,040 feet above sea level. Suck in your breath and gaze around you. The panorama from the top of Little Baldy is fantastic on a cloudless Sierra day.

You'll almost always find a wall of haze obscuring the vista to the west, but a rugged line of mountains rules the north, east, and south, poking at the heavens like a freshly painted picket fence. Settle down on a sun-warmed slab of granite, unpack a picnic and a topographic map, and feast your senses on the loveliness of the Sierra.

• •

16 TOKOPAH FALLS

Distance: 3.8 miles round trip
Difficulty: Easy
Starting point: 6,750 feet
High point: 7,380 feet
Map: USGS Lodgepole 7.5'

This pleasant family outing to Tokopah Falls is a must if you're staying at Lodgepole Campground. Those in quest of quietness should hike early in the morning, when mule deer and marmots meander along the route. Don't expect too much solitude later in the day—the trail is often busy. Even so, it offers a scenic trek beside the Marble Fork of the Kaweah River, and it's a great chance to trade the pavement and pandemonium of Lodgepole Campground for a shaded stroll away from civilization.

To reach the trailhead for Tokopah Falls, take the Lodgepole

Campground turnoff from the Generals Highway, and drive in 0.7 mile to the signed Tokopah Valley Trail. There's trailhead parking just before a log bridge across the Marble Fork. The trail begins across the water. (Park Service information on this trail lists it as 1.7 miles one way, but our measurements yielded a 1.9-mile figure.)

Set out beside the Marble Fork, with views across the river to the tentspots strung along the shore. Afternoons bring scores of swimmers and anglers to the riverbanks as well, but the crowds begin to thin as you leave the campground environs.

Climb very gently beneath a canopy of red firs, Jeffrey pines, and incense cedars, and keep an eye out for the impressive form of the Watchtower bristling above the river canyon as you hike. This 1,600-foot cliff survived the grinding passage of the Tokopah Glacier, the massive chisel of moving ice that sculpted this U-shaped canyon millions of years ago.

If you have young children with you, be sure to pause to let them sniff the trunks of the handsome Jeffrey pines along the route. They'll love the sweet butterscotch odor of these trees. Wildflowers are abundant, too. Watch for nude buckwheat and broadleaf lupine beside the trail. Closer to the water, leopard lily, Bigelow's sneezeweed, and coneflowers add spots of color to the scenery.

Pass a small waterfall and a handful of inviting wading pools at 0.6 mile. Please use caution if you plan to get your feet wet. The water is very cold, and the current can be treacherous when the early runoff is at its height.

The Tokopah Valley Trail continues at a gentle incline beside the Marble Fork. Children may require a helping hand through a few brief rocky sections, but most of the route is easy. At 1.2 miles, reach a tempting nook where the Marble Fork scoots across a bench of water-smoothed stone. Cross a feeder stream on a footbridge just after.

Views of the Watchtower unfold as you walk to a second bridge at 1.3 miles. The forest floor is green with bracken ferns through here.

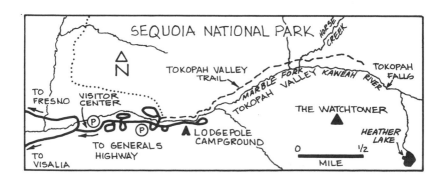

Another bridge beckons at 1.4 miles. Continue on through red firs and Jeffrey pines.

You'll get your first peek at the 1,200-foot-high Tokopah Falls at 1.6 miles. The scene's impressiveness is measured in direct proportion to the water level of the Marble Fork. Early in the season, when the runoff is abundant, Tokopah Falls is a wonderful cascade of gushing water. Later in the summer, it's simply a pretty picture, a score of rivulets trickling across a wall of rock festooned with cheery, yellow common monkeyflower.

Wind on through an increasingly rocky landscape. The trail is shadeless here, except when it ducks beneath some rather daunting overhanging boulders. You'll reach the trail's surprisingly abrupt end near the base of Tokopah Falls at 1.9 miles. Except for the view of the falls and canyon, the place is unappealing—backtrack to a favorite spot along the river to spread your picnic.

17 HEATHER LAKE

Distance: 8.4 miles round trip
Difficulty: Moderate
Starting point: 7,280 feet
High point: 9,500 feet
Map: USGS Lodgepole 7.5'

The best part of this hike is the scenery along the way. Heather Lake itself is a pleasant destination, but it's really not spectacular. The two lakes that lie beyond it are nicer. Seasoned hikers should start early in the day and continue on to Emerald Lake (1.1 miles farther) or even Pear Lake (1.0 mile past Emerald Lake) if they have the energy.

To find the trailhead for Heather Lake, take the Wolverton turn-off from the Generals Highway (2.7 miles northeast of Giant Forest Village), and drive 1.5 miles on paved road to the trailhead parking lot. Begin walking at a sign for the Lakes Trail.

Climb through a red fir forest, and reach a junction with the trail from Lodgepole Campground at 0.1 mile. Stay right with the Lakes Trail (don't take the Long Meadow Trail, which turns sharply to the right), and continue gently up through trees. The forest floor is dry and open here, scattered with chinquapin, nude buckwheat, and gayophytum.

Begin following a wildflower-lined creek at 0.9 mile. Enjoy the company of broadleaf lupine, cow parsnip, leopard lily, and arrowleaf groundsel as you climb. You'll meander through a spearmint-scented meadow at 1.7 miles. Cross the creek, and reach a trail junction at 1.8 miles. Go left here for Heather Lake.

Ascend to cross another flowery little waterway at 2.0 miles, and then endure a steady uphill to arrive at the junction of the Hump and the Watchtower trails at 2.1 miles. The route to Heather Lake via the Hump is a bit shorter, but it's also steeper and less scenic. However, it's a good option for early-season hiking (if snow is present) and for those who suffer a fear of heights. When possible, keep to the left to take the dizzying Watchtower Trail instead.

The grade mellows for a while. Make yet another creek crossing at 2.6 miles. The flowers are spectacular in July. Look for tower larkspur, common monkeyflower, arrowleaf groundsel, and broadleaf lupine. A series of switchbacks will have you breathing hard at the 3.3-mile point, and the unfolding view will have you gasping with delight.

Pause on the cliffs for an amazing vista down into the canyon cut by the Marble Fork of the Kaweah River. It's a long way down from here, so please be careful. Resist the temptation to explore the use trails that lead out toward the precipice. You'll have plenty of spectacular views from the safety of the main trail.

Look for Silver Peak and Mount Silliman in the distance. The massive prow of granite that rules the canyon wall above Tokopah Falls is the 1,600-foot-high rock formation known as the Watchtower. Climb steeply to gain a trail hewn into the cliff face above Tokopah Valley at 3.7 miles. You'll spot the Tokopah Valley Trail to Tokopah Falls below.

This is the best part of the entire hike (unless you're uncomfortable with heights). The trail is as spectacular as the view. When you can tear your eyes from the distant panorama of peaks and precipices, focus on the loveliness of mountain pride penstemon and delicate Coville's columbine in the rocks right at your feet.

Turn away from the cliffs at 4.1 miles. The Hump Trail will join in from the right as you continue on. Gain the shore of little Heather Lake at 4.2 miles. With a rocky shoreline and some nice dropoffs for would-be swimmers, Heather Lake is a pleasant picnic destination. Since it's off limits to backpacking overnighters, it should be fairly quiet.

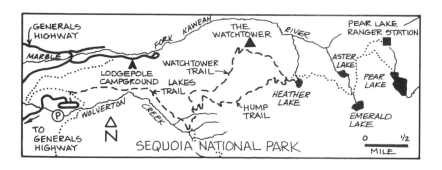

The Watchtower Trail, which leads to Heather Lake, is cut from solid stone.

Return to your starting point via either the Hump or the Watchtower trail, or press on toward lovely Emerald Lake or the shimmering Pear Lake at trail's end.

18 BIG TREES HIKE

Distance: 4.3 miles (loop)
Difficulty: Easy
Starting point: 6,900 feet
High point: 7,000 feet
Maps: USGS Giant Forest 7.5' and USGS Lodgepole 7.5'

This enjoyable family hike begins on the 2.0-mile Congress Trail, perhaps the most-often-hiked trail in Sequoia National Park. Despite the crowds, the Congress Trail is worth a visit. It takes in a handful of the world's most impressive giant sequoias. Combine the Congress Trail with the remainder of this hike and you'll have a fine mix of solitude and splendor.

To find the trailhead, drive the Generals Highway 2.1 miles east of Giant Forest Village, and turn off at a sign for the General Sherman Tree. There's a vast, paved parking area just off the highway, complete with restrooms and a lot of steaming tour buses. Informational pamphlets for the Congress Trail are available at the trailhead, for a small fee.

Begin your trek at the trail sign for the Sherman Tree—why not start with the biggest first? A brief climb leads to the base of this forest giant, where a sign proclaims the Sherman Tree to be the "largest living thing on earth" (based on a volume of 52,500 cubic feet).

You'll hear a score of foreign languages being spoken as you pause to marvel at the base of this beautiful tree. Join the crowd, and ask a

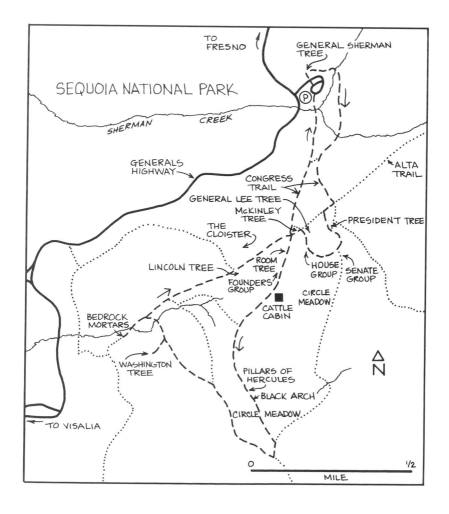

stranger to snap your photo while you linger here. From the base of the General Sherman Tree, turn right and walk to the self-guiding-pamphlet dispenser. Then continue along the sidewalk to a sign for the Congress Trail.

Go left here to begin your forest hike. You'll start by crossing shimmering Sherman Creek on a wooden footbridge and then walk past the Leaning Tree. Climb gently on an asphalt pathway, pacing beneath sequoias and scores of shade-dispensing firs.

Pause for a look at the fire-scarred sequoia marked by Signpost 6. The fact that it's still standing is a testimony to the tenacity of the species. Cross beneath a fallen tree at 0.4 mile. Then reach a junction at 0.5 mile, and keep left on the Congress Trail.

Continue climbing to a junction with the signed Alta Trail at 0.9 mile. Stay right with the asphalt pathway, and descend through a picturesque setting of broadleaf lupine and dozens of towering sequoias. Follow the Congress Trail to the feet of The President at 1.1 miles, and walk on to view The Senate shortly after. The group of sequoias known as The Senate is a lovely cluster of closely spaced giants. The trees form a picture you won't soon forget.

Stay with the signed Congress Trail at the next junction, and descend through a forest awash in broadleaf lupine and bracken ferns to find The House at 1.3 miles. Like its counterpart, The Senate, this group of sequoias is enchanting, especially when the morning sun slants through the ancient trunks, glowing more golden than the promises of a politician.

Continue on to pass the General Lee Tree, and keep left with the Congress Trail to reach a junction beside the McKinley Tree at 1.4 miles. Make your escape from the crowds as you abandon the busy Congress Trail and go left on a pathway signed for Cattle Cabin.

Descend past the Room Tree on the unpaved trail. The forest floor is spectacular here, a canvas painted with trees and sun and blossoming lupine. Pass through the Founders Group at 1.6 miles, and arrive at Circle Meadow soon after (Cattle Cabin is just beyond). Continue to the right with the trail, hiking beside flower-filled Circle Meadow as you proceed to a junction at 1.8 miles.

Go left here for Crescent Meadow, and pace an undulating trail through firs and giant sequoias. Your path will take you between two mighty stumps, called the Pillars of Hercules, at 2.1 miles. Next you'll tiptoe through the Black Arch. Descend to cross Circle Meadow just after.

Pause to enjoy the view along the meadow and listen to a symphony of blossoms, played out by California corn lily, leopard lily, arrowleaf groundsel, and Sierra rein orchid. Reach a junction at 2.2 miles, and continue to the right for Crescent Meadow. Go right again for the Washington Tree 0.1 mile later.

Descend to walk along the edge of Circle Meadow. Then angle left for the Washington Tree at 2.6 miles. Your undulating route leads to a short spur trail for the Washington Tree at 2.9 miles. Keep right at the junction, following the sign for the Alta Trail.

You'll reach a junction with the Alta Trail at 3.1 miles. A short side trip to the left leads to a scattering of bedrock mortars and an interesting glimpse into the daily lives of the Indians who inhabited this forest before the arrival of the Europeans. Return to the junction and continue on toward the Congress Trail as you begin to close your loop.

Stay with signs for the Congress Trail to reach the Lincoln Tree at 3.6 miles. Continue straight on the Alta Trail, passing the serene group of sequoias known as The Cloister along the way. You'll regain the paved and populated Congress Trail at the McKinley Tree (3.7 miles). Go left here to return to your starting point at 4.3 miles.

19 CRESCENT MEADOW

Distance: 2.3 miles (loop)
Difficulty: Easy
Starting point: 6,700 feet
High point: 6,880 feet
Map: USGS Lodgepole 7.5'

Tiger lilies run wild in the grass of Crescent Meadow.

Like the preceding Big Trees Hike, this walk in Crescent Meadow promises a visual overload of forest beauty combined with entirely too many hiking companions. However, the tourist crowds are worth enduring in exchange for the charms of Crescent Meadow. Bring along the family for fun, take a ton of film for the flowers, and douse yourself with bug juice for the often murderous mosquitoes.

To reach the Crescent Meadow trailhead, turn off the Generals Highway at Giant Forest Village, and take the paved road signed for Moro Rock and Crescent Meadow. Drive 2.7 miles to the large parking area at road's end. You'll find restrooms and drinking water here. Please be sure to cover any foodstuff in your vehicle—bears make occasional parking lot patrols.

If you have the time, be sure to pause at Moro Rock before or after your trek through Crescent Meadow (the Moro Rock turnoff is 1.3 miles off the Generals Highway on the road to the Crescent Meadow trailhead). Moro Rock provides a spectacular view down on the Kaweah River, with a vista that encompasses the Great Western Divide and the flatlands out toward Fresno. With 353 stair steps and a 300-foot elevation gain, the walk to the top of the rock is short but challenging—and definitely not for an acrophobic hiker!

From the parking lot at the Crescent Meadow trailhead, begin walking at a sign for the High Sierra Trail. (This backpackers' trail leads 70 miles east to the summit of Mount Whitney.) Your asphalt pathway skirts along the edge of Crescent Meadow, a spectacular swath of flower-speckled green, immortalized by the writings of John Muir a century ago and guarded by an encircling battalion of giant sequoias today.

Reach a junction at 0.1 mile, and go left for Tharp's Log. You'll go left again at 0.3 mile, keeping to the edge of Crescent Meadow with the trail toward the Chimney Tree. Pause often to savor the sweetness of the meadow. Pick the flowers with your camera (and *only* with your camera), sampling bistort, Sierra rein orchid, Bigelow's sneezeweed, Indian paintbrush, shooting star, tiger lily, arrowleaf groundsel, and broadleaf lupine.

Set against a backdrop of dark tree trunks, the glowing green of the sunlight-splattered meadow will almost take your breath away. Turn into the forest on a trail edged with lush ferns and broadleaf lupine, and reach a junction at 0.7 mile. You'll go right for Tharp's Log here, but first explore the short side trail to the amazing Chimney Tree.

Climb away from the junction on a winding trail, and make the short descent to Log Meadow and Tharp's Log at 1.0 mile. Hale Tharp was the first white man to taste the treasures of the Giant Forest. He brought his cattle to this hidden meadow more than 100 years ago, pass-

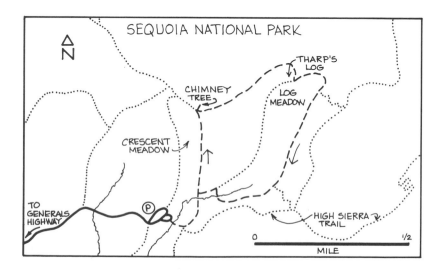

Giant sequoias and abundant wildflowers paint an exquisite picture in Crescent Meadow.

ing the sweltering months of summer living in the cool shadows of the hollowed-out Tharp's Log.

Continue on toward the High Sierra Trail as you depart Tharp's Log, tracing the perimeter of Log Meadow. This is a hauntingly beautiful scene, a hymn to the ongoing life of the forest. Massive fallen giants sprawl across the meadow floor, their long-dead trunks impervious to decay, their once-green needles replaced by sprays of living wildflowers.

Use the toppled sequoias as gangways into the center of the meadow, saving the flowers from your footsteps while you gain unforgettable vistas of the surrounding loveliness. A junction at 1.2 miles will lead you on toward the High Sierra Trail. Tiptoe along the edge of Log Meadow as you continue to another junction at 1.7 miles.

Go right here for Crescent Meadow, leaving Log Meadow for a bit of forest hiking. You'll reach the main trail and go left. Veer left once more as you regain the edge of Crescent Meadow, and keep right at the next junction to return to the parking lot at 2.3 miles.

. . . .

20 ATWELL GROVE AND PARADISE PEAK

Distance: 11.0 miles round trip
Difficulty: Strenuous
Starting point: 6,520 feet
High point: 9,360 feet
Map: USGS Silver City 7.5'

The statistics for this hike can be deceiving. Although the climb to Paradise Peak is a strenuous 11.0-mile trek, please don't let that stop you in your tracks. This hike has great potential as a family outing, especially for those staying in the adjacent Atwell Mill Campground. Simply walk as long or short a distance as you like. You'll get a look at a wonderful assortment of giant sequoias before you've gone a mile.

To find the trailhead for Atwell Grove and Paradise Peak, please refer to the driving directions for Atwell Mill Campground at the beginning of this chapter. The trailhead parking lot is just beyond the campground entrance on the Mineral King Road. It's signed "Hockett Trailhead Parking."

The trailhead itself is situated before the campground entrance, 0.3 mile from the trailhead parking lot. It's signed for Paradise Ridge and Redwood Meadow. By the way, don't believe the mileages listed by the Park Service on the trailhead sign—they're not even close!

Begin climbing in the shade of thick incense cedars and white firs, following a trail edged by fragrant mountain misery. Deer tracks are quite common here. Sharp-eyed hikers may be surprised (and a bit unsettled) by the sight of bear prints, too. Just make plenty of noise if you suspect a bear is in the neighborhood—and, whatever you do, don't flaunt your candy bars.

Ascend steadily in countless switchbacks. Jeffrey pines and sugar pines contribute to the vast variety of trees this hike has to offer. You'll gain a view across the canyon at 0.6 mile as the grade eases for a time. Then climb into the first big grouping of giant sequoias not long afterward.

The trees are beautiful, towering silently above the trail, their trunks glowing red in the filtered sunlight. The sequoias evoke a kind of reverence here. Hidden away on this forested hillside, they seem so timeless, so untouched by tourism, so unsullied by the Park Service's well-meaning but ill-advised exploitation.

Ascend through a lush ravine awash in ferns and broadleaf lupine

The view from Paradise Peak is simply heavenly. (Photo by Kay Hartley)

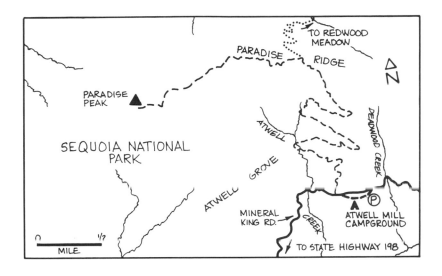

at 1.0 mile. Fallen sequoias have transformed the hillside into a giants'
cemetery. The atmosphere is almost eerie, and you may find yourself
whispering as you pass. Climb on across a more open slope with views
toward the upper reaches of the East Fork of the Kaweah River.

Manzanita, mountain misery, and assorted brambles threaten to
overrun the trail. Struggle upward to gain another treat at the 1.8-mile
point. More sequoias linger in the shadows here, guarding both sides of
the path like sentries expecting an enemy attack. Walk onward through
the trees, slipping and sliding on handfuls of grenadelike sequoia cones.
If the incline allows it, sneak a smile at the incongruity of those tiny
cones and the enormous trees.

Now the switchbacks become more serious, attacking the hill with
renewed energy. If you're doing this hike for the trees, turn back to
wander downhill with the trail. If you're en route to Paradise Peak,
heave a sigh and shift into low gear.

You'll arrive at a saddle in Paradise Ridge with 3.2 miles behind
you, legs groaning and brow damp with sweat. Unfortunately, there's not
much of a view from here. The trail to the right continues on toward
Redwood Meadow. Take the route to the left toward Paradise Peak,
tracing a lonely, difficult-to-follow trail along the tree-covered ridgetop.

Intermittent ducks will help you in your quest to find the route.
Some sections of the trail are lined with stones. Even so, you'll need
to be alert. The climb picks up steam as you continue, and views will
come and go through the nonstop blur of trees.

Skirt to the right of a granite knoll at 4.0 miles. The short scramble
to its top yields a view of Mineral and Sawtooth peaks. Push onward

with vistas of the Castle Rocks to the north. A brief level stretch melts into more steady climbing through red firs and western white pines.

Pick your way along an increasingly open, rocky ridgeline as your legs begin to falter. Suddenly you'll arrive, gaining the flat-topped pile of boulders known as Paradise Peak at 5.5 miles. Zowie!

A small weather station and a USGS marker identify the spot. It seems rather anticlimactic—until you sample the view. Peer over the edge of the rocky outcropping, and hang on! You'll be looking down the side of a cliff that drops 6,000 feet in one leap, all the way to the banks of Paradise Creek. This isn't a sight an acrophobic hiker will enjoy.

Gaze northward at the impressive vista of the Castle Rocks. Tourist-haunted Moro Rock is visible beyond, looking rather uninspiring from this angle. The view up into the heights of Mineral King is wonderful, encompassing Mineral Peak, White Chief Peak, and Hengst Peak.

Pull out a camera and a topographic map, and spend an hour matching names to the surrounding scenery. There's no doubt about it, this spot is captivating. Just remember to keep one eye on the clouds and the other on your watch—it's a long way down from Paradise.

· ·
21 LOWER MONARCH LAKE

Distance: 9.4 miles round trip
Difficulty: Strenuous
Starting point: 7,800 feet
High point: 10,380 feet
Map: USGS Mineral King 7.5'

If you're in quest of spectacular and strenuous hiking, you can't do better on the western side of the Sierra than to visit the Mineral King area of Sequoia National Park. This trek to Lower Monarch Lake is among the finest day hikes the region has to offer. Start early in the day, carry plenty of water, and prepare yourself for a visual treat and a physical challenge you'll be talking about long after.

To find the trailhead for Lower Monarch Lake, drive Highway 198 northeast from Visalia, and turn off at Hammond (3.6 miles beyond Three Rivers) at a sign for Mineral King. Follow the narrow, winding Mineral King Road 24.7 miles to arrive at the signed Sawtooth Trail parking area. Space is limited here, and you'll be in competition with bevies of backpackers on weekends. If you're staying at Cold Springs Campground, you might consider establishing a car shuttle to cover the 1.0-mile distance to the trailhead.

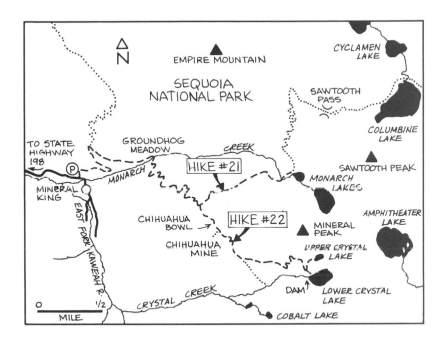

Begin hiking on the north side of the road, climbing away from the parking area on a rocky trail lined with sage and manzanita. Watch for the white faces of the diminutive mariposa lily peeking out from the dry soil.

Endure steady uphill walking through scattered Sierra junipers. You'll spot White Chief Peak on the right and 11,947-foot Vandever Mountain on the left as you curl in toward tumbling Monarch Creek. Arrive at a junction for Timber Gap at 0.6 mile (at the end of a long switchback away from Monarch Creek).

Continue to the right for Monarch Lake, ascending in moderately graded switchbacks. The 1.0-mile point brings a series of short, steep zigzags up the hillside. Climb beside Monarch Creek, enjoying the company of red penstemon, lupine, and yarrow.

Reach Groundhog Meadow at 1.3 miles. You'll be greeted by a wildflower extravaganza here. Tiger lily, corn lily, shooting star, swamp onion, and Indian paintbrush all compete for the admiration of gasping hikers. Keep to the right for Monarch Lake, and cross Monarch Creek as you push onward and upward.

A red fir forest offers welcome shade for a time. Then the terrain opens up again as the trail continues at a mellow incline. Work your way up a lush hillside in a score of switchbacks. Please be sure to stick with the main trail here. One unmarked use trail heads into the rocky reaches of Monarch Canyon—it's not a recommended shortcut!

The marvels of Sawtooth Pass await those who venture beyond Lower Monarch Lake.

You'll round a bend at 3.1 miles and be greeted with your best views yet of Vandever Mountain (on the left) and White Chief Peak (on the right). Continue up a lupine-covered hillside, and reach a junction for Crystal Lakes at 3.5 miles. Stay straight for Monarch Lake.

A steady climb leads up through Monarch Canyon, with spectacular views ahead to rugged Sawtooth Pass and 12,343-foot Sawtooth Peak. Early-season hikers often encounter snow through here. Footing can be treacherous on this steep-sided trail. Please be careful, and don't push farther than your abilities allow.

If you're free to gaze at the view, the scene is simply glorious. You'll gain a new array of wildflowers with increasing elevation, too. Look for rockfringe, mountain sorrel, myriads of Coville's columbine, and a glittering galaxy of alpine shooting star.

The trail degenerates into a pathway through loose shale at 4.1 miles. Walking is rougher and slower as you curve into the canyon. Gain a view of Monarch Creek with the needle-pointed Mineral Peak above it at 4.5 miles. You'll cross Monarch Creek at 4.6 miles, wading through a flood of alpine shooting star. Continue climbing to reach beautiful little Lower Monarch Lake at 4.7 miles. What a scene! The lake is clear and deep, overlooked by the distinctive form of 11,615-foot Mineral Peak and fed by the white-flecked cascade trickling down from Upper Monarch Lake. Wildflowers dot the shoreline of the lake, as do occasional backpackers and anglers. Although the frigid water of Lower Monarch Lake will probably cool your swimmer's ardor, you'll surely want to sample the scenic beauty of the spot while you spread your picnic lunch. There are a few possibilities for further exploring from here, if time and energy allows. A short but rocky scramble (with no defined trail) leads up to the larger of the Monarch lakes. Or you can continue with the exceedingly steep and rugged main trail to the crest of Sawtooth Pass.

The climb to Sawtooth Pass involves an additional 1,200 feet of elevation gain and will add 2.8 miles to your round-trip total for the day. It's a tough, tough haul across loose rocks—definitely not for timid or tired hikers. However, the view from Sawtooth Pass is magnificent, extending north and east to a score of peaks.

• •

22 CRYSTAL LAKES

Distance: 10.8 miles round trip
Difficulty: Strenuous
Starting point: 7,800 feet
High point: 10,850 feet
Map: USGS Mineral King 7.5'

The hike to the Crystal lakes is long and arduous, suitable only for the very fit (and perhaps the slightly masochistic). If you're in this simply for the scenery and you haven't visited Lower Monarch Lake yet, go there instead (Hike 21). The trail is better, and the lake is prettier.

But if you want to lose the hordes of Sawtooth Pass–bound back-packers that make the Monarch Lake Trail seem like a foot freeway at times, then give this challenging hike a chance. You won't be disappointed—but you will be weary at day's end.

To begin the trek to the Crystal lakes, please refer to the first eight paragraphs of Hike 21, Lower Monarch Lake. From the junction at the 3.5-mile point, go right for Crystal Lakes. Ascend on a rugged trail, gasping for oxygen as the climb quickly gains intensity.

Pass a use trail descending to the right, and continue steeply up, working your way through an open basin dotted with scrubby white-bark pines. If you glance behind you when you pause to rest, you'll be treated to a spectacular view of the mountains across the Kaweah Canyon.

The climb eases slightly at 3.8 miles as you ascend through the Chihuahua Bowl, site of the old Chihuahua Mine. Look for the mine site off to the right of the trail. It's marked by stone foundations, discarded lumber, and piled tailings.

This lofty basin was the starting point for an avalanche that demolished a building down on the valley floor in 1969, but winter snows will seem far away as you climb past an abundance of wildflowers on the rugged trail. Struggle upward past sulfur flower, meadow penstemon, and mountain heather, enduring a brutal ascent to the ridge above. The climb ends (none too soon) at 4.1 miles.

You'll pause in the shade of stout foxtail pines as you gain a lofty notch in the ridgeline. The view is magnificent from here. Continue along the hillside with the trail, descending gently for a time. Look for little Cobalt Lake below. Its outlet feeds into the chilly waters of Crystal

Lower Crystal Lake sparkles with harsh beauty.

Creek, and together they tumble down toward the East Fork of the Kaweah River.

Keep a sharp eye out for an unsigned trail junction at 4.2 miles. A piled-stone duck should help you identify the spot where the trail splits. A well-defined trail descends toward Cobalt Lake from here, luring many would-be visitors to the Crystal lakes into an unplanned detour. Keep to the left instead, following the much fainter trail along the hillside and maintaining your elevation.

Enjoy level walking through ferns and manzanita. The voice of Crystal Creek will lend its cadence to your steps. If you gaze above you, you'll see the niche where this lovely waterway spills out of the basin that cradles Lower Crystal Lake. That's the climb that's still ahead of you.

Shift into low gear as the ascent kicks in again at 4.5 miles, and pace a rocky trail lined with altitude-loving wildflowers. Alpine shooting star, purple gentian, Bigelow's sneezeweed, and swamp onion will guard your faltering steps as you continue.

Struggle upward through a set of steep and rocky switchbacks. You'll probably be questioning the wisdom of this trek by now. Cheer your groaning muscles with the songs sung by tiny wildflowers tucked into the rocks, or let your eyes listen to the melodies rung by bell-shaped Cobalt Lake below. If the gruesome incline and the meager oxygen level don't finish you, you'll hit your high note at the 5.0-mile mark.

Pass a duck and the cutoff trail to Upper Crystal Lake soon after. (It's a short side trip to the upper lake, well worth the detour.) Continue straight toward Lower Crystal Lake, and gain the dam at the lake's outlet at 5.2 miles.

Set into a lofty saucer of granite and ruled by peaks, Lower Crystal Lake is pristine and petite. The steep rock walls around the lake are flecked with patches of lingering snow, sprayed here and there like drops of milk from the tongue of a lapping cat. The lake's cold, clear water holds hungry fish for those with fishing poles and offers frigid temperatures for those with hike-heated toes.

Pause on the dam built by the Mount Whitney Power Company in 1903, and reward your day's efforts with a vista you'll long remember. You'll have a wonderful view of Mineral Peak, looming above the trail that leads toward the upper lake. The panorama of the entire Mineral King area from the dam is exquisite.

Savor the spot awhile, and then make the 0.2-mile jaunt to the smaller but lovely Upper Crystal Lake before you turn for home. Skilled scramblers may be tempted to climb to the ridgeline above Upper Crystal Lake and make the steep descent to the Monarch lakes from there, converting this hike into a challenging but extremely scenic loop. It's a wonderful route, but please don't attempt it without a good map, clear skies, and a wealth of experience.

. . . .

23 MOSQUITO LAKES

Distance: 8.4 miles round trip
Difficulty: Strenuous
Starting point: 7,800 feet
High point: 9,600 feet
Total climb: 2,400
Map: USGS Mineral King 7.5'

The hike to the Mosquito lakes is not the best trek that the Mineral King area has to offer. The trail is much less enjoyable than the route up White Chief Canyon (Hike 25), and the destination offered by Lower Mosquito Lake is much less scenic than that presented by Eagle Lake (Hike 24). But this hike pays its dividends on a sliding scale. Invest the energy in a scramble to one of the upper Mosquito lakes and you'll be amply rewarded for your efforts.

The trek to the upper lakes isn't for everyone, however. Please don't try this hike without good scrambling skills, an excellent sense of direction, a topographic map, and a bountiful supply of energy.

To reach the trailhead for the Mosquito lakes, drive Highway 198 northeast from Visalia, and turn off at Hammond (3.6 miles beyond Three Rivers) at a sign for Mineral King. Follow the narrow, winding Mineral King Road 25.0 miles to road's end and the often overflowing trailhead parking area. The Mosquito Lake–Eagle Lake–White Chief Canyon trail takes off at the far end of the parking lot.

Begin climbing on a sage-lined trail, hiking just above the East Fork of the Kaweah River. Admire the handsome form of 11,947-foot Vandever Mountain straight ahead. Just to the left of it is the pointed Tulare Peak. You'll cross columbine-edged Spring Creek on a wooden footbridge at 0.3 mile.

Continue upward, passing an unmarked side trail descending toward a pack station, and ascend along an open hillside decorated with the blossoms of mariposa lily, red penstemon, Indian paintbrush, and nude buckwheat. If you gaze directly across the Kaweah River canyon, you'll spot lovely Crystal Creek trailing down the canyon wall like a white silk ribbon.

The grade intensifies at 1.0 mile. Climb steeply through red fir shade to reach a junction at 1.1 miles. Go right here for Eagle Lake, and ascend in challenging switchbacks for a while. A meadowy hillside flanks the trail at 1.4 miles. The alpine beauty of larkspur, tiger lily, bistort, arrowleaf groundsel, and common monkeyflower will ease your pain as you continue.

Ducks lead the way to Upper Mosquito Lake.

The incline mellows mercifully at 1.7 miles, and you'll reach the shaded banks of Eagle Creek soon after. Watch for the mysterious sinkhole where Eagle Creek dives into oblivion. No one is certain where the water reappears.

Continue up beside the little waterway, enjoying the cooling shadows of red firs and lodgepole and western white pines. A trail junction awaits at 2.0 miles. Keep to the right for the Mosquito lakes, and walk a level trail for a while. Alas, the climb kicks in too soon.

Start up an open hillside where lupine, nude buckwheat, and meadow penstemon hide among the sage. Steep and rocky switchbacks yield a wonderful view across the canyon to Sawtooth and Mineral peaks. Even if you're cursing at the trail, the sight can't help but cheer you.

A brief descent at 2.3 miles leads into more mellow walking along a hillside dotted with chinquapin. The ascent regains its vigor at the 2.8-mile point, and you'll climb beneath thick trees on a trail that's deep in fallen needles. A fistful of fatiguing switchbacks leads to a tree-filled saddle at 3.0 miles.

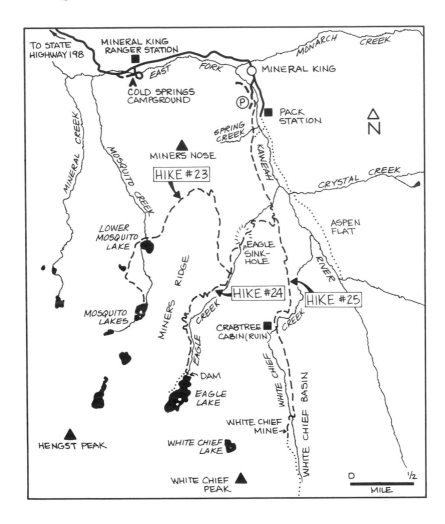

There's good news and bad news here. The good news is you're about to start downhill. The bad news is you'll have 300 unwelcome feet to climb on your way back out. Try not to think about it as you zigzag downward through a red fir forest. Purple-blossomed lupine brightens the ground beneath the trees.

The incline mellows at 3.4 miles, and you'll gain sight of Lower Mosquito Lake soon afterward. Reach the shore of this small lake at 3.7 miles. If you're visiting during mosquito season, you'll have little desire to linger here. The lake is ringed by trees and grass, and Labrador tea and mountain heather run wild on the shore.

Pause for a brief breather, and then push on toward the upper lake. Angle right along the lakeshore, and cross Lower Mosquito Lake's outlet creek. You'll pick up an unsigned use trail heading up a rocky, forested draw. Now the real work begins.

Climb steadily through lodgepole pines and red firs, watching for the ducks and blazes that mark the route. The trail is difficult to follow, but you should do fine if you use your head and your map. Piled ducks lead upward through one very rocky section. Then you'll gain a small, flat basin with a pothole lake.

Leave level ground and climb through granite once again. A wearying ascent leads up through handsome foxtail pines. You'll be breathing hard when you gain the shore of the upper lake at 4.2 miles and 9,600 feet. Wow! No matter how many times you scraped your knees or banged your shins on the climb from the lower lake, you'll agree this Mosquito lake is worth the trip.

It's spectacular—large and deep, ringed by granite and crowned with a rocky island set like a jewel in its center. Scowling Hengst Peak rules the heights above the lake, and a cool alpine breeze rushes across the water to suck the perspiration from your skin. This lake has the feel of the High Sierra. It has the look of it, too.

More Mosquito lakes await above, if you have the time and the strength to look for them. But even if you choose to end your day of exploring here, you'll turn homeward with the taste of the Sierra forming a smile on your lips.

. . . .

24 EAGLE LAKE

Distance: 6.8 miles round trip
Difficulty: Strenuous
Starting point: 7,800 feet
High point: 10,050 feet
Map: USGS Mineral King 7.5'

This scenic trek to Eagle Lake is one of the easier hikes in the Mineral King area of Sequoia National Park. Even so, it's still very challenging, with inclines made more difficult by the lofty elevation. If you're planning to do several day hikes in the area, this is a good warm-up trip.

To begin your trek to Eagle Lake, please refer to the beginning of Hike 23, Mosquito Lakes. From the trail junction at the 2.0-mile point, continue with the left-hand branch for Eagle Lake. A short stretch of level walking provides a breather before another climb begins at 2.2 miles.

Eagle Lake is a picture-perfect Sierra destination.

Ascend on a steep, rocky, and shadeless trail, and feast your eyes on the expanding views. The incline eases briefly at 2.6 miles, but this is just the introduction to another challenging assault on the seemingly unending hill.

Endure slow going on an extremely rocky trail, and console yourself with wonderful views across the canyon to Sawtooth Pass and Mineral Peak. Tear your gaze from the distant scene to feast on the banquet of mountain pride penstemon nestled among the rocks. You'll escape the worst of the terrain at 3.0 miles, working into a more moderate ascent paced by the song of Eagle Creek. Reach the shore of lofty Eagle Lake at 3.4 miles.

The headwall behind the lake is a fortress of shining granite flecked with tenacious patches of unyielding snow, even in late July. Wander out onto the dam at the close end of the lake to gain a perfect photo or picnic spot. The views are great in both directions.

You'll probably see a few backpackers camping at Eagle Lake and you might hear the voice of a visiting angler. But this lovely corner of the wilderness is usually uncrowded, and it invites you to enjoy a leisurely afternoon of quietness.

25 WHITE CHIEF CANYON

Distance: 7.0 miles round trip
Difficulty: Strenuous
Starting point: 7,800 feet
High point: 9,600 feet
Map: USGS Mineral King 7.5'

Like the trek to Eagle Lake (Hike 24), the walk up White Chief Canyon is one of the less-demanding hikes the Mineral King area has to offer. If you're looking for a pleasant family outing, consider putting White Chief Canyon on your itinerary. Just remember, this hike is far from easy.

Wildflower lovers will be delighted with the canyon's meadow finery early in the season, and would-be spelunkers will find the canyon's array of abandoned mine shafts tantalizing. Be sure to carry a strong flashlight if you plan to do any exploring, and please proceed with the utmost caution.

To begin your White Chief Canyon walk, please refer to the beginning of Hike 23, Mosquito Lakes. From the junction at the 1.1-mile point, keep to the left for White Chief Canyon. You'll climb steadily from here, and the hill gains fury with every step. This is the worst section of the trek—known in hiking circles as a "grunt." Don't be afraid to take it slow and indulge in frequent rest stops.

Console yourself with views across the Kaweah Canyon, or count the pack horses and hikers on the trail to Farewell Gap. The punishing uphill continues mercilessly, but heavy-branched red firs offer much-needed shade as you ascend. Gain sight of the little waterway coming out of the White Chief Basin just before a short switchback offers some respite from the exhausting climb.

Peaks begin to pop out everywhere as you gain altitude. Continue up on an increasingly rocky trail, and marvel at the haunting shapes of twisted Sierra junipers among the stones. You'll pick up the company of bushy foxtail pines as well, a testimony to the lofty elevation here. Pause for a postcard view back the way you've come. The scene encompasses pointy-topped Mineral Peak and the rugged Sawtooth ridgeline.

Press on and ease into an open, rocky bowl ringed by mountains. This is the start of the White Chief Basin, famed in Mineral King history as the site of the Crabtree Cabin and the White Chief Mine. James Crabtree claimed the White Chief Mine in 1873, and the news that silver had been discovered here soon transformed this corner of the Sierra into a miners' paradise.

Devastating winters and disappointing yields turned the mining

The old White Chief Mine tempts a hiker with a flashlight and a taste for adventure.

A lone Sierra juniper guards the trail toward the White Chief Basin.

boom into a major bust, leaving broken dreams and abandoned mine shafts in its wake. You'll find the ruins of the Crabtree Cabin 20 yards to the right of the trail, just before you cross the rocky creekbed that holds White Chief Creek. Stand beside the decaying timbers and toppled stovepipe of James Crabtree's home, its walls long fallen, with his dreams, onto the harsh Sierra ground.

Return to the trail and cross the creek at 2.4 miles, and then cruise on across the basin. Wildflowers are abundant early in the year, and the chorus of blossoms blends the colors of alpine shooting star, cinquefoil, yarrow, and lupine. Late-summer hikers must be content with the songs of meadow birds and the antics of fat marmots for their entertainment.

Continue with your gentle passage through the basin. Weathered tree trunks lie like scattered matchsticks on the meadow floor, long-dead victims of the avalanches that roar down from the heights each winter. Ease into a mellow ascent along a ridgeline ruled by red firs and foxtail pines. Things open up once more as you press onward.

Look for the often waterless gully cut by White Chief Creek below you on the right, its water swallowed by the marble-riddled bed of stone it travels. The meadow flowers return with new variety as you continue. Sharp-eyed hikers will spot purple gentian and little elephant heads just above ground level.

Approach the waterfall-decorated headwall of the basin at 3.4 miles. The trail makes a 90-degree turn to the right at this point, diving steeply downhill to cross the creek. (A use trail continues straight ahead but fades into confusion not long afterward.)

This is a good spot to pause and savor your surroundings. If you have the time and energy, the brief climb up the opposite hillside to the White Chief Mine is well worth it. The shaft opening is visible from the trail, marked by a pile of glowing white tailings. Scramble up the steep incline to gain the mine opening at 3.5 miles.

A cool blast of air will meet you at the entrance. Click on your flashlight and probe the darkness. The walls of the shaft hold the marks of tools that fought the stone more than 100 years ago, and park rangers talk of graffiti dating back to 1900 that's hidden in the shadows here. The shaft ends at a wall of solid stone after less than a football field's length.

Return to the basin to savor the sweetness of the meadow flowers, or press onward with the trail as it climbs steeply from the White Chief Mine. The upper reaches of the canyon will repay your efforts with increasing wildness and beauty, but the trail is faint and the way is rugged.

CHAPTER FOUR
· · · · · · · · · · ·
Mount Whitney Ranger District

Trails in the Mount Whitney Ranger District offer spectacular but strenuous hiking to those who wish to explore this section of the Sierra Nevada. All trailheads are accessed via Highway 395, which runs along the hot and desolate Owens Valley. The Owens Valley is the deepest valley in North America (based on the difference in elevation between the 14,496-foot summit of Mount Whitney and the valley floor). Provisions, gasoline, lodgings, and information are available in the towns of Independence and Lone Pine.

The ascent from the often stifling Owens Valley to the Whitney district trailheads is arduous and steep. Please be sure that your vehicle is equipped with a good radiator for the trip up and a dependable braking system for the drive down. From the trailheads, your route on foot will continue to ascend, climbing to lofty passes, alpine lakes, or perhaps a mountaintop. Altitude sickness is an immediate danger. Try to allow yourself a day or two to get acclimated before attempting one of the more strenuous outings.

A stop at the Mount Whitney Ranger District office located in the heart of Lone Pine (on the east side of Highway 395) is a good way to begin your exploration of the area. The office staff can provide you with maps, guidebooks, wilderness permits (for overnight visits), and campground and trail information. For advice in advance, write to Mount Whitney Ranger District, PO Box 8, Lone Pine, CA 93545.

You might also want to visit the excellent Inter-Agency Visitor Center (just south of Lone Pine off Highway 395) when you're in the area. Revel in an "information overload" as you prepare to satiate your senses with the natural beauty the nearby trails provide.

Trails in this section explore the Inyo National Forest, an area stretching 175 miles from Owens Lake in the south to Lundy Canyon, north of Mono Lake. You'll touch the boundaries of Kings Canyon and Sequoia national parks (see chapters 2 and 3) on Hike 30, Mount Whitney, and Hike 32, Kearsarge Pass.

Wilderness areas accessed in this section are the John Muir Wilderness (please see background information in chapter 1) and the

Golden Trout Wilderness. The 306,916 acres of the Golden Trout Wilderness are named for California's elusive and much-prized state fish.

The Kern River golden trout and the Little Kern golden trout are both threatened by nonnative species. Because of this, special fishing regulations are in effect within the wilderness, allowing only artificial lures or flies with single, barbless hooks and a five-fish limit. Check with the Forest Service or the California Department of Fish and Game if you're an angler. The Cottonwood Creek drainage (hikes 26 and 27) is also restricted to a five-fish limit and artificial lures or flies with single, barbless hooks.

CAMPGROUNDS

Horseshoe Meadow Campground *(Hike 26, Cottonwood Lakes; Hike 27, Cottonwood Pass Loop)* This isolated walk-in campground is designed for the convenience of hikers using the Cottonwood Creek trails. You'll have to leave your car in the parking lot and haul your gear into a site, but the short trudge is worth it. And the campground's lofty elevation (10,000 feet) makes it a cool escape from the lowland heat.

To find the campground, turn west off Highway 395 in Lone Pine for Whitney Portal. Drive 3.2 miles on Whitney Portal Road, and veer left at a sign for Horseshoe Meadow. Travel the paved Horseshoe Meadow Road 19.3 miles, enduring a twisting, arduous ascent, and turn right at a sign for the Cottonwood Lakes trailhead. You'll find water and toilets here.

Horseshoe Meadow Campground is open June to October. No reservations. Moderate fee.

Tuttle Creek Campground *(Hike 26, Cottonwood Lakes; Hike 27, Cottonwood Pass Loop; Hike 28, Meysan Lake; Hike 29, Lone Pine Lake; Hike 30, Mount Whitney)* This free Bureau of Land Management campground is a good option for those who want to avoid the overnight crowds around the Mount Whitney trailhead. However, Tuttle Creek Campground is definitely not a spot for those who want to linger around camp all day. It's right on the valley floor, and it's desolate and hot when the sun is high.

Spend your days hiking in the mountains, and return to Tuttle Creek Campground to watch the sun set behind picturesque Lone Pine Mountain. If you're an early riser, you'll be awed by the beauty of the sunrise here. The surrounding Alabama Hills are stark and lovely against the scenery of the Sierra crest. These ancient rock formations look exactly like a rugged backdrop for a spaghetti western—and, indeed, several movies have been filmed here!

To find the campground, turn west off Highway 395 in Lone Pine for Whitney Portal. Drive 3.2 miles on Whitney Portal Road, and veer left at a sign for Horseshoe Meadow and Tuttle Creek Campground. Continue 1.6 miles on this paved road, and go right for Tuttle Creek Campground. An additional 1.0 mile of unpaved road will take you to the campground entrance.

Tuttle Creek Campground's 85 sites for tents or motorhomes offer picnic tables, fireplaces, and non-flush toilets. There is no drinking water here, and the only shade will be underneath your picnic table. Little Tuttle Creek provides a ribbon of coolness through the campground, though.

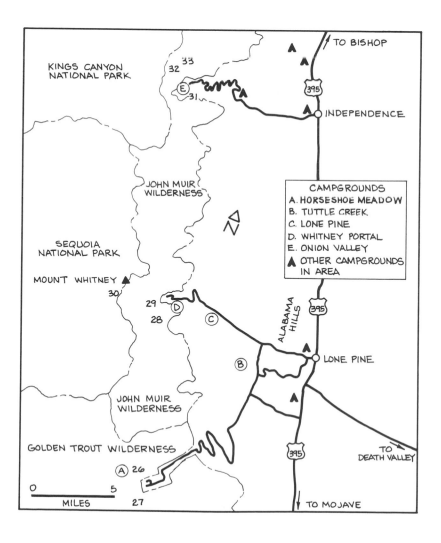

Tuttle Creek Campground is open April to October. No reservations. No fee.

Lone Pine Campground *(Hike 26, Cottonwood Lakes; Hike 27, Cottonwood Pass Loop; Hike 28, Meysan Lake; Hike 29, Lone Pine Lake; Hike 30, Mount Whitney)* Lone Pine Campground is another, less desolate option for lowland camping, an alternative to the windswept Tuttle Creek Campground. Its 44 sites for tents or motorhomes are situated along Lone Pine Creek. In addition to a bit of shade, sites offer drinking water (available May through October only), fireplaces, picnic tables, and non-flush toilets.

To find Lone Pine Campground, turn west off Highway 395 in Lone Pine for Whitney Portal, and drive 6.7 miles to a sign for Lone Pine Campground.

Lone Pine Campground is open all year. Reservations accepted. Moderate fee.

Whitney Portal Campground *(Hike 28, Meysan Lake; Hike 29, Lone Pine Lake; Hike 30, Mount Whitney)* What this popular campground lacks in solitude and serenity, it makes up for in convenience and scenic beauty. The campground has wonderful views of majestic Mount Whitney, and it's a great jumping-off spot for the Whitney-area trailheads. Unfortunately, it's often difficult to find an available campsite at Whitney Portal. Come early in the day, and avoid weekends whenever possible.

Whitney Portal Campground's 44 shaded campsites for tents or motorhomes perch at a lofty 8,000 feet. Nights are chilly here, so bring lots of blankets. Campsites offer fireplaces, picnic tables, drinking water, and flush toilets—plus a host of opportunities to chat with fellow hikers.

To reach the campground, turn west off Highway 395 in Lone Pine for Whitney Portal, and drive 11.1 miles on the paved Whitney Portal Road. You'll see the campground sprawled along the left side of the road.

Whitney Portal Campground is open May to October. Reservations accepted. Moderate fee.

Onion Valley Campground *(Hike 31, Robinson Lake; Hike 32, Kearsarge Pass; Hike 33, Dragon Peak Lakes)* With a spectacular setting and superior trailhead access, Onion Valley Campground has just about everything going for it—and everyone going to it. You'll really have to scramble to find a weekend campsite here. Weekdays can be busy too, so come as early as possible.

The campground's 29 tentsites are tucked into a starkly beautiful mountain canyon at an elevation of 9,200 feet. Picnic tables, fireplaces, drinking water, and flush toilets are provided. Bears are frequent campground raiders, so be careful with your foodstuff here.

To find Onion Valley Campground, turn west off Highway 395 in

Independence for Onion Valley. Drive 13.0 miles on the paved but punishing Onion Valley Road to reach the campground at road's end. In the summer months, a campground host and a resident trail ranger are usually stationed here.

Onion Valley Campground is open June to September. Reservations accepted. Moderate fee.

26 COTTONWOOD LAKES

Distance: 11.5 miles (loop)
Difficulty: Strenuous
Starting point: 10,040 feet
High point: 11,100 feet
Map: USGS Cirque Peak 7.5'

Although the mileage for this trek to the Cottonwood lakes basin is somewhat daunting, the route is not too punishing. With an early start and a leisurely lunch break halfway through, this could be a manageable outing for even an average hiker. Best of all, the delights to be found in the Cottonwood basin are far from mediocre!

To reach the trailhead for Cottonwood Lakes, turn west off Highway 395 in Lone Pine for Whitney Portal. Drive 3.2 miles on Whitney Portal Road, and veer left at a sign for Horseshoe Meadow. Travel the paved Horseshoe Meadow Road 19.3 miles, enduring a twisting, arduous ascent, and turn right at a sign for the Cottonwood Lakes trailhead.

Continue 0.6 mile to an immense, paved parking area, complete with drinking water, toilets, and a one-night backpackers' camping area. You'll quickly realize the popularity of this trail if you arrive on a weekend, as you may have to scramble for a parking spot.

Begin walking at a sign for Cottonwood Lakes, pausing at a Forest Service information board along the way. The sandy trail slices through a scattering of foxtail pines to arrive at the boundary of the Golden Trout Wilderness at 0.2 mile.

Continue with your mostly level route, traversing a rocky, open landscape through handsome foxtail and lodgepole pines. The red-hued trunks of the foxtails are particularly lovely in the early-morning light.

Cross the South Fork of Cottonwood Creek at 1.5 miles, and wander on through platoons of pines. You'll begin to hear the murmur of Cottonwood Creek as it rushes through a willow-filled gully at 2.3 miles. Climb gently beside a creek-fed meadow as you continue, and entertain yourself by testing your familiarity with the wildflowers that you'll find.

Hikers pace the scenic trail through the Cottonwood Lakes Basin.

Pass a short cutoff trail to Golden Trout Camp (an outdoor-education facility) at 2.9 miles, and proceed gently uphill with the main trail. Arrive at an entry sign for the John Muir Wilderness at 3.1 miles. The surrounding meadow is aflame with Indian paintbrush, yampah, little elephant heads, and cinquefoil.

Cross Cottonwood Creek at 3.2 miles, and begin climbing more noticeably, ascending to a trail junction at 3.7 miles. The trail to the right (signed for Cottonwood Lakes) will be your return route if you're making this a loop. Veer left for South Fork Lakes.

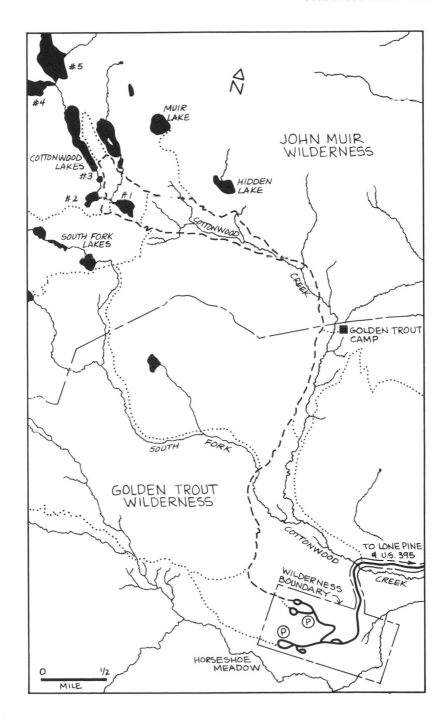

#5
#4

MUIR
LAKE

JOHN MUIR
WILDERNESS

COTTONWOOD
LAKES
#3

HIDDEN
LAKE

#2   #1

COTTONWOOD

CREEK

SOUTH FORK
LAKES

■ GOLDEN TROUT
CAMP

SOUTH   FORK

GOLDEN TROUT
WILDERNESS

COTTONWOOD

TO LONE PINE
& U.S. 395

WILDERNESS
BOUNDARY

CREEK

P
P

HORSESHOE
MEADOW

0   1/2
MILE

Some nifty rock hopping will keep your feet dry as you recross Cottonwood Creek. Continue climbing very gently with the trail, enjoying meadow views and glimpses of anglers working the banks of the little waterway. The grade intensifies at 4.5 miles as you climb toward a canyon headwall decorated with the streamers of trickling waterfalls.

Reach a junction at 5.0 miles, and angle right for New Army Pass (the route to the left leads to South Fork Lakes). Continue steadily uphill through trees and rocks, and gain sight of Cottonwood Lake 1 at 5.2 miles. Keep left for New Army Pass at another junction, and enjoy level walking past the open, meadowy shore of saucerlike Cottonwood Lake 1.

Delve deeper into this vast and windswept alpine lake basin as you continue, savoring vistas of surrounding granite slopes and guardian peaks. Watch carefully for a faint use trail on the right as you approach Cottonwood Lake 2 at 5.5 miles. The use trail cuts off the main trail just before a little knoll. Follow it across the meadow, fording the stream between lakes 1 and 2.

Please try to stay on the trail as you wander through this pristine meadow. The delicate primrose monkeyflower, meadow penstemon, and hikers gentian that make the meadow so enchanting will thank you for your careful footsteps.

Keep Cottonwood Lake 2 on your left as you head for a low jumble of boulders sprinkled with foxtail pines. Just beyond the little mound is the small pothole lake that marks the lower reaches of Cottonwood Lake 3. Follow the footpath along the right-hand shore, and reach the lake proper at 5.9 miles.

Cottonwood Lake 3 is long and lovely, set against a breathtaking backdrop of cliffs. A meadowy shoreline boasts an assortment of alpine wildflowers. If you're still looking for a picnic spot, this is it.

To begin your trek back toward the parking lot, proceed with the lakeside trail about 50 yards past the sign for Cottonwood Lake 3, and then veer right at a 90-degree angle from the shore. A brief (0.1-mile) cross-country scramble will take you to the main Cottonwood Trail beside a pair of pothole lakes. Go right on this trail, and enjoy a gentle descent toward the lower reaches of the lake basin.

You'll get another peek at Cottonwood Lake 1 (from the opposite side) as you continue. Be sure to turn back once for a view of Cirque Peak dominating the basin. Pass a cutoff trail for Muir Lake at 6.8 miles, and bid a regretful farewell to the Cottonwood lakes as you start into the meat of your descent.

A fistful of rocky switchbacks evolves into a mellower downhill at 7.2 miles. You'll regain sight of Cottonwood Creek less than 0.5 mile later. Hit the junction with the trail to South Fork Lakes at 7.8 miles. Continue straight here, and backtrack to your starting point at 11.5 miles. (Be sure to follow signs for hiker parking—not the pack station—as you near the finish.)

27 COTTONWOOD PASS LOOP

Distance: 11.4 miles (loop)
Difficulty: Strenuous
Starting point: 9,950 feet
High point: 11,250 feet
Map: USGS Cirque Peak 7.5'

*Trails in the Cottonwood Lakes area
probe the Golden Trout Wilderness.*

This hike lacks the stunning scenery of Hike 26 to Cottonwood Lakes, but it also lacks the weekend crowds that trample that exceedingly popular trail. If you have a couple of days in the area, try this trek when the crowds are thick, and visit the Cottonwood lakes when things calm down a bit.

To find the Cottonwood Pass trailhead, turn west off Highway 395 in Lone Pine for Whitney Portal. Drive 3.2 miles on Whitney Portal Road, and veer left at a sign for Horseshoe Meadow. Travel the paved Horseshoe Meadow Road 19.6 miles to reach the signed Golden Trout hiker parking area at road's end. The lot has drinking water and toilets to accommodate visitors.

Set out at a sign for Cottonwood Pass at the far end of the parking lot. The wide, flat trail leads to an entry sign for the Golden Trout Wilderness at 0.1 mile. Continue on past scattered lodgepole pines and purple-hued patches of mat lupine. You'll arrive at a trail junction at 0.3 mile (the trail to the left is your return route).

Proceed straight ahead from the junction, staying with the sandy trail signed for Cottonwood Pass. Climb gently with the vast Horseshoe Meadow on your left. Enter a more concentrated stand of lodgepole pines at 1.0 mile. The walking is level and easy to a creek crossing at 1.4 miles. You'll touch the edge of Horseshoe Meadow here. Look for yampah, shooting star, little elephant heads, meadow penstemon, and ranger buttons.

Angle sharply right with the trail to ascend beside the water. Angle right again to cross another branch of the creek soon after, and continue gently up through pines. The climb gains momentum at 1.9 miles as you approach the base of a foxtail-sprinkled hill.

Your zigzagging ascent to Cottonwood Pass begins in earnest at 2.1 miles. Eighteen switchbacks climb at a steady pace, traversing a hillside characterized by chinquapin, rocks, and pines. Views expand to take in Horseshoe Meadow and the Inyo Mountains to the east of the Owens Valley.

The switchbacks cease at 2.9 miles. You'll walk through a willow-filled meadow, delighting in the blossoms of mountain pennyroyal, fireweed, nude buckwheat, spreading dogbane, larkspur, and California corn lily. Leave the meadow at 3.1 miles, and climb in several more switchbacks before a final uphill push leads to the 11,150-foot crest of Cottonwood Pass.

Turn east to look back on the 4 miles of trail behind you. The view extends to the dark faces of the distant Inyo Mountains. Gaze westward from the pass and you'll see the peaks of the Great Western Divide as well as the hidden reaches of the Golden Trout Wilderness and Sequoia National Park.

Cottonwood Pass is often cool and windswept, so you'll want to don a jacket if you linger. If you'd prefer a lake hike to a loop hike, little Chicken Spring Lake lies less than a mile farther, to the west of Cottonwood Pass.

To stay with the route, veer left at the trail junction just beyond the pass, and join the Pacific Crest Trail toward Trail Pass. Pick up a view of 12,900-foot Cirque Peak to the north as you skirt along a rocky slope, enjoying level walking and expanding mountain vistas. Angle left with the trail to cross a ridgeline at 4.7 miles, and then descend into a meadowy basin with fine views of surrounding peaks.

A mostly level trail leads into a brief climb at 5.9 miles. Watch for a rocky outcropping to the right. From here, you'll get a look into the heart of the Golden Trout Wilderness, with views of Olancha Peak, Templeton Meadow, and Kern Peak.

Another 15 or 20 minutes of walking winds on toward Poison

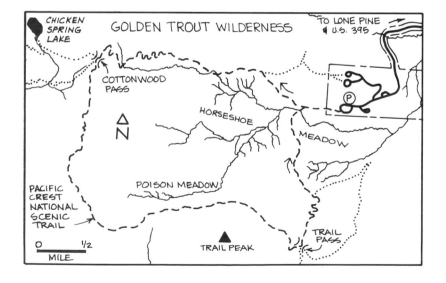

A father and son gain the crest of Cottonwood Pass.

Meadow. You'll gain your first view of this long swath of green at 7.2 miles. The "poison" doesn't seem to bother the scores of cattle that wander here in August. Hike a level trail above the meadow. Horseshoe Meadow appears in the distance at the 7.8-mile point, and tall Mount Langley dominates the view to the north.

A half mile of gentle uphill leads into the descent to a signed trail junction at 9.2 miles. Abandon the Pacific Crest Trail here as you go left for Horseshoe Meadow. Continue steeply down on a very sandy trail. The passage of platoons of horses is "fragrantly" apparent.

Keep left with a sign for "Trailhead–pack station" at 9.8 miles. Your descent will be more gradual from here. The level expanse of Horseshoe Meadow spreads before you at 10.7 miles. Start across the flatland with pleasing views of Mount Langley, Cirque Peak, and Cottonwood Pass.

Once across the meadow, regain your entry route as you go right at a sign for "Hiker parking" at 11.1 miles. The final 0.3 mile is an easy backtrack to the parking lot.

28 MEYSAN LAKE

Distance: 11.6 miles round trip
Difficulty: Strenuous
Starting point: 7,900 feet
High point: 11,600 feet
Total climb: 3,950 feet
Maps: USGS Mount Langley 7.5' and USGS Mount Whitney 7.5'

The trek to Meysan Lake is not for those in search of a pleasant, relaxing day hike. It's not for children, and it's definitely not for those who are even slightly out of shape. This is a tough, tough hike on an infrequently maintained trail. But if you like a challenge, and if you're willing to work hard for your scenery, this may be the hike for you.

If you're staying at Whitney Portal Campground, the trek to Meysan Lake will begin right from your campsite. To drive to the trailhead for Meysan Lake, turn west off Highway 395 in Lone Pine for Whitney Portal, and proceed 11.2 miles on the paved Whitney Portal Road. Look for a sign for Meysan Lake parking. You'll need to leave your vehicle on the road shoulder, just above Whitney Portal Campground.

Please be sure to bring extra clothes and water for this trek. It begins at nearly 8,000 feet and finishes well above 11,000 feet. Also, start as early in the day as possible. This will ensure that you beat the heat, and it will provide wonderful early-morning light on the mountains.

Begin walking at the closed-off asphalt road that descends into Whitney Portal Campground. You'll need to keep a sharp eye out for trail signs as you traverse the camping area, crossing the campground's lively Lone Pine Creek and gaining the trail proper at 0.2 mile.

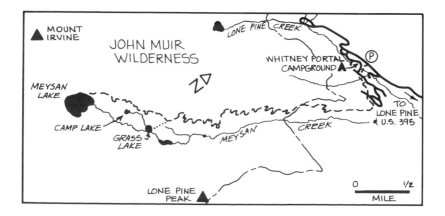

Lofty Meysan Lake is harsh but beautiful.

Start uphill through a rock- and sage-sprinkled landscape, and enjoy the first of many views out toward the Alabama Hills, the Owens Valley, and the Inyo Mountains. Join an asphalt road through a handful of summer cabins at 0.4 mile. Then abandon the asphalt soon after as you turn back onto the signed footpath.

Climb steadily (the story of this hike) with an enchanting vista of 12,943-foot Lone Pine Peak overhead. Ascend through a series of dry switchbacks to arrive at an entry sign for the John Muir Wilderness at 0.9 mile. From here, you'll begin a long, straight ascent toward the canyon headwall, tracing the course of a well-graded trail.

Intermittent sets of switchbacks interrupt the steady climb past scattered white firs, Jeffrey pines, and an abundance of bushy chinquapin. You'll be glad for your early start through here, as there is very little shade to fend off the persistent sun.

Cross a seasonal creek at 1.9 miles, and gain sight of Meysan Creek soon after. Meysan Creek tumbles downward, leaping off a shelf of granite. There's an unmarked side trail leading toward the water's edge, but surplus detours may be ill-advised on this lengthy trek.

Climb in switchbacks, enjoying a cooling breeze and the company of handsome foxtail pines as you gain elevation. The roar of Meysan Creek intensifies as the increasingly rugged trail leads into a small basin at 3.6 miles. If you're hiking early in the season, you'll be treated to a host of alpine shooting star through here.

Leave the basin to climb in steep switchbacks on a markedly deteriorating trail. The way is difficult to follow, so you'll need to pay close attention. Gain more open, rocky terrain once more, continuing a steep and punishing ascent. A sandy slope will confront you with the most brutal section of your climb thus far.

The punishment abates at 4.5 miles, and you'll climb more gently to reach a breathtaking vista of the valley floor soon after (watch for a granite shelf just to the left of the trail). Arrive at a fork in the trail at 4.7 miles. To the left, a 0.3-mile jog leads to Grass Lake. If you're feeling the strain of this difficult trek, Grass Lake makes a worthy early stopping point.

To continue on for Meysan Lake, make a very sharp right turn with the trail (signed for Camp and Meysan lakes). Climb steadily into an exquisite amphitheater of peaks. Working from left to right, look for Mount LeConte, Mount Mallory, and Mount Irvine, all above 13,500 feet. And watch for serene Grass Lake in the basin just below the trail.

A fascinating passage by weather-sculpted foxtail pines leads on to meadow-surrounded Camp Lake at 5.1 miles. This petite beauty is nearly overwhelmed by the avalanche of alpine shooting star and mountain heather that rules its shores. Pause to enjoy the wildflowers, and then press on toward your destination.

The trail from here is very difficult to follow. Start into the small draw to the right of Camp Lake, keeping an eye out for the ducks that mark the way. Hop across Camp Lake's inlet creek at the base of the draw, and follow the ducks up a steep and rocky slope. You'll gain the plateau above Meysan Lake at 5.7 miles.

Gaze down on lofty Meysan Lake, a harsh and rugged saucer set into the shadow of the mountain headwall. The barren plateau above Meysan Lake is the high point of your trek. You may choose to skip the 0.1-mile descent to Meysan Lake's severe shoreline and return to friendlier Camp Lake before spreading your picnic.

Pause to absorb the awesome beauty of the surrounding mountains. Chortle, "I made it!" Then turn back toward your starting point with weary but exultant steps.

· ·
29 LONE PINE LAKE

Distance: 6.0 miles round trip
Difficulty: Moderate
Starting point: 8,300 feet
High point: 10,040 feet
Maps: USGS Mount Langley 7.5' and USGS Mount Whitney 7.5'

No doubt about it, the Mount Whitney trailhead is a Sierra Nevada phenomenon. This trail attracts thousands of people during every hiking season. Some might say it's not a trail at all—it's a Sierra superhighway. Despite the drawbacks of overuse and overexposure, the Mount Whitney trail is worth exploring. Just don't do it on a weekend!

For a taste of the Mount Whitney experience without the torment of the entire trek to the summit (see Hike 30, Mount Whitney), try this pleasant hike to attractive Lone Pine Lake. Pack a picnic lunch, and make a day of it.

To find the Lone Pine Lake–Mount Whitney trailhead, turn west off Highway 395 in Lone Pine for Whitney Portal, and drive 11.9 miles on the paved Whitney Portal Road. There's a vast hikers' parking lot here, complete with walk-in campground, drinking water, and several non-flush toilets. If you visit at a particularly busy time, you may have to leave your vehicle in the overflow parking area, 0.2 mile short of the trailhead.

Pause at the trailhead information board before beginning, and add your name to the thousands scrawled on this trail register each year. With that business taken care of, set out on the Mount Whitney trail, climbing in well-graded switchbacks lined with chinquapin, mountain mahogany, sage, and manzanita.

The jagged outline of the Sierra crest will draw your gaze upward as you ascend. Cross a small creek awash in fireweed, yarrow, and Indian paintbrush at 0.6 mile, and continue up a hillside dotted with Jeffrey and single-leaf pinyon pines. A second stream crossing awaits at 0.8 mile. Look for wood rose, ranger buttons, angelica, and spreading dogbane here.

Reach an entry sign for the John Muir Wilderness at 0.9 mile. The subsequent switchbacks yield a lovely view out to the Alabama Hills, the Owens Valley floor, and the distant Inyo Mountains. The grade intensifies at 1.3 miles, and you'll get a glimpse of Lone Pine Creek tumbling downhill in a white cascade.

Continue up beneath white firs and Jeffrey pines. Then gain more switchbacks and mellower climbing as you traverse a sun-washed slope. Your steady uphill grind will lead to the banks of Lone Pine

Creek at 2.7 miles. After the long ascent from the parking lot, you'll sigh happily as you enter this cool cloister of creekside air, decorated with the reverent blue blossoms of monkshood.

Cross the creek shortly afterward, and pick up the company of altitude-loving foxtail pines. Arrive at a junction at 2.9 miles. From here, the main trail continues on toward Mirror Lake, Trail Camp, and the summit of Mount Whitney (see Hike 30). Veer left to take the short

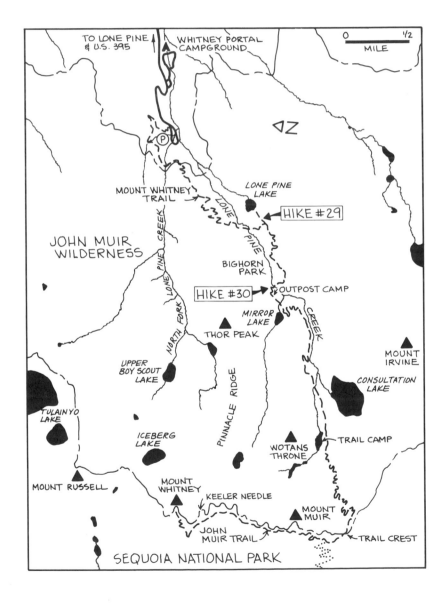

side trail to the shore of Lone Pine Lake.

Lone Pine Lake does a watery balancing act on the lip of the canyon, clinging to the precipice like some vista-seeking daredevil. This pretty lake has a lovely setting, and it's a great spot for a midday picnic and a cooling splash. You'll probably share the lakeshore with several backpackers, as the route to Whitney's summit is almost always crowded. Nonflush toilets are available at Outpost Camp, approximately 0.7 mile beyond Lone Pine Lake.

· ·
30 MOUNT WHITNEY

Distance: 21.8 miles round trip
Difficulty: Strenuous
Starting point: 8,300 feet
High point: 14,496 feet
Maps: USGS Mount Langley 7.5' and USGS Mount Whitney 7.5'

OK, OK, so the 21.8-mile journey to Mount Whitney's summit is stretching the day-hike category just a bit. Be forewarned, this monster day trek is only for the able-bodied, the tenacious, the fleet of foot...and perhaps the slightly masochistic. Even so, it's a wonderful way to reach the highest point in the contiguous United States without going through the hassle of making overnight arrangements for this exceedingly busy trail.

Backpacking permits for the Mount Whitney Trail are always at a premium, and the trailside campsites are seriously overburdened. You'll be doing this trail a favor by doing it in a day. And the obese, marauding marmots that ransack every Whitney backpacker's camp won't miss your meal a lick—we guarantee it.

So, how do you prepare for the Whitney marathon? First, don't try it unless you're in excellent condition. If at all possible, allow yourself a few days to get acclimated to the trailhead elevation before you begin to hike. Altitude sickness is a common malady on Mount Whitney's summit, and the bill for the rescue helicopter will definitely blow your vacation budget.

Clear skies and an early-morning start are both essential to a summit-seeker's success. Try to be on the trail by 7:00 A.M. Carry plenty of fluids or a water-purification system (don't even think about drinking untreated water in this populated corner of the wilderness). You'll need sunscreen, a jacket, and a flashlight. Go heavy on the munchies, too—this trail burns up a ton of calories.

Please remember one more thing before you try this hike: safety and enjoyment are more important than reaching Mount Whitney's summit. Listen to your body, and use common sense. Don't push farther than you should. If the distance or the altitude begins to take its toll on you, simply bag it. This trail is beautiful all along the way. Your day won't be wasted with an early stop—nor will your life.

Please refer to the beginning of Hike 29, Lone Pine Lake, to get you started on the Mount Whitney trek. From the junction at 2.9 miles, keep to the right with the main trail, and continue on into a granite-dominated canyon. A set of switchbacks carved into the cliff will lead you upward as you depart from the canyon.

Emerge into the meadowy vale known as Bighorn Park at 3.6 miles. This wildflower-filled wonderland is watered by Lone Pine Creek. You'll enjoy level walking amid an abundance of early-season shooting star as you stay with the trail along the meadow's edge. Reach the busy Outpost Camp at 3.9 miles. Campsites and toilets make this a haven for backpackers.

The climb resumes with more switchbacks from here, leading on to quiet Mirror Lake at 4.5 miles. This petite lake has a pleasant, shaded shoreline, overhung by lodgepole and foxtail pines. There's no camping at Mirror Lake, so it's an uncrowded spot to take a breather, if you're in need of one. You'll have a view of the needlelike Whitney Pinnacles from the lakeshore.

Leave Mirror Lake and climb in switchbacks, savoring terrific views down to Bighorn Park and Lone Pine Lake. Watch for mountain sorrel and alumroot hiding in the rocks as you continue uphill with a rugged trail, ascending beside Lone Pine Creek once more.

Arrive at the tiny Trailside Meadow at 5.3 miles. This pretty pocket of alpine extravagance is ankle deep in shooting star and crimson columbine. Push onward through a series of short switchbacks to gain your first look at deep blue Consultation Lake at 5.8 miles. An unrelenting climb leads to the lakeshore (camping allowed) at the 6.0-mile point.

A smaller, more barren, windswept lake is the site of the infamous Trail Camp at 6.4 miles. Otherwise known as "Marmot City," Trail Camp is the spot where scores of Whitney backpackers leave their packs and tents for the final assault on the summit. In their absence, the marauding marmots move in. You haven't lived until you've seen a rotund marmot lumbering homeward with a bag of potato chips in its jaws.

Trail Camp is a good spot to take a break and assess your physical condition. From here, the grinding climb to the Whitney ridgeline begins with a vengeance. Your elevation will increase markedly now. If you're feeling any symptoms of altitude sickness (drowsiness, nausea, mental fuzziness), please call it a day. Check out the weather situation, too. Once you make the ridgeline, you'll be extremely vulnerable. If thunderclouds are gathering, don't continue.

To press on toward the summit, leave Trail Camp and start into a series of more than 90 well-graded switchbacks. This trail is absolutely

ENTERING
SEQUOIA NATIONAL PARK
TRAIL CREST
& JOHN MUIR TRAIL
PETS AND FIREARMS
PROHIBITED

U.S. DEPT. OF THE INTERIOR
NATIONAL PARK SERVICE

A switchback-laden ascent leads to the ridgeline above Trail Camp.

The summit of Mount Whitney provides a fantastic 360-degree vista.

amazing, hewn into the solid granite of the cliff face. Watch for clumps of elusive sky pilot as you climb. The handsome blue flower thrives at altitudes above 10,000 feet. You'll have fantastic views east into Nevada as you snake up the rocky trail.

The grade will intensify (as will your weariness) as you near the crest of the ridge. Top out at 13,600 feet and 8.8 miles. If the altitude doesn't make you dizzy, the panorama will. The view is awesome from the crest, extending for countless miles to both east and west. A trail sign here marks the eastern boundary of Sequoia National Park.

Revel in a brief descent as you follow your rocky path to a junction with the John Muir Trail at 9.0 miles. Continue straight for "Whitney Summit," following the famous John Muir Trail toward its finish at the top of Mount Whitney. This 212-mile trail begins in Yosemite National Park and winds its way along the scenic Sierra Crest, leading long-haul backpackers to the Whitney summit from the west side of the mountains.

Resume climbing from the junction, keeping an eye out for glowing alpine gold and soaring sky pilot among the rocks. Tear your gaze from the trail, and marvel at the lakes far below the crest. This fistful of brilliant blue gems looks as though it spilled out of a jewel thief's pocket while he made a hasty getaway.

The trail levels out at 9.4 miles. It's a remarkable feat of work, hacked out of the solid stone. Tightrope-walk across the first awesome gap between the jagged Whitney pinnacles at 9.6 miles. The death-defying view will make you gasp.

A final section of the ridgeline leads into the rough-and-rocky scramble to Whitney's summit. You may lose the trail through here, but your course is obvious. Continue upward on aching legs, and reach Mount Whitney's lofty "flat top" at 10.9 miles. You made it!

There's a hikers' register to sign here, as well as a stout stone shelter offering respite from the often chilly wind. You won't stay inside for long, however. The view is too tremendous. Drink your fill of this matchless moment, shoot all your film and munch most of your munchies, and then turn happily for home.

31 ROBINSON LAKE

Distance: 2.8 miles round trip
Difficulty: Moderate
Starting point: 9,200 feet
High point: 10,530 feet
Map: USGS Kearsarge Peak 7.5'

The uphill push to Robinson Lake is a bit too brief to earn a strenuous rating, but don't let the distance fool you—this hike will give you a heaving chest in no time. Console yourself with the knowledge that the hill is short, and then poke along and enjoy the scenery. One bit of advice: despite its brevity, this is best done as a morning hike. The hill is horrendous in the afternoon heat.

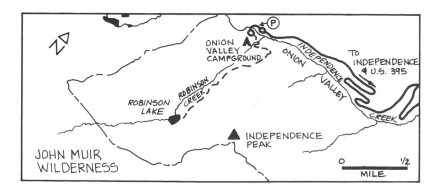

To reach the trailhead for Robinson Lake, turn west off Highway 395 in Independence for Onion Valley. Drive 13.0 miles on the paved but punishing Onion Valley Road to reach the hikers' parking lot at road's end.

This hike description starts from the trailhead inside Onion Valley Campground. If you're leaving your vehicle in the hikers' parking lot, add 0.2 mile each way (for a 3.2-mile total distance). Walk through Onion Valley Campground to the trail's start between sites 6 and 7. A sign for Robinson Lake trailhead marks the spot.

Begin by crossing rambunctious Robinson Creek, and take the footpath that ascends along the far shore of the little waterway. The creek ravine is riotous with flowers. Look for fireweed, lupine, ranger buttons, monkshood, angelica, and Indian paintbrush.

The gradual climb quickly escalates into a punishing ascent. Push upward across a rocky hillside characterized by sage and wildflowers. Whitebark and foxtail pines offer occasional patches of much-needed respite from the sun.

The steady uphill is punctuated by some extremely steep sections.

A wind-sculpted pine stands beside the trail to Robinson Lake.

Be sure to take breathers as they're needed, especially if you're unaccustomed to the elevation. The incline mellows slightly at 0.5 mile as you wander across an avalanche-blighted hillside strewn with uprooted trees. This slide in the early 1980s went all the way to the Onion Valley floor, destroying the ranger cabin at the bottom.

Regain the voice of Robinson Creek at 0.7 mile. The waterway is on your right, hidden in a willow-shrouded cleft. Cross a small feeder creek, and then continue up beside another, larger creek. The ascent picks up momentum as you weave through whispering willows. Be careful of your footing here—gravel and granite make a slippery combination.

Climb across a rocky, open slope strewn with massive boulders at 1.0 mile. The sight of delicate Sierra primrose tucked into the rocks will cheer you as the sweat drips off your nose. Just when you begin to wonder if the hill will ever end, the incline abates at 1.4 miles.

Continue on your (mercifully) level path to reach the shore of Robinson Lake soon after. This alpine beauty is shallow and petite, guarded by a battalion of encircling peaks. A shoreline shaded by whitebark and foxtail pines offers plenty of nice places for picnics or midday naps, and the lip of the little basin that cradles Robinson Lake will delight you with its view down to the Onion Valley floor.

• •

32 KEARSARGE PASS

Distance: 9.6 miles round trip
Difficulty: Strenuous
Starting point: 9,200 feet
High point: 11,823 feet
Maps: USGS Kearsarge Peak 7.5' and USGS Mount Clarence King 7.5'

If you must choose only one of the three hikes leaving from the trailheads at Onion Valley Campground, the trek to Kearsarge Pass is the one to take. This is definitely a "don't-miss" hike. The trail is good, the inclines are mostly moderate, and the vista from Kearsarge Pass is a Sierra Nevada masterpiece.

Be sure to get an early-morning start on this challenging day hike. Carry plenty of liquids for the climb and a windbreaker for the pass. And avoid weekends whenever possible. The word is out about this fantastic trail; as a result, it's sadly overcrowded from Friday through Sunday.

To reach the trailhead for Kearsarge Pass, follow the driving directions for the preceding hike, Robinson Lake. Park in the hikers' lot

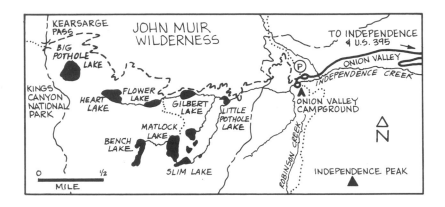

adjacent to Onion Valley Campground, and begin walking at the far end of the lot. Look for a trailhead information board and a sign denoting the Kearsarge Pass Trail.

Start with a gentle ascent beside charming Independence Creek, and climb across a sage-covered hillside flecked with sulfur flower and scarlet penstemon. You'll pass an unmarked trail descending to the right at 0.3 mile. Continue straight from here, climbing steadily with expanding views.

A sign marks the boundary of the John Muir Wilderness at 0.7 mile. A peek across the canyon will yield a view into the little basin that cradles Robinson Lake (see Hike 31). Puff through a series of switchbacks, and pick up the company of scattered foxtail and lodgepole pines as you gain elevation.

A meadowy menagerie of wildflowers will greet you at 1.1 miles as you hike beside Independence Creek. Watch for swamp onion, Bigelow's sneezeweed, bistort, mountain pennyroyal, death camas, and alpine shooting star. You'll swear the switchbacks outnumber the wildflowers as you continue up beside the water.

Pass Little Pothole Lake to the left of the trail at 1.5 miles. The moderate incline continues unabated, as do the seemingly endless switchbacks. Console yourself with views of the surrounding mountains, dominated by the distinguished form of 13,632-foot University Peak.

The climb eases at 2.2 miles as you arrive at pretty Gilbert Lake. This lake provides an excellent destination or picnic spot for those in quest of an easy hiking day. Ringed by willows and foxtail pines, Gilbert Lake is particularly picturesque against the backdrop of University Peak.

Continue with the trail along the lakeshore, and keep right when the path branches (the trail to the left leads to lakeside campsites). You'll climb the hillside at the far end of the lake in—guess what—more switchbacks.

Shapely Heart Lake shows off its name.

Zigzag up to a signed junction for Matlock Lake at 2.6 miles. (This lake makes a lovely destination, too. It's 0.7 mile from the junction.) Continue straight for Kearsarge Pass and look for Flower Lake to your left soon after.

Yet another installment of switchbacks leads up through open, rocky terrain. If it's not too late in the flower season, you'll see meadow penstemon, Sierra primrose, and alpine buckwheat thriving beside the trail. Enchanting little Heart Lake will steal your affections, as you gain a look down into its aquamarine water from the swiftly climbing path at 3.5 miles.

More rocky switchbacks will take you within sight of your goal at 3.8 miles. Round a bend and there it is. You'll see Kearsarge Pass in the distance, tied to your feet by a long ribbon of trail.

Except for scattered clumps of shrubby whitebark pine, the route from here is almost desolate. Although the grade is moderate, the climb is unrelenting. Press on to gain a look down onto Big Pothole Lake at 4.2 miles. It's just a water-filled basin in a bed of rocks, a barren testimony to its lofty elevation.

Climb on and on with your goal in sight. The cheery blossoms of Sierra primrose will lift your spirits when your gaze falls to your aching feet. Reach the 11,823-foot crest of Kearsarge Pass at 4.8 miles. If the altitude and the exertion don't have you hyperventilating by the time you reach the pass, the exploding vista will. It's awesome!

Weary hikers celebrate atop 11,823-foot Kearsarge Pass.

Explore the depths of Kings Canyon National Park with wondering eyes, drinking in a vision of a host of mountains. You'll see North Guard, Mount Brewer, South Guard, and a multitude of other peaks. To the left, University Peak and the Kearsarge Pinnacles rule the scene. To the right, the bulk of massive Mount Gould overwhelms everything.

Just below, the route leads on to Bullfrog and Kearsarge lakes, luring backpackers by the score. Behind you, you'll see the tale of your long journey toward the pass, told by a tenacious trail that cuts across rocks and barren ground. Find a flat boulder, sit down and rest, and enjoy the view from Kearsarge Pass.

33 DRAGON PEAK LAKES

Distance: 6.2 miles round trip
Difficulty: Strenuous
Starting point: 9,200 feet
High point: 11,400 feet
Map: USGS Kearsarge Peak 7.5'

This challenging hike leads to a pair of unnamed lakes near the more popular Golden Trout lakes. But who wants to dub a hike description "Unnamed Lakes"? And who would want to choose such a nondescript spot for a destination? So, we've named these lofty lovelies the Dragon Peak lakes, in honor of the peak that rules the scene above them.

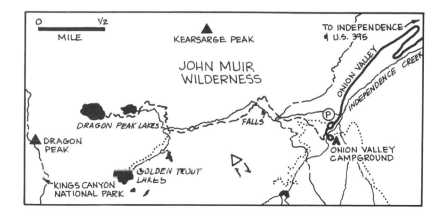

With that bit of business out of the way, here's a warning: this is a very tough hike on an unmaintained trail. If you're not in shape, don't try it. And if you're apt to get lost when the way is faint, opt for another outing. If, however, you like a challenge, want a bit of solitude, and love lonely alpine lakes, be sure to devote a day to visiting the Dragon Peak lakes.

Many Sierra Nevada trails are suitable for tennis shoes; this one isn't. The way is rocky, and the incline is often gruesome. Wear sturdy boots, and carry a double dose of water.

To reach the trailhead for the Dragon Peak lakes, follow the driving directions for Hike 31, Robinson Lake. Park in the hikers' lot adjacent to Onion Valley Campground, and begin walking at the far end of the lot. Look for a trailhead information board and a sign denoting the Kearsarge Pass Trail. (You'll abandon this busy trail after 0.3 mile.)

Start with a gentle ascent beside Independence Creek, and climb along a sage-covered hillside flecked with sulfur flower and scarlet penstemon. Watch closely for an unmarked trail descending to the right at the 0.3-mile point (if you reach a sign announcing the upcoming national park boundary, you've gone too far).

Take the side trail to the right, and descend briefly to join another trail ascending from the pack station and ranger cabin. Go left on this trail to resume your climb toward Dragon Peak lakes. The warm-up period is over now. Almost everything is steep from here.

Ascend on a punishing trail lined with sage, sulfur flower, Indian paintbrush, and angelica. The slope eases slightly at 0.5 mile. Continue up beside a creek with banks aflame in fireweed, and cross the creek at 0.7 mile. The climb continues unabated.

Lift your gaze from the hill before you to admire a lacy waterfall far above. This is the goal of your initial bout of heavy breathing. Labor through a rough and rocky section where encroaching chinquapin threatens to overwhelm the trail. Then trade the struggle with the underbrush for a war with steep and open ground.

Struggle upward until your calves beg for mercy, and then take a break to ease your heaving lungs. You'll reach the end of this unfriendly introduction to the "Dragon Peak Lakes Trail" at 1.0 mile. Pause at the crest of the hill to savor a stunning view across the canyon. The regal form of the 13,632-foot University Peak dominates the scene.

Continue on a rough trail lined with pungent mountain penny-royal, and recross the creek (above the waterfall) at 1.1 miles. The ascent resumes much too quickly. You'll be glad for the drops of shade spilled by scattered foxtail pines as your heart rate soars again.

Ascend along a rocky ridgetop where weather-tormented foxtails are grotesquely beautiful against a blue Sierra sky. The trail continues at an unrelenting grade. The way is indistinct in places, so don't let your attention wander.

Push upward with the creek on your right. The bright blossoms of crimson columbine and alpine shooting star make the way lovely. Draw in toward the creek's banks at 1.7 miles. A trail visible on the far shore will tempt you to hop across the water. The best route stays along the left bank, however. Keep your feet dry and stick with it.

Continue climbing beside the torrent, groaning through a rocky, exhausting ascent. You'll arrive at what appears to be an insurmountable jumble of boulders at 1.9 miles. Look for a small rock cairn beside the creek (there may be one on both banks). This marks your crossing point.

Skip across the creek, and keep climbing with the rocky path. You'll recross the water at 2.0 miles (just as you come to a dense willow thicket), and yet more uphill going will bring you to a beautiful grassy basin at 2.1 miles.

This is an enchanting spot when the wildflowers are in full swing. Look for hikers gentian, primrose monkeyflower, cinquefoil, alpine shooting star, and meadow penstemon springing from the creek-fed soil. Follow an indistinct trail along the left side of the meadow, working your way through an avalanche-blighted patch of trees.

When the trail turns away from the basin to begin its climb toward the Golden Trout lakes, abandon the route and keep to the right along the meadow's perimeter. Descend into the lush center of the meadow shortly after, and cross the creek again.

Be sure to pause here for a fantastic view out toward the distant lowlands. It appears as though someone pushed the world off a precipice at the meadow's edge. Search for an indistinct path through galaxies of alpine shooting star (they're incredible in early season), continue across the meadow, and begin climbing on the rocky trail that leads out of the basin.

Your legs will complain bitterly as you work your way up a rugged hillside strewn with wildflowers. The two-humped crest of Dragon Peak comes into view as you continue, as does the basin that shelters the Golden Trout lakes. A pocket-sized meadow offers respite from your climb at the 2.5-mile point, but the break is brief.

Climb along the right-hand shore of the lower lake's outlet stream, and reach your goal at last, with 2.8 miles behind you. The lower of the Dragon Peak lakes is small but crystal clear and lovely, held in place by a rim of mountains. A beautiful shoreline boasts mountain heather, little elephant head, and Sierra primrose, as well as a handful of tempting campspots.

To continue on to the upper lake, explore the left-hand shore of the lower lake with a sometimes indistinct trail. Then ascend the small ridge to the left of the inlet stream to approach the upper lake at 3.1 miles. Another treat awaits you here.

The upper of the Dragon Peak lakes is a gorgeous little alpine beauty, hidden in a bowl of granite. Although the lake's shoreline is less inviting than that of its neighbor, its ruggedness only serves to accentuate its unspoiled loveliness.

Fanciful stories often cast dragons as hoarders of precious gems. If there's any truth to these legends, then these two often-overlooked, unnamed lakes are certainly the most prized jewels of Dragon Peak's collection. Spend an hour delighting in this corner of the wilderness, and then turn your weary footsteps homeward.

CHAPTER FIVE
· · · · · · · · ·
White Mountain
Ranger District

Like its counterpart to the south, the Mount Whitney Ranger District, the White Mountain Ranger District holds a score of opportunities for extremely rugged hiking. Trailheads are often above 9,000 feet, and day hikers in the district will soar as high as 11,980 feet (see Hike 38, Bishop Pass).

Pacing yourself is very important at these lofty elevations. If at all possible, allow your lungs a few days to get acclimated before attempting the more strenuous outings. Concentrate on breathing deeply while exerting, and pause for regular rest breaks when climbing steeply. Sunscreen, sunglasses, drinking water, and a windbreaker are required equipment on all high-elevation excursions.

Trailheads in the White Mountain Ranger District are often very busy. As with all heavily used Sierra areas, weekday visits are preferable whenever possible. If you plan an overnight visit to the backcountry, you'll need to obtain a permit.

Advance permits for eastside entries into the John Muir Wilderness (see background information in chapter 1) or Sequoia and Kings Canyon national parks (chapters 2 and 3) may be requested by mail. Write to White Mountain Ranger District, 798 N. Main Street, Bishop, CA 93514.

Wilderness permits may also be obtained at the entrance stations located on the main access roads into the Bishop Creek and Rock Creek areas. (Currently, the Forest Service plans to staff these stations during daylight hours from the end of June to the middle of September.)

Once in the area, it's a good idea to stop at the ranger station for current trail information, maps, and camping recommendations. The office is just off Highway 395 in the heart of Bishop.

If you're planning to camp in the White Mountain Ranger District, be advised that campgrounds here are seldom empty. Make advance reservations through the Forest Service's 280-CAMP number if you can. And remember, the practice of free camping on Forest Service land is not allowed in the Big Pine Creek, Bishop Creek, or Rock Creek drainages.

CAMPGROUNDS

Upper Sage Flat Campground *(Hike 34, Big Pine Lakes; Hike 35, Brainard Lake)* To find the recently enlarged Upper Sage Flat Campground, turn west off Highway 395 in Big Pine at the sign for Big Pine Creek. Proceed 9.0 miles on this paved thoroughfare to reach the midsize campground.

Upper Sage Flat Campground offers several pleasant sites shaded by quaking aspens and Jeffrey pines. Drinking water is provided, as are fireplaces, picnic tables, and non-flush toilets. A small section of the campground is available on a first-come, first-served basis. The remainder of the sites may be reserved through the Forest Service.

Sage Flat Campground is open May to November. Reservations accepted. Moderate fee.

Big Pine Creek Campground *(Hike 34, Big Pine Lakes; Hike 35, Brainard Lake)* This wonderfully situated campground is just a stroll away from the trailhead for hikes 34 and 35. Perched near charming Glacier Lodge on Big Pine Creek, the campground boasts fantastic mountain scenery and a pleasant, shaded setting. More than 30 sites for tents or motorhomes provide drinking water, fireplaces, picnic tables, and non-flush toilets.

To reach Big Pine Creek Campground, turn west off Highway 395 in Big Pine at the sign for Big Pine Creek. Proceed 10.5 miles on the paved thoroughfare, and veer left for Glacier Lodge. Cross Big Pine Creek, and go left again to arrive at the campground soon after.

Roughly one-half of the campsites are available on a first-come, first-served basis, but you'll need to show up early to get a spot. The remainder of the sites may be reserved through the Forest Service.

Big Pine Creek Campground is open May to November. Reservations accepted. Moderate fee.

Four Jeffrey Campground *(Hike 36, Tyee Lakes; Hike 37, Green Lake; Hike 38, Bishop Pass; Hike 39, Treasure Lakes; Hike 40, Blue Lake; Hike 41, Lamarck Lakes; Hike 42, Piute Pass; Hike 43, Horton Lake)* This well-equipped campground on the South Fork of Bishop Creek is one of the few campgrounds in the area that consistently has available sites. Four Jeffrey's limited popularity is probably due in part to its distance from the trailheads and largely to the meager fishing opportunities here.

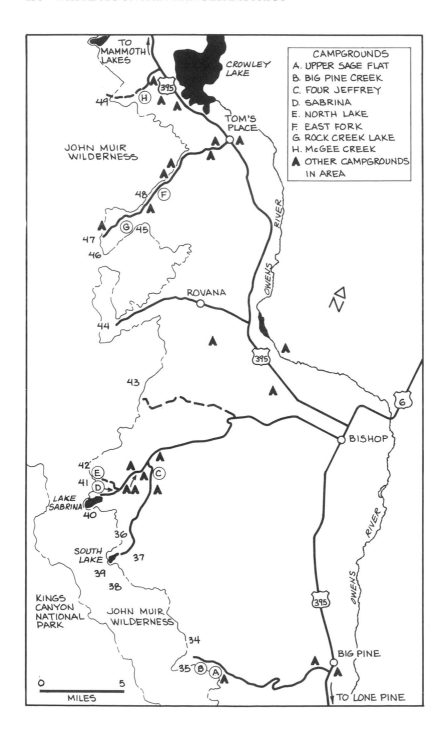

The campground's more than 100 sites for tents or motorhomes provide drinking water, fireplaces, picnic tables, and non-flush toilets. Some sites are shaded, but most are exposed to the sun. The campground's namesake four Jeffreys are by far the dominant trees in the vicinity.

To find the campground, turn west off Highway 395 in Bishop onto Highway 168 (signed for Lake Sabrina and South Lake). Reach a junction signed for South Lake 15.1 miles from Bishop. Veer left at the junction, and continue 1.1 miles to the signed entrance for the campground.

Four Jeffrey Campground is open April to November. Reservations accepted. Moderate fee.

Sabrina Campground *(Hike 40, Blue Lake; Hike 41, Lamarck Lakes; Hike 42, Piute Pass; Hike 43, Horton Lake)* Open campsites are a valuable commodity on the North Fork of Bishop Creek. You'll probably have to take whatever you can get, but the rustic Sabrina Campground is a good choice if you like a bargain: it's free. Convenient trailhead access and excellent fishing opportunities combine to make Sabrina Campground especially popular with people familiar with the area.

To find the campground, turn west off Highway 395 in Bishop onto Highway 168 (signed for Lake Sabrina and South Lake). Drive 9.7 miles to the Bishop Creek Entrance Station, and pause to pick up your campground permit. (You need a permit, even though there is no camping fee.) The entrance station is open from 6:00 A.M. to 9:00 P.M., July 1 through Labor Day.

Reach a junction signed for South Lake 15.1 miles from Bishop. Continue straight 3.4 miles from the junction, and look for a sign for Sabrina Campground on the right. Be sure to post your permit when you claim your spot.

Sabrina Campground's more than 30 sites for tents or motorhomes are sprinkled along the fish-filled North Fork of Bishop Creek. Be prepared to listen to campground conversation centered on trout, bait, and fishing holes if you decide to stay here. Campsites offer picnic tables, fireplaces, and non-flush toilets. There is no drinking water, so you'll have to bring your own.

Sabrina Campground is open May to September. Reservations accepted. Moderate fee.

North Lake Campground *(Hike 40, Blue Lake; Hike 41, Lamarck Lakes; Hike 42, Piute Pass)* This pleasant little campground boasts wonderful access to trailheads on the North Fork of Bishop Creek. In fact, it's within walking distance of two of them. North Lake Campground is especially popular with families, as it's a bit less rustic than nearby Sabrina Campground.

Drinking water is provided at North Lake Campground, as are flush toilets, picnic tables, and fireplaces. About a dozen sites (less than half are suitable for motorhomes) lie along lively Lamarck Creek, not far from the fisherman-flocked North Lake. A few walk-in sites are available as well.

To reach North Lake Campground, follow the driving directions given for Sabrina Campground, but check your mileage at the junction for South Lake (15.1 miles from Bishop). Continue straight 3.1 miles from the junction, and go right at a sign for North Lake. Follow this intermittently paved road 2.0 miles to the campground entrance.

North Lake Campground is open June to October. Reservations accepted. Moderate fee.

East Fork Campground *(Hike 45, Dorothy Lake; Hike 46, Chickenfoot Lake; Hike 47, Mono Pass; Hike 48, Hilton Lakes)* This large campground sprawled along the edge of Rock Creek offers more than 20 sites for tents or motorhomes. Picnic tables, fireplaces, drinking water, and flush toilets are available, and scattered quaking aspens drop their shade on the roomy campsites.

East Fork Campground makes a great launching pad for the many hikes in Rock Creek Canyon. To find the campground, turn off Highway 395 for Rock Creek Lake 15.0 miles south of Mammoth Junction. Drive 6.0 miles on the paved road, and go left at a sign for the campground.

East Fork Campground is open May to October. Reservations accepted. Moderate fee.

Rock Creek Lake Campground *(Hike 45, Dorothy Lake; Hike 46, Chickenfoot Lake; Hike 47, Mono Pass; Hike 48, Hilton Lakes)* This extremely popular campground boasts a scenic situation near the shore of Rock Creek Lake. Although it's cramped and overrun with anglers, the campground is an excellent home base for Rock Creek Canyon day hikers. Hike 45, Dorothy Lake, leaves right from the campground, and the other canyon trailheads aren't far away.

The campground's 47 sites for tents or motorhomes offer picnic tables, fireplaces, drinking water, and flush toilets. Several walk-in sites are a late-comer's best chance of claiming an open spot.

To find the campground, turn off Highway 395 for Rock Creek Lake 15.0 miles south of Mammoth Junction. Continue on the paved road 8.7 miles, and then go left for Rock Creek Lake. Drive the lakeside road 0.4 mile to reach the edge of the campground sprawled along the lakeshore.

Rock Creek Lake Campground is open May to October. Reservations accepted. Moderate fee.

McGee Creek Campground *(Hike 49, McGee Creek)* To find McGee Creek Campground, turn off Highway 395 for McGee Creek 8.5 miles south of Mammoth Junction, and drive the paved road 1.9 miles to the campground entrance. A portion of the campground's 34 sites for tents or motorhomes are available on a first-come, first-served basis. The remainder are reservable through the Forest Service's 280-CAMP number.

Campsites situated right on the banks of McGee Creek are quite pleasant; however, the sage-surrounded sites that bake in the sun a short distance from the water are bleak at best. All sites offer picnic tables and fireplaces. Drinking water and flush toilets are available as well.

McGee Creek Campground is open June to October. Reservations accepted. Moderate fee.

Sparkling McGee Creek flows past tree-covered slopes and grassy meadows.

• •

34   BIG PINE LAKES

Distance: 13.1 miles (loop)
Difficulty: Strenuous
Starting point: 7,800 feet
High point: 10,810 feet
Maps: USGS Coyote Flat 7.5', USGS Mount Thompson 7.5', and USGS Split Mountain 7.5'

There are few trails in the Sierra that have more lake and mountain scenery packed into a 13-mile loop than this Big Pine Lakes jaunt. Not only will you get a peek at the Palisade Glacier, the largest in the Sierra Nevada, but you'll also pass a handful of enchanting lakes. And you'll be courted by the company of rugged mountain peaks throughout your hiking day.

Now that we've sung the praises of this trail, here's one drawback: it's exceedingly crowded. Not only is it a popular backpacking route, but it's also used by scores of climbers seeking access to the mountaintops. Avoid making a Friday, Saturday, or Sunday visit and you'll encounter fewer hikers.

To find the trailhead for Big Pine Lakes, turn west off Highway 395 in Big Pine at the sign for Big Pine Creek. Drive this paved road 10.6 miles to reach a limited day-use parking area at road's end. Drinking water and restroom facilities are available here.

There's additional day-use parking on the spur road to Glacier Lodge, 0.1 mile short of road's end. Backpackers must use the overnight lot near the pack station.

Begin at a sign for the Big Pine Trail, circumventing a gate across the road and walking beside rip-roaring Big Pine Creek. You'll pass a handful of private cabins as you pace beneath Jeffrey pines and Fremont cottonwoods.

Look for the frothy junction of the north and south forks of Big Pine Creek, and then climb to a sturdy bridge across the North Fork at 0.3 mile. The foaming cascade here is titled First Falls. Continue to a signed junction, and go right for the North Fork Trail.

Ascend in several switchbacks, traversing a rugged hillside dotted with sage and mountain mahogany. Fine views into the canyon of the South Fork of Big Pine Creek will entertain you as you climb. The switchbacks end at 0.9 mile, and level walking will take you to a reunion with your abandoned roadbed. Go right on the old road to continue.

Recross the North Fork on another sturdy footbridge, and stay with the road to ascend beside the creek. Second Falls comes into view at 1.2 miles. Your admiration for the lofty waterfall may dim when you realize you'll be climbing to the top of it.

The old road narrows to a trail in a quaking aspen grove at 1.5 miles. Angle right with the trail as your ascent picks up momentum.

Labor up a shadeless hillside in long switchbacks, and reach a junction signed for the pack station (right), Baker Creek (straight), and Big Pine Lakes (left). You may pick up some fellow hikers here, as the pack station trail leads to the overnight parking area. Hikers starting from this trailhead will pace essentially the same distance, but the route is dry and boring.

Go left for Big Pine Lakes, ascending at a steady pace. A sign marks the boundary of the John Muir Wilderness at 2.2 miles. Climb close to the creek once more, as you leave Second Falls behind and saunter in the shade of Jeffrey and lodgepole pines. Look for spreading dogbane and manzanita huddled on the forest floor.

Pass several use trails leading down to fishing holes and campsites on the creek, and stay with the main trail up above. Your climb eases at 2.6 miles as you hike through a meadowy area inhabited by monkshood, ranger buttons, arrowleaf groundsel, and legions of lupine.

Watch for a handsome, rock-walled cabin set near the creek at 2.9 miles. Built by film star Lon Chaney, the building stands empty now.

Resume climbing as the creek's downhill tumble picks up steam. You'll be treated to a fine view of the imposing face of Temple Crag as you round a bend at 3.8 miles. Next, the peaks to the right of Temple Crag come into view. Look for the 14,242-foot North Palisade and then Thunderbolt Peak, Mount Winchell, and Mount Agassiz.

Enjoy level going until you cross Black Lake's outlet creek at 4.2 miles, and then ascend in switchbacks once again. You'll be greeted with a junction (and a decision) at the 4.6-mile point. This 13.1-mile loop route makes the jog to Black Lake from here and returns via Fourth, Third, Second, and First lakes on the trail that continues straight from this junction.

If you feel your energy or time is running low, you can shorten

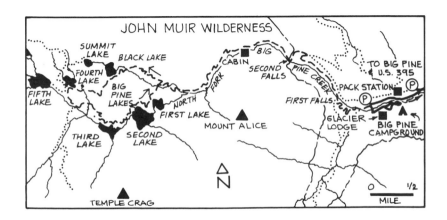

your trek to 9.8 miles by cutting out the Black Lake loop and proceeding straight toward the Big Pine lakes. Go as far as the delightfully scenic Second Lake, and then backtrack to your starting point.

To stay with the longer, loop route, go right for Black Lake as you leave the junction. Climb in steady, unrelenting switchbacks, and enjoy your first peek at First Lake at 4.8 miles. The lake's unusual turquoise hue will startle you at first—it's so unlike the color of a "normal" lake. But you're in glacier country now, and this shocking blue lake is a testimony to the presence of glacial runoff.

If the lake color doesn't make you gasp, the ascent from here surely will. Grind upward at a punishing incline, and pause to suck in lungfuls of air as you pick up sight of Second Lake not long after. Vistas of Temple Crag and surrounding peaks will cheer you as you labor up the hill once more.

The climb finally eases at 5.4 miles, and a willow-filled ravine leads gently upward to the shore of Black Lake at 5.7 miles. You'll know this lake isn't glacier fed at once. Its dark water looks as though it was filmed in black and white, compared with the blazing technicolor of First Lake. Even so, Black Lake is pretty, tucked into a granite slope and edged with Labrador tea and mountain heather.

Leave the scattered campers and anglers on Black Lake's shore, and climb with the trail once more. At the 6.0-mile point, just as the trail begins a brief descent, watch for a rock outcropping on the left. There's a nice view of area peaks and (if you use your imagination) the edge of the famed Palisade Glacier from here.

A gentle downhill trek leads to the edge of Fourth Lake at 6.3 miles. This lovely little gem is also out of the path of descending glacial silt, so it has a more "traditional" color. Leave the company of Fourth Lake to descend to a four-way junction at 6.4 miles. Go left here to begin your trek toward home.

Wonderful views of the mountains, coupled with the roar of the rowdy North Fork of Big Pine Creek, will accompany you as you descend. Reach a junction with the Palisade Glacier trail at 6.7 miles, and continue straight through a meadowy basin awash in wildflowers. Shooting star rules the scene in early season, with California corn lily taking over later on.

The switchback-laden descent to Third Lake kicks in at 7.0 miles. Third Lake is the milkiest of the trio of lakes you'll pass from here, simply because it's first in line for the glacier's handouts. Walk beside Third Lake at 7.4 miles, and continue on to the edge of Second Lake soon after.

If these three lakes were siblings, First and Third lakes would probably be jealous of Second Lake's looks. Second Lake is gorgeous. With statuesque granite shores and a flawless turquoise complexion, Second Lake is framed perfectly by the surrounding peaks.

Leave the charming company of Second Lake at 8.2 miles (be sure to turn back for one last view), and catch a peek at First Lake soon after.

The trail will allow you only a quick look at this lake before you turn away to continue your descent. Reach the junction for Black Lake at 8.5 miles, and keep right here to close the loop to your starting point.

35 BRAINARD LAKE

Distance: 11.4 miles round trip
Difficulty: Strenuous
Starting point: 7,800 feet
High point: 10,260 feet
Maps: USGS Coyote Flat 7.5' and USGS Split Mountain 7.5'

Let's not mince words—this hike to Brainard Lake is punishing. It's long and steep and rugged, and if you get a late start, you'll probably bake for the first few miles.

With those warnings out of the way, consider the positives of this trek: it's much lonelier than the hike to Big Pine Lakes (Hike 34), and it's filled with fantastic mountain scenery. Ideally, you'll have time to sample both of the routes that share this trailhead. Your legs will forgive you—eventually.

To begin the journey to Brainard Lake, please refer to the beginning of the preceding hike (Big Pine Lakes). From the junction just beyond the bridge across the North Fork of Big Pine Creek (0.3-mile point), continue straight for the South Fork Trail. Follow a gentle uphill route along a sage-covered hillside, with the rumble of the South Fork of Big Pine Creek filling the ravine below.

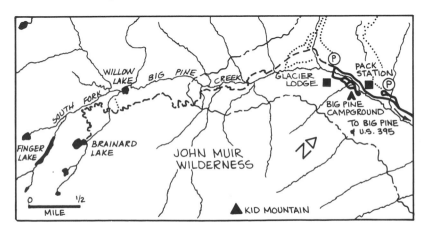

A pair of energetic backpackers braves the punishing trail to Brainard Lake.

Views of the Palisade Crest and Norman Clyde Peak fill the way ahead, while sulfur flower and mountain pennyroyal frolic in your footsteps. Reach an abandoned roadbed at 0.6 mile. Cross the road, and continue with the trail on the far side. Hike gradually uphill on a sometimes rocky, continually weaving path, winding through sage, blue elderberry, and a host of heavenly angelica.

Come in beside the South Fork of Big Pine Creek once more at 1.2 miles, and meander to a creek crossing at the 1.8-mile point. The wooden planks that span the South Fork can be treacherous when the water level is high—be very careful of your footing.

The steady climb eases for a time as you savor a view of the South Fork spilling down the canyon wall ahead. Alas, the ascent renews with a vengeance at 2.0 miles. Before it's over, you may swear it's never going to end.

Climb in scores of steep and rocky switchbacks, consoling yourself with the sight of bright spirea, hearty mountain sorrel, and the enchanting blossoms of crimson and Coville's columbine. You'll pick up the company of sturdy limber pines with added elevation. Unfortunately, the climb only intensifies as you approach the crest.

Stagger to the ridgetop at last, with 3.6 miles and who knows how many switchbacks sweltering behind you, and revel in a dramatic mountain panorama that will make all your sweating seem worthwhile. This is a gorgeous view.

From left to right, marvel at the sight of Disappointment Peak, Middle Palisade Peak and the Middle Palisade Glacier, the Palisade Crest and the Clyde Glacier, and Mount Jepson.

Another 0.1 mile of climbing improves the view even more, yielding what may be the finest vista this hike has to offer. If your legs have had all the uphill going they can take, you might do well to make this viewspot your day's stopping point. Break out the lunch fixings, and "taste" the scenery for an hour.

To continue on to Brainard Lake, revel in a gentle downhill walk through willows and wildflowers. You'll catch sight of Willow Lake at 4.0 miles as you negotiate a steeper descent through rocks.

The cutoff trail to Willow Lake awaits at 4.2 miles. Continue straight for Brainard Lake instead, wading through a stream of wildflowers. Fragrant swamp onions will flood your senses with their odor.

Follow an undulating trail through whitebark and lodgepole pines, and hop across Brainard Lake's outlet creek at 4.4 miles. Now the final climb begins. Ascend through a lush meadow, and then start up a lodgepole-shaded hillside. Expanding views of slowly silting Willow Lake will greet you as you climb.

Struggle up beside Finger Lake's outlet creek, doing your best to ignore the protests of your aching thighs. Abandon the creek at 5.2 miles, pass a small pothole lake, and continue up. The trail dips into a shady, willow-filled ravine at 5.3 miles. Unfortunately, this brief descent is just a teaser.

The climb resumes with sadistic glee from here, and a final steep assault will lead you, gasping, to the shore of Brainard Lake at 5.7 miles. Beautiful Brainard Lake is tucked right into the bosom of the mountains, its lofty situation a testimony to the ascent behind you.

The waters of this pretty, midsize lake are home to much-prized golden trout, and the lakeshore is edged with mountain heather, Labrador tea, and willows. The water is frigid, but not too cold for overheated toes. Scattered campsites tempt overnighters, and possibilities for exploration to higher lakes abound.

Best of all, Brainard Lake is wonderfully secluded, and if you're heading home from here, it's as high as your legs will have to carry you today!

36 TYEE LAKES

Distance: 7.6 miles round trip
Difficulty: Moderate
Starting point: 9,080 feet
High point: 11,020 feet
Map: USGS Mount Thompson 7.5'

The delicate blossoms of Labrador tea add their own unique beauty to Sierra hiking.

Among the wealth of hiking opportunities on the South Fork of Bishop Creek, this trek to the Tyee lakes offers one of the best opportunities for solitude. A string of lakes along the way and a scenic lakeside destination make this an entertaining outing, full of "perks" for younger hikers. Perhaps the hike's one drawback is the hill—it's not exactly gruesome, but it is seemingly eternal.

To reach the trailhead for Tyee Lakes, turn west off Highway 395 in Bishop onto Highway 168 (signed for Lake Sabrina and South Lake). Drive 15.1 miles to the junction signed for South Lake, and go left. Continue 5.0 miles on this paved road, and look for a deluxe footbridge across the South Fork of Bishop Creek (it's just before Willow Campground).

The bridge marks the start of the Tyee Lakes trek. There's shoulder parking available nearby. Cross the South Fork on the footbridge, and leave the creek with the trail continuing straight ahead. Anglers' use trails trace the shoreline to the right and left.

A small, unofficial trail sign for Tyee Lakes will greet you just before your climb begins. Ascend through sage and quaking aspens, and pick up the welcome shade of lodgepole pines as you gain elevation. Start into a series of more than 20 switchbacks at the 0.7-mile point.

This challenging section of the trail will lead you up nearly 1,000 feet. The grade intensifies along the way, but the views expand as well. Enjoy the company of chinquapin and perky Labrador tea as you puff up the hill. Cross little Tyee Creek at 1.9 miles, and continue up through a pine forest.

At 2.2 miles, the trail flattens out at last. Approach the first of the Tyee lakes soon after. This midsize lake has a wildflower-decked shoreline bright with Indian paintbrush, fireweed, larkspur, and ranger buttons. Brightly colored common monkeyflower will "ape" for your attention as you loop around the lakeshore with the trail. The climb resumes at 2.4 miles.

More steep switchbacks slice uphill through the trees, and you'll be ready for another break by the time you reach the second lake at 2.9 miles. This lake is a smaller version of the first. Push onward, as the best is yet to come.

The ascent never breaks its stride as you grunt uphill in more steeply sloped switchbacks. When the hillside opens up to boulders and scrubby whitebark pines, look for the cheery faces of Sierra primrose smiling among the rocks. Blessed level ground will greet you at the 3.2-mile point, and you'll find the third lake 0.2 mile later.

Now the climb begins to seem worthwhile. This lake is an alpine beauty, with a rocky shore and a deep, cold center. Fishing opportunities abound here. (What else would you expect from a string of lakes named

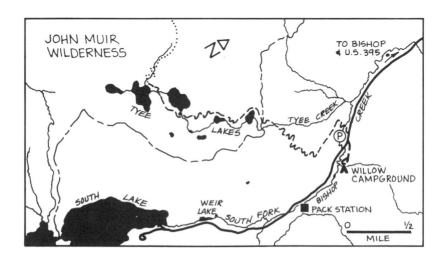

for a brand of salmon eggs?) Area anglers boast of the abundance of rainbow and brown trout in the lakes' cool waters.

Stay with the trail to push on toward the fourth and final lake. If your legs begin to grumble, just ignore them--this lake is the prettiest of the lot.

Swarms of Sierra primrose, Coville's columbine, and mountain sorrel hover in the rocks beside the path, and a brief climb ceases at 3.8 miles, as you emerge on the fourth lake's lovely shoreline.

The lake has a sandy shore that will tempt anglers and toe dippers alike. (Of course, the water is nothing short of frigid.) Visitors in quest of wildflowers will revel in lakeside meadows bursting with hikers gentian, primrose monkeyflower, and little elephant heads. Weary hikers who simply want a place to sit and rest will find this scenic perch amid the mountains to be a delicious picnic for their senses.

37   GREEN LAKE

Distance: 5.8 miles round trip
Difficulty: Moderate
Starting point: 9,800 feet
High point: 11,080 feet
Map: USGS Mount Thompson 7.5'

Like the hike to the Tyee lakes (Hike 36), this trek to Green Lake is one of the least crowded outings on the South Fork of Bishop Creek. It boasts some impressive mountain vistas as well as a host of opportunities for wildflower watching. The hike's unique beginning (the first mile is along an abandoned pipeline) may rule it out for younger hikers, as the footing is frequently unsteady on the pipe.

To find the Green Lake trailhead, turn west off Highway 395 in Bishop onto Highway 168 (signed for Lake Sabrina and South Lake). Drive 15.1 miles to the junction signed for South Lake, and go left. Continue 7.2 miles on this paved road to reach South Lake and the road's end. Park in the day-use parking area near the trail board for Bishop Pass. Toilets and drinking water are available here.

(An alternate trailhead leaves from Parcher's Rainbow Village near the pack station, 6.0 miles from the junction on Highway 168. This trail avoids the pipeline walk but has an additional 500 feet of elevation gain as a drawback.)

From the day-use parking lot at South Lake, walk to the upper end of the overnight wilderness-users' parking lot. Gain a gated, unpaved road that leaves from here. Follow this road a short distance to find the start of your pipeline prowl.

The beaten, old pipe that once carried creek water to South Lake is about 18 inches in diameter. The pipe is sometimes buried, sometimes raised. At times, you'll be able to follow use trails beside it; at other times, encroaching ground cover will force you to tightrope-walk the pipe itself. It's not bad going—just be alert for spots where the metal has collapsed.

Trace a gentle uphill angle with the pipe, walking in the shade of quaking aspens and lodgepole and whitebark pines. You'll hear the whisper of the water still running through the pipe as your footsteps echo on the rusted metal path. The Green Lake Trail ascends the hillside from the pack station at 1.0 mile, meeting the pipeline here.

Look for the resort and pack station below, and abandon your pipeline prowl to join the trail toward Green Lake as it continues steeply up the hill. You'll come in beside a tumbling creek at 1.1 miles. Steep switchbacks climb beside a creekbed choked with willows and wildflowers. Cross the creek at 1.3 miles.

Hike upward through an avalanche-blighted ravine, marveling at the devastated landscape overrun by fireweed. The trail can be difficult to follow here, as rerouting efforts are not well marked. Watch your way carefully for a time.

The grade eases mercifully at 1.5 miles. Enjoy easy walking as you wind into a green lake basin. Early in the season, the trail is lined with brilliantly colored shooting star. Look for little elephant heads, primrose monkeyflower, and Sierra arnica as well.

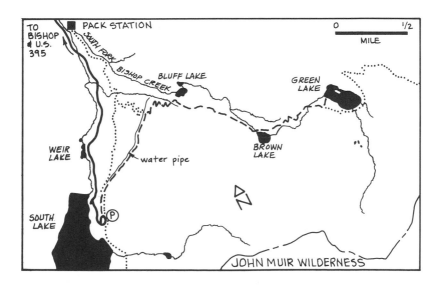

Cross Brown Lake's outlet stream at 2.0 miles, and arrive at little Brown Lake not long afterward. This homely little lake is certainly no beauty queen, but anglers can't take their eyes off it when the trout are jumping. Resume climbing as you leave Brown Lake, enjoying lovely views of the South Fork of Bishop Creek across the canyon.

A gentle uphill leads to a crossing of Green Lake's outlet stream at 2.4 miles. Pause to revel in the view down along the lake basin. Climb onward through a rocky landscape brightened by Coville's columbine and lacy white angelica.

A short, steady up eases as you near Green Lake. The trail branches at the 2.8-mile point. Stay to the left to arrive at Green Lake at 2.9 miles. This large, attractive lake boasts a meadowy shore awash in wildflowers.

Flower lovers will find a host of blossoms early in the year. Scrubby whitebark pines offer spots of shade, and the rocky slopes behind the lake heighten the beauty of the setting. Green Lake is popular with backpackers and anglers, but you shouldn't have any trouble finding the perfect peaceful picnic spot.

38 BISHOP PASS

Distance: 12.0 miles round trip
Difficulty: Strenuous
Starting point: 9,800 feet
High point: 11,980 feet
Maps: USGS Mount Thompson 7.5'
and USGS North Palisade 7.5'

A blaze leads hikers toward Bishop Pass.

It's impossible to say too much about the hike to Bishop Pass. This hike is in a class all by itself. It's fantastic! The bad news is, the word is out about Bishop Pass. This trail attracts a multitude of day hikers, backpackers, and horseback riders. No matter—it's worth the crowds.

Allow yourself an entire day to complete this hike. Not only does the trek to Bishop Pass involve both considerable mileage and a hefty elevation gain, but it boasts so many tempting lakes, so many photo opportunities, and so many sights to linger over, that you won't want to hurry through any part of it.

If you do happen to get a late start on the hike, or if you feel daunted by the length of the walk to the crest of Bishop Pass, you can at least get a taste of this delicious trek by simply making the 4.4-mile

The view from lofty Bishop Pass is one of the Sierra Nevada's finest.

round-trip jaunt to beautiful Long Lake.

To locate the trailhead for Bishop Pass, turn west off Highway 395 in Bishop onto Highway 168 (signed for Lake Sabrina and South Lake). Drive 15.1 miles to the junction signed for South Lake, and go left. Continue 7.2 miles on this paved road to reach South Lake and the road's end. Park in the day-use parking area near the trail board for Bishop Pass. Toilets and drinking water are available here.

Begin walking on the footpath beside the trail board, starting your day with a stroll along the shore of South Lake. This section of the trail is exceedingly busy, and you'll surely encounter anglers, horses, picnickers, and others. Please be sure to step aside for the many tourist pack trains on the trail—skittish horses and inexperienced riders often make a volatile mix.

Views of the surrounding peaks frame South Lake perfectly as you pace an aspen-lined trail, claiming bits of shade from scattered whitebark and lodgepole pines. Turn away from the lakeshore at 0.5 mile to continue ascending through a willow-filled ravine. Shooting star runs rampant here early in the summer.

Wind onward through the trees to arrive at a junction with the trail for Treasure Lakes at 0.8 mile. Keep left for Bishop Pass, and ascend more gently with a view to the right of bulky Hurd Peak. A small stream and a wooden footbridge mark the 1.0-mile point of your trek.

Cross the stream and continue climbing, passing a cutoff trail for

Marie Louise Lake at 1.4 miles. A series of short, well-graded switchbacks yields views down onto Hurd Lake at 1.7 miles. Ascend to a junction with the trail for Bull and Chocolate lakes at the 1.9-mile mark.

Continue straight from the junction, pushing on for Bishop Pass. A wildflower wonderland follows. Watch for hikers gentian, little elephant heads, ranger buttons, and mountain heather as you climb. You'll reach the crest of your ascent at 2.1 miles and then descend to the shore of Long Lake.

This lanky lake is deep and lovely, pointing like a watery arrow toward Bishop Pass. You'll see tall Mount Agassiz to the left of the pass. The Inconsolable Range is the high ridgeline on your left as you cruise the curving shoreline of Long Lake, a popular destination for anglers and campers alike.

Follow an undulating route along a lakeshore bright with Coville's columbine and cinquefoil, and pass the cutoff trail for Ruwau Lake at 2.8 miles. Stay with the main trail, and leave Long Lake soon afterward. Then ascend once more, savoring spectacular views of nearby peaks.

Your path will take you past little Spearhead Lake, another popular haunt of fishermen. Then the climb intensifies along a rocky hillside scented with hearty mountain pennyroyal. Turn back for a scenic farewell to Long Lake before the trail levels off at 3.7 miles.

An easy stream crossing leads into the brief climb to Saddlerock Lake. You'll find this midsize lake studded with rock islands at the 4.0-mile point of your hiking day. Handsome Mount Goode lends its presence to the scene at Saddlerock Lake.

Ascend gently from the lake, and pass the unsigned spur trail to Bishop Lake at 4.5 miles. Continue straight with the main trail, gaining a peek at bite-size Bishop Lake soon after. Now the climb begins to pick up steam.

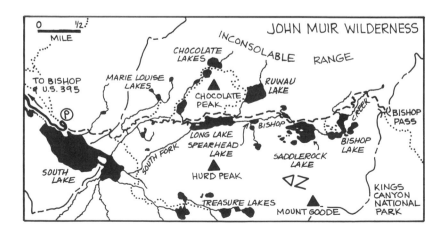

Labor uphill on a rocky trail lined with mountain heather and shrubby whitebark pines. The small stature of the whitebarks is a testimony to the lofty elevation here.

Rocks take over the trail completely at 5.2 miles. Pick your way through several short switchbacks, looking back frequently to savor the sight of Bishop and Saddlerock lakes. The ascent eases at 5.7 miles, as you wind into a notch in the ridgeline.

Continue up across a rock-strewn ridgetop. Nothing grows on this windswept spot but tiny alpine plants and flowers, and it's not unusual to find snow here, even in late August. Massive Mount Agassiz looms just above your left shoulder, and the Inconsolable Range probes the skyline to the left of that.

Reach the crest of Bishop Pass at 6.0 miles. A trail sign marks the boundary of Kings Canyon National Park. You'll want to leave the trail to find the best view from here.

Scramble up the low ridge to the right (north) to gain a panorama that will suck the air out of your lungs. Look out over Bishop, Saddlerock, and Long lakes, mounts Tom and Humphreys, and the Inyo Valley floor. This has to be one of the most gorgeous scenes in the whole Sierra Nevada.

Wander to the left (south) of the Kings Canyon sign, and you'll get a peek down on the Dusy Basin, ruled by Columbine and Giraud peaks. Distant mountains form a backdrop more beautiful than any an artist could conceive. If you have any film left in your camera, shoot it out, and then turn happily for home.

39 TREASURE LAKES

Distance: 6.0 miles round trip
Difficulty: Moderate
Starting point: 9,800 feet
High point: 10,680 feet
Total climb: 1,280 feet
Map: USGS Mount Thompson 7.5'

Those in quest of a friendly family hike around the South Fork of Bishop Creek will do well to investigate this trek to the Treasure lakes. Its name is certainly appropriate—this hike is a gem!

Although the trail to the Treasure lakes gets its share of visitors, it's always less crowded than the Bishop Pass Trail. Weekday hikers may even find it somewhat lonely.

Older hikers enjoy the easy trail to the Treasure Lakes.

Grades are mostly moderate and the footing is good, so the hike is perfect for walkers of all abilities. And anglers, picnickers, and scenery lovers alike will be delighted with the hike's destination, a lake-sprinkled basin that's a Sierra treasure.

To begin your trek to the Treasure lakes, please refer to the beginning of Hike 38, Bishop Pass. From the junction at the 0.8-mile point, go right for Treasure lakes. You'll notice a change in your surroundings when you leave the junction: you'll lose the Bishop Pass–bound pack animals, and the air quality will improve enormously.

Descend on a delightfully horseless trail, crossing a small stream on a rickety bridge and continuing down the hill. Look for the hulking form of 12,237-foot Hurd Peak on the left. On the right, 12,871-foot Mount Johnson dominates the view. A short climb leads into the meat of your descent at 1.1 miles.

Endure a steady drop on a gravel-sprinkled trail. Please be careful of your footing here, as it's very slick. Cross the South Fork of Bishop Creek at 1.4 miles, and enjoy a lupine-lined view up the canyon toward Hurd Peak. More downhill walking leads to the banks of the Treasure lakes' outlet creek not long afterward.

Continue downstream beside the sparkling water, delighting in the company of mountain heather and Labrador tea. Anglers' use trails trace both shores, but stick with the main trail to reach a stream crossing at 1.8 miles. Once across the creek, you'll leave the water and begin to climb again.

Work through a steady, challenging ascent on a winding trail. An expanding view of South Lake will greet you as you climb. The grade mellows across an open granite hillside, and you'll regain the song of the Treasure lakes' outlet stream soon afterward.

Recross the tempestuous little waterway at 2.3 miles, wading through an overflow of mountain heather and leafy lupine. Lovely views of nearby peaks await in all directions. Continue uphill on a rocky trail, snatching bits of shade from hearty whitebark pines. The climb intensifies into

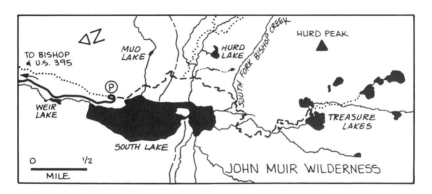

a wearying set of switchbacks and then eases at 2.8 miles.

Push on to reach the first of the Treasure lakes at 2.9 miles. It's a beauty—a deep blue jewel perched on the lip of a rugged lake basin. Surrounding peaks appear to guard the lake from would-be thieves, but campers, anglers, and picnickers are welcome.

Follow the path as it winds on along the lakeshore. Then look for an unsigned use trail departing to the left at 3.0 miles (it passes near a snow marker, also on the left). The use trail will lead you to the second Treasure lake, just a stone's throw from the first.

This little gem is tucked into the protecting shadow of Hurd Peak. It's smaller than the first lake, but it's just as deep and lovely. The shoreline offers wildflowers, willows, and pines for a pleasant picnic setting. Choose a comfortable spot, and settle in.

If you're in the mood for more exploring, additional lakes await you in the watery treasure chest formed by this alpine lake basin. With a topographic map, a little excess energy, and some scrambling skills, you can "treasure-hunt" all afternoon.

40 BLUE LAKE

Distance: 6.2 miles round trip
Difficulty: Moderate
Starting point: 9,070 feet
High point: 10,380 feet
Map: USGS Mount Thompson 7.5'

The Bishop Creek Canyon boasts so many fabulous hikes, this trek to Blue Lake does well simply to be named among them. But put this delightful trek in any other area, and you just couldn't rave enough about it. Blue Lake is undoubtedly one of the most scenic lakes you'll find in the Sierra.

To reach the trailhead for Blue Lake, turn west off Highway 395 in Bishop onto Highway 168 (signed for Lake Sabrina and South Lake). Drive 15.1 miles to the junction signed for South Lake, and continue straight another 3.7 miles to a sign for the Sabrina Basin Trail, on the left. There is limited off-road parking here as well as a parking lot at the Lake Sabrina Lodge, just 0.3 mile farther on.

This trail attracts a multitude of backpackers. However, these overnight wilderness users must park before Sabrina Campground, 0.3 mile short of the trailhead.

The trail toward Blue Lake offers awesome mountain scenery.

Begin walking near the sign for the Sabrina Basin Trail, setting off on a wide, willow- and aspen-lined route. The trail narrows as you climb above the dammed Lake Sabrina, and you'll quickly realize this is also a popular horse-packers' trail. Step carefully as you parallel the lakeshore, pausing to admire the surrounding peaks.

Look for handsome Mount Wallace and needle-nosed Mount Haeckel at the far end of the lake. Closer in, wildflowers try to overrun the trail. Brush past angelica, fireweed, Indian paintbrush, and lupine as you hike. Scrappy whitebark pines are abundant here as well.

Begin climbing away from Lake Sabrina at the 1.0-mile point. You'll have a steady ascent to a junction at 1.3 miles. The swiftly ascending trail that exits to the left leads to George Lake and then over the ridgeline to the Tyee lakes (see Hike 36). Continue straight for Blue Lake.

Cross a stream soon afterward, and reach a second tumbling water-way at 1.6 miles. A series of short, steep switchbacks lies beyond. Labor through the rock-strewn ascent, consoling yourself with expanding vistas of Lake Sabrina and the haze-softened White Mountains to the east.

Round a bend at 2.3 miles, and gain a magnificent view of Mount Haeckel ahead. A peek downhill yields a look at a ribbonlike cascade on the swiftly descending Middle Fork of Bishop Creek. Curve in toward the ruggedly impressive Thompson Ridge as you continue up toward Blue Lake.

This painstakingly stair-stepped section of the trail is the handi-work of the California Conservation Corps. Granite and gravel make for tricky footing, though, so please be careful.

Start up the rocky course of a dry streambed at 2.9 miles, delighting in a flood of Coville's columbine and mountain sorrel. You'll arrive at picture-perfect Blue Lake soon afterward. The scene is done in wonder-ful Sierra technicolor, filled with snow-flecked mountains and sparkling

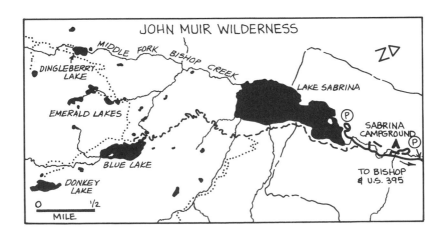

water. Gaze across Blue Lake toward the awesome backdrop formed by the 13,494-foot Mount Thompson and the Thompson Ridge.

Once you've caught your breath again, cross Blue Lake's little outlet creek, and follow the undulating trail along the rugged shore. You'll find your ideal picnic spot with 3.1 miles behind you. Claim a slab of granite with an angle on the view. Plunk in a fishing line or brave a bracing swim. Then get friendly with a sandwich before you turn for home.

If you feel you just can't get enough of this fantastic scenery, the trail continues on an easy route to Dingleberry Lake (via the tiny Emerald lakes). There's very little elevation gain between Blue and Dingleberry lakes, and the ridgeline above Dingleberry (4.7 miles from the trailhead) yields an awesome view of the Clyde Spires and Mount Haeckel. Dingleberry Lake isn't nearly so nice as Blue Lake, however.

41 LAMARCK LAKES

Distance: 6.4 miles round trip
Difficulty: Moderate
Starting point: 9,250 feet
High point: 10,920 feet
Map: USGS Mount Darwin 7.5'

Monkshood lingers in the shadows on the trail to the Larmarck Lakes.

Although this trek to the Lamarck lakes involves a challenging ascent, the distance is quite manageable. Families staying at North Lake Campground near the trailhead will find it a delightful outing. Pack along a picnic and a fishing pole, and plan to spend the day.

If you're driving to the trailhead for Lamarck Lakes, turn west off Highway 395 in Bishop onto Highway 168 (signed for Lake Sabrina and South Lake). Proceed 15.1 miles to a junction signed for South Lake.

Continue straight 3.1 miles from the junction, and go right at a sign for North Lake. Follow this intermittently paved road 1.6 miles to a sign for trailhead parking, and veer right to find a large parking area 0.2 mile farther.

You'll see why this hike is particularly convenient for campers at North Lake Campground when you have to walk the roadway 0.7 mile from the hikers' parking lot to reach the trailhead at the far end of the camping area. Tiptoe past the walk-in sites to find the signed trailhead with nearly a mile already behind you.

Take the trail to the left for "Lamarck," and cross the North Fork of Bishop Creek soon after. This lovely waterway is bright with monkshood, yampah, and swamp onion. Climb away from the creek on a trail lined with quaking aspens, and then start into a passel of switchbacks shaded by tall lodgepole pines.

The hillside opens up at 1.4 miles as you continue upward on a rocky trail. A punishing incline eases slightly at 1.6 miles, and you'll hit the Grass Lake junction shortly afterward. Keep to the right with the trail toward Lamarck lakes, sighing as the climb regains momentum.

Slice back and forth across a sage- and aspen-sprinkled slope. You'll be glad for an early start (if you got one), as the sun can be relentless here. Distract yourself with views of North Lake and the Inyo Valley floor. The peaks to the south form the rugged Thompson Ridge.

The ascent is unrelenting, and you may wonder if you've somehow entered an eternal set of switchbacks as your thighs begin to scream. Don't despair—the crest of the climb awaits at the 2.5-mile point. Let loose a whoop of triumph, and then pass a small pothole lake as you continue on your delightfully level way.

Reach the short spur trail to Lower Lamarck Lake 0.1 mile later. Muriel Peak rules the skyline to the west, while Mount Lamarck dominates the view to the southwest. Lower Lamarck Lake is large and deep, and anglers won't be able to resist taking a shot at its cool waters. A shoreline dotted with rocks and willows makes this the superior picnic destination of the two Lamarck lakes.

Don't stop short without a look at the upper lake, however—it's too beautiful to miss. Continue with the trail, and cross the lower lake's outlet creek. Climb on a rough and rocky route, enjoying the company

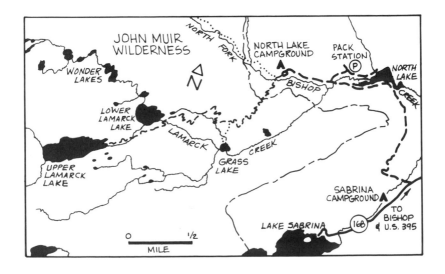

of intricately formed Coville's columbine. A handful of challenging switchbacks leads to the banks of Upper Lamarck Lake's outlet creek. Cross the creek and ascend beside it, watching for resident ranger buttons and sassy shooting star. You'll gain the edge of the upper lake at 3.2 miles. Fed by the snowfields just above, the lake is achingly cold. It boasts a brilliant aqua hue, set off by the glowing granite on an exceedingly rocky shore. A massive moraine rules the farthest shore, and the bulk of Mount Lamarck completes a picture-perfect scene.

. . . .

42 PIUTE PASS

Distance: 11.0 miles round trip
Difficulty: Strenuous
Starting point: 9,250 feet
High point: 11,423 feet
Map: USGS Mount Darwin 7.5'

The trek to Piute Pass is one of those unusual hikes where the journey itself is more remarkable than the destination. It's not that Piute Pass isn't beautiful—it boasts a rewarding view to the east and west—it's just that getting to the pass is absolutely wonderful. This is a hike that has mile after mile of delightful scenery.

You'll heighten your enjoyment of this trek considerably if you're able to avoid doing it on a weekend. Saturdays and Sundays bring hordes of horses and backpackers to the trail. It's often difficult to find an open parking spot at the sprawling trailhead lot.

If the distance to the pass seems a bit daunting, don't rule out the Piute Pass hike. A handful of lovely destination spots offer options for a shorter day.

To find the trailhead for Piute Pass, please read the early paragraphs of the preceding hike, Lamarck Lakes. From the trail's start at the far end of North Lake Campground (the 0.7-mile point), go right at the sign for "Piute." Begin climbing through quaking aspens and lodgepole pines while the North Fork of Bishop Creek lends its cadence to your walk.

Ascend on a rocky trail lined with mountain pennyroyal, nude buckwheat, and red penstemon, and come in beside the North Fork at 1.2 miles. You'll cross the creek at 1.3 miles, climb with the falling water, and cross the creek again. Watch for ranger buttons, Bigelow's sneezeweed, monkshood, and the elusive Sierra rein orchid along the trail.

Scattered lodgepole pines offer their shade as you ascend steadily on an often rugged trail. Pass below a rocky, red-hued slope ruled by the

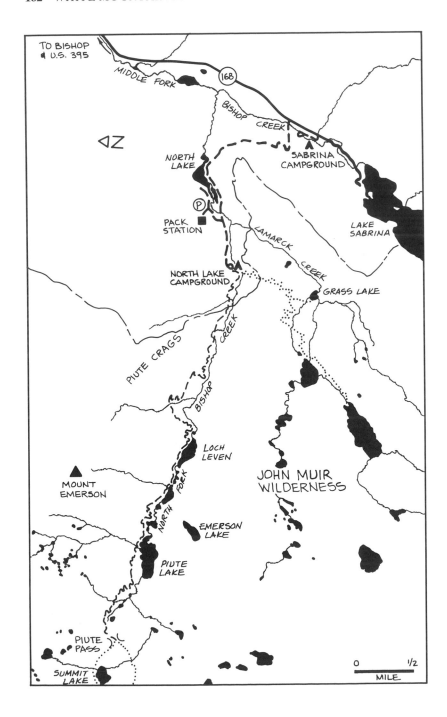

TO BISHOP
◀ U.S. 395

MIDDLE FORK

168

BISHOP CREEK

◁Z

NORTH
LAKE

SABRINA
CAMPGROUND

P

PACK
STATION

LAKE
SABRINA

LAMARCK CREEK

NORTH LAKE
CAMPGROUND

GRASS LAKE

PIUTE CRAGS

BISHOP CREEK

LOCH
LEVEN

JOHN MUIR
WILDERNESS

MOUNT
EMERSON

NORTH FORK

EMERSON
LAKE

PIUTE
LAKE

PIUTE
PASS

SUMMIT
LAKE

0   ½
MILE

The crest of Piute Pass welcomes young hikers.

stern Piute Crags at the 2.0-mile point, savoring the sparkling expanse of shooting star that blooms beside the trail. A series of switchbacks awaits just ahead.

Your steep and rocky uphill push will finally ease at 2.9 miles. Enjoy an easy uphill finish to arrive at Loch Leven Lake at 3.1 miles. This rock-edged little lake is overpowered by the cliffy peaks that peer down into its depths. Camping, fishing, and picnicking spots are scattered along the shore, inviting an early stop for those who need a rest.

Gaze upward along the lake basin from your perch at Loch Leven Lake and you'll spot Piute Pass beckoning in the distance. That should be enough to get your legs in gear again. Continue with the trail along Loch Leven's shore, and begin climbing gently toward Piute Lake.

Stubby whitebark pines, hearty mountain heather, and scattered willows line the way as you wind through a meadowy basin sprinkled with small ponds. Wildflowers are abundant early in the season. Meadow penstemon and little elephant heads delight those who pause to hunt for them.

Ascend a low ridgeline at 3.8 miles, and then descend into a pocket-sized meadow filled with hikers gentian. Another gentle climb leads to the edge of Piute Lake at 4.2 miles. While much larger than Loch Leven Lake, Piute Lake may be less inviting—its rocky shores are often cold and windswept. Still, they tempt their share of campers and anglers.

Climb away from Piute Lake on a winding trail, weaving through a carpet of tiny alpine wildflowers. You'll hit a series of swiftly ascending switchbacks at 4.8 miles. Pause along the way to savor satisfying vistas of Piute and Loch Leven lakes.

The climb mellows quickly, melting into more lovely meadow walking, with Piute Pass ahead. These high, alpine meadows are home to brilliantly colored wildflowers. Primrose monkeyflower, Lemmon's paintbrush, and little elephant heads thrive in this lofty setting above 10,000 feet.

The final ascent to Piute Pass kicks in at the 5.3-mile mark in your day. Zigzag uphill on an exceedingly rocky trail, pausing often to glean extra oxygen from the thinning air. Each stop will yield an increasingly fantastic panorama of the lake basin below, with Piute and Loch Leven lakes looking distant and pure and cold.

The most gorgeous vista comes just before the summit. Gaze back on your path a final time, and then push on to Piute Pass at 5.5 miles. After all the prepass loveliness, you may find your goal to be somewhat anticlimactic. Most people expect an 11,423-foot pass to make them a little dizzy; Piute Pass doesn't.

The terrain falls gently away on either side of the crest, making the spot seem more like a hilltop than an 11,423-foot ridgeline. Even so, it's often brutally cold and windy on the pass. Perhaps that will give thrill seekers some satisfaction. The view is satisfying, too. Pull out a jacket and a camera, and enjoy!

Face toward the west, and look down on the trail that leads toward Summit Lake. Beyond that, a rim of ragged peaks rips the Sierra skyline, with Glacier Divide and The Pinnacles reigning supreme. The mass of Mount Humphreys rules in the north, while Muriel Peak guards the southern sky.

Still, the best view to be found is the one you'll have when you turn homeward and gaze out over the treasure-filled lake basin you've just walked through.

· · · · · · · · · · · · · · · · · · · ·

43 HORTON LAKE

Distance: 9.8 miles round trip
Difficulty: Strenuous
Starting point: 7,750 feet
High point: 10,040 feet
Maps: USGS Tungsten Hills 7.5' and USGS Mount Tom 7.5'

The hike to Horton Lake is not for everyone. First of all, it's very difficult to reach the trailhead. The unpaved access road is long and extremely rough—definitely unsuited for an ordinary passenger car.

Next, the hike begins at a low elevation. Late starters or those who don't do well in heat will probably want to avoid this trek. Finally, the trail to Horton Lake is often rocky, and the climb is long. This is not an easy walk.

With those warnings out of the way, just what does Horton Lake have going for it? It's beautiful, and it's largely undiscovered. Invest a day in the hike to Horton Lake, and you'll reap dividends of scenic mountain vistas, abundant wildflowers, and a lovely lakeside destination. And, with any luck, you'll have the whole adventure to yourself!

To find the trailhead for Horton Lake, turn west off Highway 395 in Bishop onto Highway 168 (signed for Lake Sabrina and South Lake). Drive 7.3 miles, and veer right onto the unpaved Buttermilk Road. The road splits after 4.0 miles. Keep to the right and stay with the main dirt road another 2.0 miles (6.0 miles from Highway 168). Then turn right onto an unsigned (as of 1989) and extremely rough spur road.

Continue 0.8 mile to where the road splits. If you're driving an appropriate vehicle, it's possible to keep right from the junction and drive another 0.6 mile to a gate across the road. Our woefully "inap-

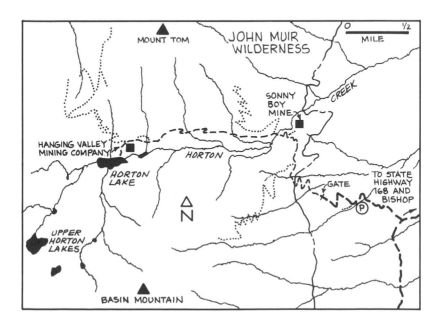

propriate" passenger car was rubbing its belly and complaining, so we parked 0.6 mile short of the gate and began the hike mileage here.

Stay to the right from the junction, and ascend on a rocky road through sage and shadeless ground. Reach the gate across the road at 0.6 mile. Circumvent the barrier, and continue on with the rocky mining-access road. The bulk of towering Mount Tom is straight ahead.

Climb in long, rugged switchbacks. Even in this dry terrain, sulfur flower, scarlet gilia, mountain pennyroyal, lupine, and mule ears brighten the harsh landscape. Reach the edge of a murmuring grove of quaking aspens at 1.6 miles, and continue steadily uphill.

Views expand to take in the Bishop Creek canyon, the Owens Valley, and the distant White Mountains as you climb. You'll top a rise at 2.2 miles and then delight in a brief descent. Pass a short spur road that leads to the abandoned Sonny Boy Mine settlement at 2.3 miles. (This is fun to explore, if you have the time.)

Resume climbing much too soon. You'll cross crystal clear Horton Creek on an old wooden bridge at 2.5 miles, and then enjoy level walking through a broad meadow that's overwhelmed with wild iris early in the season. The ascent kicks in again as you head up into Horton Creek's canyon.

Look for Basin Mountain, the Four Gables, and Mount Tom as you hike. Endure a steady, challenging climb on a sage-lined road, tracing the hillside above Horton Creek. You'll finally hit a pair of switchbacks at 3.4 miles. Gain some extra elevation here, and then continue on the straight-arrow path toward Horton Lake.

Sulfur flower, red penstemon, crimson columbine, and snatches of sweet-smelling wood rose decorate the route, and a pleasing view of a small waterfall on Horton Creek will take you into another set of short switchbacks at 3.8 miles. Negotiate the subsequent straight and steady stretch of roadway, and then hit another switchback at the 4.4-mile point.

You can avoid this zigzag by watching for a faint footpath marked by a small pile of stones (it takes off from the roadway as the switchback begins). The path cuts through a stand of quaking aspens and rejoins the road at 4.5 miles. You'll get your first look at the small, marshy lake below Horton Lake soon after you regain the road.

Continue up to earn a peek at Horton Lake not long after. Horton Lake balances boldly on the lip of its alpine basin, just above a long cascade in Horton Creek. The rocky road branches at 4.6 miles. Keep left to make the short descent to Horton Lake, and pass the abandoned buildings of the Hanging Valley Mining Company along the way.

Reach the flower-covered shore of Horton Lake at 4.9 miles. No carpet could be lovelier than this weave of alpine shooting star, primrose monkeyflower, and hikers gentian. And the picture formed by Horton Lake, embraced by a close-knit brotherhood of surrounding peaks, is a wonderful climax to any hiking day.

44 PINE LAKE

Distance: 9.4 miles round trip
Difficulty: Strenuous
Starting point: 7,400 feet
High point: 9,950 feet
Map: USGS Mount Tom 7.5'

Day hikers are a rare commodity on the trail to Pine Lake, probably because of the hike's difficulty and the isolated trailhead. The route is popular with backpackers and horse riders, though. You certainly won't lack for company on weekends.

Pine Lake is definitely a worthy goal   it's large and beautiful. But you'll want to keep some things in mind before you go. First of all, an early start is very important, as the first few miles of this hike can be punishing in midday heat. Second, if you're not in the habit of wearing boots on your Sierra outings, you may want to wear them here. Much of the trek traces the route of an old mining road. It's extremely rocky walking.

Finally, this hike really isn't convenient to any organized campground. Free camping is possible on Forest Service land along Pine Creek; otherwise, you'll have a bit of a drive from your base of operations.

To find the Pine Creek trailhead, drive Highway 395 north of Bishop, and turn off at the sign for Pine Creek Road and Rovana. Follow the

Overheated hikers give in to the temptations of Pine Creek.

paved Pine Creek Road 9.4 miles to road's end and a sign for the Pine Creek trailhead. There's a pack station and a pair of woeful outhouses here. There is no drinking water, so be sure to fill up before you come.

Begin walking at the trailhead sign, taking the unpaved road past the pack station. Gain the trail proper just beyond. Climb on a dusty roadway edged with sage and rocks, sinking the cadence of your footsteps into the roar of Pine Creek. The road narrows to trail width just before a creek crossing at 0.3 mile.

Ascend steadily from here, grateful for the shade of white firs and quaking aspens. Pink-petaled wood roses paint the air with sweetness. Another stream crossing at 0.6 mile offers a cool sanctuary from the sun, populated by a choir of glowing monkshood.

Trade fir trees for Jeffrey pines and Sierra junipers as you continue up. You'll see the buildings of the sprawling Pine Creek Tungsten Mill across the way as you pant across a sage-covered hillside at 0.9 mile. Views extend to the valley floor and the White Mountains in the distance.

Ascend in well-graded switchbacks and join an old mining road at 1.1 miles. It's rugged walking, steep and rough and hot. The road snakes uphill in long, punishing switchbacks, its edges strewn with mountain mahogany, sulfur flower, phlox, and unexpected explosions of giant blazing star.

You'll get a brief break at 1.7 miles as the road levels off to cross a creek. Then climb again, enjoying the sight of stout Sierra junipers. Pass an old mine shaft probing the hill's belly at 1.9 miles, and look for the abandoned tram line nearby.

More grim climbing leads to your first look at the upper reaches of Pine Creek at 2.2 miles. The water paints a lovely picture as it slides downhill through a series of granite chutes. Unfortunately, the ascent continues unabated as you work upward toward the headwall of the canyon.

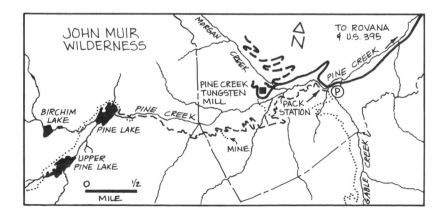

Leave the rock-strewn mining road (with absolutely no regrets) at 2.8 miles, and continue upward on a—guess what—rocky trail. Note the appearance of whitebark pines along the hill as you gain elevation. Cross a small creek at 3.5 miles, its banks awash in Labrador tea and willow. Then endure more switchbacks to reach a sign for the John Muir Wilderness at the 3.8-mile point in this exhausting day.

Good news: the gruesome climb will soon be over! Reach the crest of your ascent just past the sign, and cruise onward through a sparse pine forest with the rumble of Pine Creek on your right. Come in beside the creek at 4.2 miles, and ascend gently beside the water.

This lovely waterway will tempt you with scores of inviting pools and petite waterfalls. If you don't stop to wriggle your toes at least once, you don't know how to live!

Make your leisurely way toward Pine Lake, strolling through a creekside paradise. The trail crosses glowing expanses of polished granite here, the handiwork of a long-departed glacier. Reach an unsigned fork in the trail at 4.5 miles. Keep to the right to find a log ford across Pine Creek (the branch to the left is the horse route).

From the creek crossing, a gentle climb will take you to the edge of Pine Lake at 4.7 miles. An awesome mountain backdrop gives this large lake a delightful setting. And broad slopes of variegated stone add a Sierra "art deco" influence.

The lake's deep, clear water will tempt overheated hikers (at least those who haven't already succumbed to Pine Creek's attractions). Fishing, picnicking, and camping spots abound on the spacious shoreline, too. An additional 1.1 miles of easy walking will take the energetic traveler on to Upper Pine Lake. It's another lovely spot.

45 DOROTHY LAKE

Distance: 6.0 miles round trip
Difficulty: Easy
Starting point: 9,700 feet
High point: 10,560 feet
Map: USGS Mount Morgan 7.5'

When compared with some of the higher trails in Rock Creek Canyon, this trek to Dorothy Lake is downright lonely. Yet it leaves from an immensely popular family campground, and it's a pleasant, easy hike. The Dorothy Lake hike is at its best early in the season, when the meadows that line the trail are still green from winter snows.

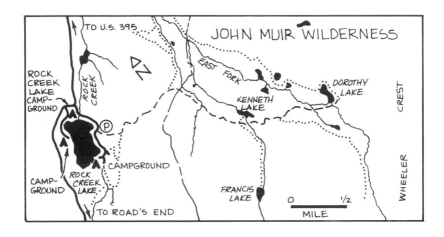

To reach the trailhead for Dorothy Lake, turn off Highway 395 for Rock Creek Lake 15.0 miles south of Mammoth Junction. Drive the paved road 8.7 miles, and then go left for Rock Creek Lake. Follow the lakeside road 0.4 mile to enter Rock Creek Lake Campground, and watch for a sign for trailhead parking. Leave your vehicle in one of the hiker slots on the left side of the road.

Begin at the trailhead information board near the parking area, setting out on a rough, swiftly climbing trail. A steady up through quaking aspens leads to a junction at 0.2 mile. Continue straight for Dorothy Lake, enjoying expanding views of Rock Creek Lake as you labor up a challenging incline.

At 0.4 mile, pause for an outstanding vista of Rock Creek Canyon, with the triple treat of Mount Dade, Mount Abbot, and Mount Mills ruling the horizon. All three peaks are above 13,000 feet. Continue uphill on a trail lined with angelica, mountain pennyroyal, and red penstemon.

The climb eases a bit as you press onward, and scattered whitebark and lodgepole pines distribute patches of cooling shade. Nearly level walking leads to a trail junction at the 1.0-mile point. Go right here for Kenneth Lake.

Enter a meadowy basin guarded by the rocky Wheeler Crest, and hike gently uphill on a sandy trail edged with sage and whitebark pines. The climb intensifies at 1.4 miles and then eases once again. You'll find another junction at 1.8 miles. The trail to the right goes to Francis Lake, while the left-hand trail leads to what's left of Kenneth Lake. (Several low-snow years had nearly done in Kenneth Lake by 1990.)

Continue straight for Tamarack Lake, and pay homage to the parched remnants of Kenneth Lake as you pass. Wander through another meadow brightened by early-season wildflowers, and then start into a series of swiftly climbing switchbacks at 2.1 miles.

Pause, panting, at yet another junction 0.3 mile later. Go left here for Dorothy Lake. Wind onward with an undulating trail to emerge in a broad meadow after 2.6 miles. Admire the rugged shoulders of the Wheeler Crest as you walk a grass-edged trail across the meadow.

Reach the marshy shore of little Dorothy Lake at 3.0 miles. Although it's shallow and petite, Dorothy Lake is attractive, with a shoreline shaded by scattered pines. A lakeside meadow hides a treasure of hikers gentian, with the jewel-like blossoms of alpine gentian an even rarer treat.

Picnickers and anglers will have no trouble passing an afternoon at Dorothy Lake, while energetic day hikers or backpackers may decide to explore the trails to other lakes in the area.

Hikers relax after a swim in Dorothy Lake.

46 CHICKENFOOT LAKE

Distance: 5.8 miles round trip
Difficulty: Easy
Starting point: 10,240 feet
High point: 10,810 feet
Maps: USGS Mount Morgan 7.5' and USGS Mount Abbot 7.5'

This delightful walk to Chickenfoot Lake is undoubtedly the finest
family outing Rock Creek Canyon has to offer. First of all, the hike begins above 10,000 feet, so you'll be starting out with one foot in heaven.
Then the trail climbs gently past a handful of alpine lakes, all potential
stopping points for weary walkers. Finally, spectacular mountain scenery
accompanies every footstep, making this trek a treat from start to finish.

Of course, with all that going for it, this trail is painfully popular in
July and August. Avoid weekend visits like the plague: you'll find the
crowds daunting and empty parking spaces nearly nonexistent. Weekdays make the masses much more manageable—and the hiking infinitely
more enjoyable.

To reach the trailhead for Chickenfoot Lake, turn off Highway 395
for Rock Creek Lake 15.0 miles south of Mammoth Junction. Drive the
paved road 10.5 miles to road's end and a sign for hiker parking. There are
non-flush toilets here.

Begin walking on the closed-off road at the far end of the parking
lot, continuing straight at a sign for the Mono Pass Trail. Climb very
gently beside rushing Rock Creek, sharing your way with schools of
eager anglers. Lovely alpine scenery unfolds at once, as a handful of
13,000-foot peaks frames the trail.

Reach an entry sign for the John Muir Wilderness at 0.3 mile. The
ascent picks up from here, and you'll climb on a rocky trail lined with
willows and leafy lupine. Arrive at a signed junction at 0.5 mile, and keep
left for Morgan Pass.

A brief ascent is rewarded with a wonderful view of Little Lakes
Valley, backed by its encircling peaks. Descend to cross a creek at 0.7
mile, and gain a look at Mack Lake to the left. Climb again, pacing a wide,
rocky trail. The craggy form of Bear Creek Spire claws the sky ahead.

You'll spot grassy Marsh Lake to the left of the trail at the 1.0-mile
point. Continue on to cross a small feeder creek at 1.2 miles. Descend
toward Heart Lake, tiptoeing across Ruby Lake's outlet creek along the
way. Heart Lake is petite and pretty, pulsing within willow-sprinkled
shores.

Enjoy level walking as you pace beside Heart Lake, and then keep
to the right with the main trail, climbing gently past a flower-filled

The trail toward Chickenfoot Lake winds through a spectacular alpine basin.

meadow. Delight in the cheery company of little elephant heads and hikers gentian as you continue.

The ascent mellows past spacious Box Lake at 1.7 miles. You'll climb beside Rock Creek before rock hopping across the water. Continue gently up to reach the lower end of Long Lake at 2.1 miles. This lake is the most beautiful yet, deep and sprawling and framed by peaks.

Gain a wide roadbed along the lakeshore, and watch for a flock of alpine flowers roosting in the rocks that line the way. Coville's columbine, mountain sorrel, and phlox thrive in the thin mountain atmosphere of this lofty lake basin. Lovely level walking leads to the far end of Long Lake. Then the climb resumes.

Endure a steady ascent on a wide and rocky trail, and reach the junction for Chickenfoot Lake at 2.8 miles. The main route continues straight for Morgan Pass and the adjacent Pine Creek Canyon (see Hike 44, Pine Lake). Go left at the junction to press on toward Chickenfoot Lake.

Climb straight toward the granite face of Mount Morgan, and reach a rocky ridgeline and the end of your ascent. You'll have a wonderful vista of Mount Mills just across the Little Lakes Valley as you pause for a glance back the way you've come. Descend to the shore of Chickenfoot Lake at 2.9 miles.

This beautiful alpine lake scratches at the underbelly of massive Mount Morgan, clinging to the hillside on a 10,789-foot perch. It's a satisfying spot to end a hiking day filled with panoramic pauses. Spread your picnic on the meadowy shoreline, or wiggle your toes awhile in the ice-cold water. Then turn happily for home, watching Rock Creek Canyon's scenery unfold from a host of new angles.

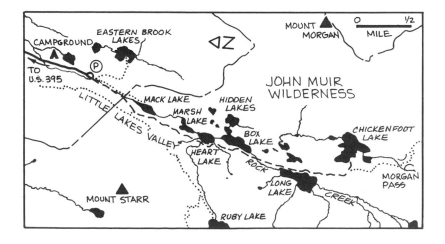

Jubilant hikers rejoice at the crest of Mono Pass.

• •

47 MONO PASS

Distance: 8.0 miles round trip
Difficulty: Strenuous
Starting point: 10,240 feet
High point: 12,120 feet
Maps: USGS Mount Morgan 7.5' and USGS Mount Abbot 7.5'

The hike over Mono Pass is a popular backpackers' route into the Pioneer Basin and on to the Pacific Crest Trail. A healthy distance and a hefty elevation gain make Mono Pass a challenging day-hike destination, but the trek is worth the work for the enchanting scenery along the way.

Famed Sierra naturalist and explorer William Brewer paused at the crest of Mono Pass in 1864. The vista he saw then is the one you'll see today, extending to the Mono Recesses and the lake-sprinkled Pioneer Basin. This 12,040-foot pass is barren and exposed. Bring a jacket for the cold, and don't linger if thunderclouds are present.

To get started on your hike to Mono Pass, please refer to the beginning of Hike 46, Chickenfoot Lake. From the junction at the 0.5-mile point, stay to the right for Mono Pass. Switchbacks slice uphill through scrubby whitebark pines, and a trail will join you from the pack station at 0.7 mile.

Continue for Mono Pass, accompanied by the blossoms of nude buckwheat, phlox, and angelica. The trail straightens out before a nice viewpoint at 0.9 mile. Pause for a look out over the Little Lakes Valley, threaded by the watery stream of sparkling Rock Creek. You'll see Mack Lake, Marsh Lake, Heart Lake, and Box Lake, serenaded by a symphony of peaks.

Climb steadily, with expanding views of the lake basin, and pass a small pothole lake at 1.6 miles. The grade intensifies and then eases once again. Watch for perky hikers gentian in the meadowy spots beside the trail, while pungent mountain pennyroyal dominates the drier sections.

Arrive at a junction with the spur trail to Ruby Lake at 2.0 miles. A short stroll leads to this alpine beauty, set like a precious stone within its ring of mountains. You'll get a look down on Ruby Lake from the main trail. Unless you have a lot of time and energy, skip the detour and continue to the right for Mono Pass.

Start into the meat of your ascent, picking up a view of Mount Dade and Mount Abbot to the south as you continue. A series of short and steady switchbacks attacks the hill, yielding a vista of Ruby Lake at the

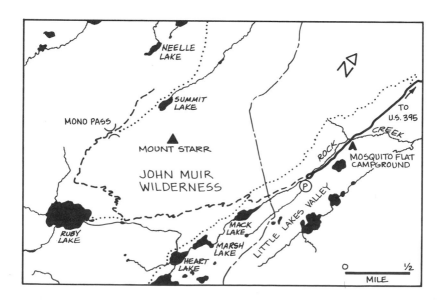

2.4-mile mark. Continue up without a break, consoling yourself with wonderful alpine scenery. The sudden presence of lively purple rockfringe is a testimony to the increasing elevation. Round a bend at 3.1 miles, and gaze up the draw toward Mono Pass. Stifle a weary sigh and struggle on. The final climb kicks in from here.

The setting is pure High Sierra as you push on—barren, bleak, and oh, so beautiful. You'll finally see the crest ahead, 3.4 miles from the trailhead. Stagger onward through an achingly steady climb, and win Mono Pass at 3.7 miles. A sign proclaims the elevation and your victory.

The view from the trail is wonderful, offering a peek downhill toward Summit Lake, but a little extra effort on your part will yield an even more spectacular vista. Leave the main trail at the sign, and angle uphill to the left. A faint use trail leads the way to the windswept ridgeline above the pass.

You'll hit 4.0 miles here and discover a view that's truly magnificent. Gaze down on Pioneer Basin and its lakes. Then look out toward Mount Stanford, Mount Crocker, Red and White Mountain, and Mount Baldwin. Linger as long as time and the icy wind will let you. Then scramble downhill to the trail, and turn back for the trailhead.

• •

48 HILTON LAKES

Distance: 8.8 miles round trip
Difficulty: Strenuous
Starting point: 9,840 feet
High point: 10,370 feet
Total climb: 1,730 feet
Maps: USGS Mount Morgan 7.5' and USGS Mount Abbot 7.5'

If you've done many hikes in the Sierra, the trail to the Hilton lakes won't be one of your favorites. It's a roller-coaster affair, less than scenic, and dusty with the passage of horse-packers. However, the Hilton lakes themselves are delightful. And, compared to the busy lakes reached by the Mono Pass Trail (see hikes 46 and 47), the Hilton lakes are downright isolated.

To find the trailhead for Hilton lakes, turn off Highway 395 for Rock Creek Lake 15.0 miles south of Mammoth Junction. Pass the permit station after 0.2 mile, and continue 8.9 miles on the paved road to a sign for the Hilton Lakes–Davis Lake trailhead. There's limited parking just

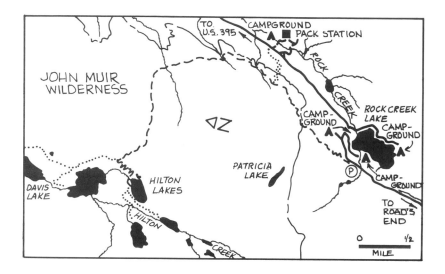

beyond, on the right side of the road. (Rock Creek Lake is just across the way.)

Begin climbing on an aspen-lined trail, enjoying views down to Rock Creek Lake and up Rock Creek Canyon to the lovely peaks beyond. Trees obscure the vista before long. Continue up the hillside in the shade of lodgepole pines.

Reach the crest of the initial ascent at 0.4 mile, and ease into more level walking with some gentle ups and downs. Look for sage, lupine, nude buckwheat, sulfur flower, and scarlet gilia in the dusty ground along the way. Arrive at an entry sign for the John Muir Wilderness at 0.7 mile.

More undulating terrain follows, and small meadows boast bright fireweed, California corn lily, and yarrow. At the 1.3-mile point, a feeder trail joins in from the pack station, adding more horses to an already trampled trail. Continue straight for the Hilton lakes.

A long, gentle downhill levels off at 1.6 miles, and then you'll glide across an open hillside studded with Sierra junipers. Start into a steady climb at 2.0 miles. You'll end it, panting, atop a lodgepole-covered ridge at the 2.3-mile mark.

Stay to the right as the trail branches, and continue on a wide, sandy route beneath the trees. At 2.9 miles, the gentle ascent becomes a full-fledged assault on a tree-sprinkled hillside. A half mile of climbing leads to yet another dry ridgetop.

Continue through an avalanche-blighted area littered with the corpses of uprooted trees, and then start into a steep descent at 3.7 miles. You'll groan inwardly as you pick your way downhill on a steep, switchback-studded trail, knowing that this little "detour" means more climbing on your homeward journey. Pause for a peek at distant Davis Lake through the trees as you descend.

Reach a junction at 4.1 miles and go left toward the Hilton lakes (the sign calls out "3rd–6th Lake"). The trail to the right leads toward Davis Lake and the second Hilton lake.

Climb in short, steep switchbacks, breathing threats against the person who laid out this roller-coaster ride the Forest Service calls a trail. Your muttering will end with a happy sigh at 4.3 miles as you arrive at a wonderful viewpoint of Davis Lake and the second Hilton lake. Beyond Davis Lake, the view extends to the valley floor and the distant White Mountains.

Continue with a level trail to reach the shore of the third Hilton lake at 4.4 miles. This lovely alpine lake will win you over right away, and you'll quickly forget your griping at the trail as you admire a startling granite backdrop that tumbles right into the lake's cool waters.

Best of all for hungry hikers, the lake boasts a meadowy shoreline that's perfect for picnicking. Find a spot beside a blossoming mountain heather bush, or plunk yourself down in a nook filled with Labrador tea. Wiry whitebark pines offer shade to those who want to flee the sun.

Anglers can explore the depths of the third Hilton lake and its nearby neighbors for brook trout and the much-prized golden trout. The high elevation guarantees a chilly dip for hikers with swimming on their minds.

The mountain-backed Hilton Lakes are a scenic day-hike destination.

49 McGEE CREEK

Distance: 6.0 miles round trip
Difficulty: Easy
Starting point: 8,100 feet
High point: 9,080 feet
Map: USGS Convict Lake 7.5'

Pleasant creekside walking, lovely mountain scenery, and very little company—these are the treats a walk along McGee Creek has to offer. Those in quest of a lake will find the distance daunting (the first lake this trail accesses is Steelhead Lake, about 7 miles in), but if you can be satisfied with an easy stroll along a pretty waterway, give this hike a look.

To reach the trailhead for McGee Creek, turn off Highway 395 at the sign for McGee Creek (8.5 miles south of Mammoth Junction), and drive the paved road 1.9 miles to McGee Creek Campground. The trailhead access road is unpaved past the campground.

Proceed an additional 2.1 miles on gravel to reach road's end and the trailhead parking area. There's a free, walk-in campground here (non-flush toilets, no drinking water).

Begin walking beside the trail-information board, and climb through a dry, sage-sprinkled landscape with views up the canyon to Mount Abbot and Mount Baldwin. Arrive at an entry sign for the John Muir Wilderness at 0.1 mile.

A trail joins in from the pack station soon afterward. Continue to the left with the main route, ascending gradually along the hillside. You'll

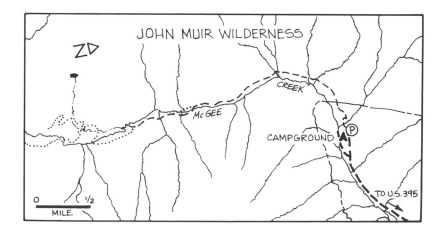

see McGee Creek rushing headlong through its green ravine just below. At 0.6 mile, the climb eases as you hoof it through a herd of yellow-blossomed mule ears. The face of 12,458-foot Mount Crocker comes into the picture on the left as you continue. A gentle ascent leads through quaking aspens and blue elderberry bushes. Cross a small stream edged with cavorting common monkeyflower at 1.2 miles.

Climb steadily for a time. Then come in close to McGee Creek at 1.9 miles, and enjoy more level walking. You'll have Sierra junipers and limber pines for company as you press on. Angle left with the trail at 2.3 miles, and run smack into McGee Creek soon after.

You'll face a couple of options here: you can wade across the water, wondering what happened to the bridge while your toes do a quick freeze, or you can try the boulder-hop crossing that's just upstream from the ford (watch for a use trail leading to the right before you hit the creek). You'll probably get your feet wet either way, but please be careful at both spots—McGee Creek's water really moves early in the summer.

If you choose to wade, continue gently uphill on numb but invigorated toes. The trail from the rock ford joins in from the right soon after. The ascent gains intensity at 2.7 miles, as you work your way upward through a narrowing in the canyon.

Enjoy an unfolding vista at 3.0 miles. The route levels off as McGee Creek meanders through a broad, green meadow. Long meadow grasses hide a host of wildflowers early in the season. Unless you're planning to push on (and up) toward Steelhead Lake, now's the time to begin searching for your picnic spot. Take the side trail exiting on the right, and descend into the meadow.

This is a lovely spot. You'll see McGee Creek tumbling down through a rocky chute at the upper end of the little valley, while the foreground boasts clumps of willows, waving wildflowers, and a winding waterway. Behind it all, bulky Mount Crocker rules the scene, peeking down from the heavens to see what you packed in your picnic bag.

CHAPTER SIX
· · · · · · · ·

Mammoth and Mono Lake Ranger Districts/ Devil's Postpile National Monument

The hiking region encompassed by the Mammoth and Mono Lake ranger districts is probably the most heavily used area on the east side of the Sierra Nevada and south of Yosemite National Park. Weekends are zooish here, and open camping sites can be difficult, if not impossible, to find. Fortunately, a wide variety of camping options are available.

If you're not familiar with the area, make a Forest Service office your first stop upon arriving. The Mammoth Ranger District Office–Mammoth Visitor Center, in the town of Mammoth Lakes, is well signed from Road 203. Be sure to pause here for campground listings, overnight wilderness permits, or information on entry regulations for the Devil's Postpile National Monument.

This office boasts a good supply of free literature as well as a wide selection of books and maps for purchase. This is a good place to do your research on the Devil's Postpile National Monument, too. The mailing address is Mammoth Ranger District, PO Box 148, Mammoth Lakes, CA 93546.

If you're venturing into the Agnew Meadows–Red's Meadow area and Devil's Postpile National Monument, be advised that vehicle access is restricted for the area. Those staying at one of several campgrounds in the area must pay camping fees and obtain vehicle permits at the Devil's Postpile entrance station. Entrance-station personnel keep a running total on vacancies at the nonreservation campgrounds within the boundaries, and you won't be allowed to drive into the area if there aren't any open sites.

Even with a vehicle permit, it's best to take advantage of the intra-valley shuttle bus when traveling to and from area trailheads. The shuttle is free to those staying within the Devil's Postpile National Monument boundaries. The shuttle runs frequently, is easy to use, and reduces traffic on the twisting, narrow Devil's Postpile road.

Day visitors to Devil's Postpile National Monument must leave their vehicles at the Mammoth Mountain ski area and pay to use the intravalley shuttle bus. Ask at either the Mammoth Ranger District Office–Mammoth Visitor Center or at the Mammoth Mountain ski area for a bus schedule and fee information.

If you're exploring the area slightly to the north of Mammoth Lakes, visit the Mono Lake Ranger District office in Lee Vining. The office is just west of the junction of Highway 120 (Tioga Pass Road) and Highway 395. The mailing address is Mono Lake Ranger District, PO Box 429, Lee Vining, CA 93541.

Day hikes in the Mammoth and Mono Lake ranger districts explore both the John Muir and Ansel Adams wildernesses. Please refer to chapter 1, Huntington Lake and Kaiser Pass, for background information on these protected areas.

CAMPGROUNDS

Convict Lake Campground *(Hike 50, Convict Lake)* This extremely popular campground near the shore of Convict Lake is packed with anglers, families, and water lovers of every shape and size. It offers great access to pretty Convict Lake, where boaters, swimmers, and anglers abound. The campground is not on a reservations system at present, so an early arrival is essential to your chances of claiming a site.

To find Convict Lake Campground, turn west off Highway 395 at the sign for Convict Lake, 4.5 miles south of Mammoth Junction. Drive the paved road 2.3 miles, and then angle left for "Day use parking." Continue 0.1 mile, and veer left again to enter the campground.

Convict Lake Campground's 88 sites for tents or motorhomes provide picnic tables, fireplaces, drinking water, and flush toilets. Shade is a scarce commodity here. Some of the nicest sites are scattered along Convict Creek.

Convict Lake Campground is open April to October. No reservations. Moderate fee.

Sherwin Creek Campground *(Hike 51, Valentine Lake)* Secluded Sherwin Creek Campground is an excellent camping option for the often filled-to-overflowing Mammoth Lakes area. When you can't find an open campsite at other places, you might find one here. The campground is pleasant and attractive, set on singing Sherwin Creek and shaded by tall Jeffrey pines.

To reach Sherwin Creek Campground, turn off Highway 395 at Mammoth Junction. Follow Road 203 through the town of Mammoth

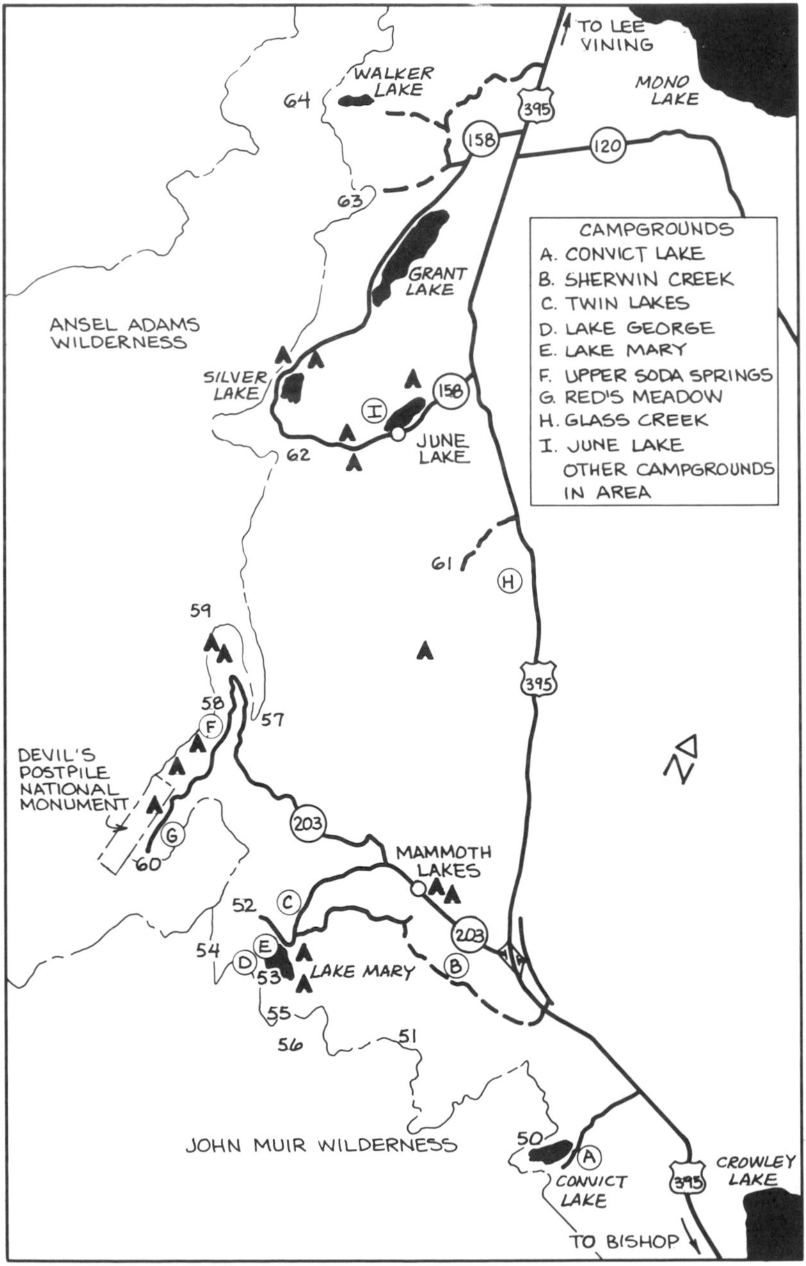

TO LEE VINING
MONO LAKE
WALKER LAKE
64
395
158
120
63
GRANT LAKE
CAMPGROUNDS
A. CONVICT LAKE
B. SHERWIN CREEK
C. TWIN LAKES
D. LAKE GEORGE
E. LAKE MARY
F. UPPER SODA SPRINGS
G. RED'S MEADOW
H. GLASS CREEK
I. JUNE LAKE
OTHER CAMPGROUNDS IN AREA
ANSEL ADAMS WILDERNESS
SILVER LAKE
JUNE LAKE
62
61
59
58
57
DEVIL'S POSTPILE NATIONAL MONUMENT
203
60
MAMMOTH LAKES
52
54
53
LAKE MARY
55
56
51
JOHN MUIR WILDERNESS
50
CONVICT LAKE
CROWLEY LAKE
TO BISHOP

Lakes, and go south on Old Mammoth Road. Drive 0.8 mile, and then veer left onto Sherwin Creek Road. You'll lose the pavement 0.2 mile later. Continue an additional 1.7 miles on gravel to gain the campground entrance.

Sherwin Creek Campground's 27 sites for tents or motorhomes offer picnic tables, fireplaces, drinking water, and flush toilets. The majority of sites are on a first-come, first-served basis, but some sites can be reserved through the Forest Service's 280-CAMP number.

Sherwin Creek Campground is open May to October. Reservations accepted. Moderate fee.

Twin Lakes Campground *(Hike 52, McLeod Lake; Hike 53, TJ Lake and Lake Barrett; Hike 54, Crystal Lake and Mammoth Crest; Hike 55, Emerald Lake and Sky Meadows; Hike 56, Duck Pass; Hike 57, San Joaquin Ridge)* This developed campground adjacent to the people-packed Twin Lakes absorbs a large portion of the camping crowd that floods the Mammoth Lakes area on every summer day. With 97 sites for tents or motorhomes, Twin Lakes Campground comes equipped with horseback riding, boat rental, and a grocery store as well as the more mundane features of picnic tables, fireplaces, and flush toilets. Drinking water is available as well.

To find Twin Lakes Campground, turn off Highway 395 at Mammoth Junction, and drive Road 203 through the town of Mammoth Lakes. Reach the signed Lake Mary Road after 3.7 miles. Continue straight onto this paved thoroughfare, and proceed 2.3 miles to a sign for Twin Lakes Campground. Veer right onto a paved side road, and reach the campground entrance after 0.5 mile.

Despite its size and hectic atmosphere, Twin Lakes Campground is quite pleasant, with many scenic, shaded sites to choose from. While you're staying here, be sure to make the short drive to the Twin Lakes overlook at Twin Falls (1.9 miles farther on Lake Mary Road). Park at the signed Twin Falls Picnic Ground, just across from Lake Mamie.

Lake Mamie's outlet stream tumbles downhill more than 300 feet from this spot, creating Twin Falls along the way and feeding the basin that holds Twin Lakes. You can't see much of Twin Falls from the overlook, but you will have a great view down to the jewel-like Twin Lakes. Take a pair of binoculars, and perhaps you'll spot your tent!

Twin Lakes Campground is open June to October. No reservations. Moderate fee.

Lake George Campground *(Hike 52, McLeod Lake; Hike 53, TJ Lake and Lake Barrett; Hike 54, Crystal Lake and Mammoth Crest; Hike 55, Emerald Lake and Sky Meadows; Hike 56, Duck Pass; Hike 57, San Joaquin Ridge)* The always-busy Lake George Campground is a favorite spot for families and anglers, and it's an ideal launching pad for day

The scenic hike along the San Joaquin Ridge commences with an awesome panorama of Mount Ritter and the Minarets.

hikes in the Mammoth Lakes area. Set on the shore of pretty Lake George, the campground's 21 sites for tents or motorhomes offer picnic tables, fireplaces, drinking water, and flush toilets.

An early arrival time is essential if you hope to claim a vacant site at Lake George Campground. If you're fortunate, you'll find a spot with a view of the lake. To find Lake George Campground, turn off Highway 395 at Mammoth Junction, and drive Road 203 through the town of Mammoth Lakes. Reach the signed Lake Mary Road after 3.7 miles.

Continue straight onto this paved thoroughfare, and proceed 3.9 miles before veering left onto Road 4S09 (signed for Lake Mary and Lake George campgrounds). Drive Road 4S09 0.3 mile, and go right for Lake George. Arrive at the campground 0.3 mile later.

Lake George Campground is open June to October. No reservations. Moderate fee.

Lake Mary Campground *(Hike 52, McLeod Lake; Hike 53, TJ Lake and Lake Barrett; Hike 54, Crystal Lake and Mammoth Crest; Hike 55, Emerald Lake and Sky Meadows; Hike 56, Duck Pass; Hike 57, San Joaquin Ridge)* Like the nearby Lake George Campground, Lake Mary Campground is an exceedingly popular spot. Its more than 50 sites for tents or motorhomes are set near the shore of spacious Lake Mary. Some sites have a fine view of the lake, and the campground boasts the usual selection of picnic tables, fireplaces, drinking water, and flush toilets.

To find Lake Mary Campground, turn off Highway 395 at Mammoth Junction, and drive Road 203 through the town of Mammoth

Lakes. Reach the signed Lake Mary Road after 3.7 miles. Continue straight onto this paved thoroughfare, and proceed 3.9 miles before veering left onto Road 4S09 (signed for Lake Mary and Lake George campgrounds). A brief 0.1 mile on Road 4S09 leads to Lake Mary Campground.

Lake Mary Campground is open June to October. No reservations. Moderate fee.

Upper Soda Springs Campground *(Hike 58, San Joaquin Trail to Devil's Postpile National Monument; Hike 59, Shadow Lake; Hike 60, Rainbow Falls)* Upper Soda Springs Campground is located within the Agnew Meadows–Red's Meadow area of the Mammoth Ranger District, making it subject to the special camping setup discussed in this chapter's introductory paragraphs. It's one of the less busy campgrounds in the area and is usually the best bet for late arrivers.

The campground's 22 roomy sites for tents or motorhomes are set near the San Joaquin River and provide excellent access to the San Joaquin Trail. Sites offer picnic tables, fireplaces, drinking water, and non-flush toilets.

To find Upper Soda Springs Campground, turn off Highway 395 at Mammoth Junction, and drive Road 203 through the town of Mammoth Lakes. Reach a junction signed for Lake Mary Road and Mammoth Mountain–Devil's Postpile after 3.7 miles.

Angle right for Devil's Postpile, and continue 5.6 miles to the Devil's Postpile entrance station. You'll need to pause here to check on site availability and obtain your vehicle pass. While you're in the vicinity, be sure to check out the Minaret Vista (the paved entry road exits to the right just before the entrance station).

A short 0.3-mile detour leads to the vista parking area. Climb out of your car to marvel at a fantastic view of Mount Ritter, Banner Peak, and the Minarets. A plaque beside the parking area provides names for the peaks. You'll feel like you're standing in the heavens as you gaze at the surrounding mountains from your 9,265-foot perch. A self-guiding nature trail leaves from the vista point (this is also the start of Hike 57, San Joaquin Ridge).

To continue your drive to Upper Soda Springs Campground, leave the entrance station and proceed 5.0 miles on the paved road toward Devil's Postpile National Monument. Turn off the pavement at a sign for Upper Soda Springs Campground, and gain the campground entrance 0.2 mile later.

Upper Soda Springs Campground is open June to October. No reservations. Moderate fee.

Red's Meadow Campground *(Hike 58, San Joaquin Trail to Devil's Postpile National Monument; Hike 59, Shadow Lake; Hike 60, Rainbow Falls)* This is probably the most popular campground in the Agnew

Meadows–Red's Meadow area of the Mammoth Ranger District—and for good reason. It boasts a bonus many seasoned hikers would give their eyeteeth for: a bathhouse with hot showers!

No, the U.S. Forest Service hasn't suddenly decided to pamper its campers—these free showers are provided by a higher power: they're fueled by a natural hot spring.

Even if you aren't able to get a site at Red's Meadow Campground, you can use the showers while you're camping in the area. There's a small visitors' parking lot beside the bathhouse. Of course, the showers are usually busy, but they're always worth the wait.

Additional features of Red's Meadow Campground seem anti-climactic after such a treasure, but here they are. The campground's 54 sites for tents or motorhomes are pleasantly situated in a shady grove of Jeffrey pines. Campsites offer picnic tables, fireplaces, drinking water, and flush toilets.

To find Red's Meadow Campground, turn off Highway 395 at Mammoth Junction, and follow Road 203 through the town of Mammoth Lakes. Reach a junction signed for Lake Mary Road and Mammoth Mountain–Devil's Postpile after 3.7 miles. Angle right for Devil's Postpile, and drive 5.6 miles to the Devil's Postpile entrance station. You'll need to pause here to check on site availability and obtain your vehicle pass.

From the entrance station, continue 7.7 miles on the paved road toward Devil's Postpile National Monument, and turn left at the sign for Red's Meadow Campground. If you have a choice, try to select a site away from the hot-spring bathhouse. Your walk to the showers will still be short, and you'll avoid some of the bathhouse noise and traffic.

Red's Meadow Campground is open June to October. No reservations. Moderate fee.

Glass Creek Campground *(Hike 61, Glass Creek Meadow; Hike 62, Fern Lake; Hike 63, Parker Lake; Hike 64, Lower Sardine Lake)* This easy-to-miss campground just north of the Mammoth Lakes junction is probably the best accommodation bargain to be found in the entire Mammoth Lakes area. Granted, Glass Creek Campground lacks certain "luxuries" like flush toilets and running water; however, the campground is free, and it's so large and unstructured that one can almost always find a site here.

To join the dozens of bargain-seeking motorhome residents that frequent Glass Creek Campground, turn west off Highway 395 6.0 miles south of the more southerly of the two June Lake junctions (the turn is just across from a sprinkling of highway department buildings). Drive in a short distance to reach the sprawling camping area, strung out along tiny Glass Creek.

The campground's more than 50 sites for tents or motorhomes offer picnic tables, fireplaces, and non-flush toilets. You'll have to provide your own drinking water, though.

Believe it or not, the little ribbon of water (Glass Creek) that trickles through the campground yields many fish. The creek is stocked at least once a week during the summer. Even if you're not an angler, you'll probably be offered a few fish for your supper. Anglers' creels are almost always bigger than their stomachs.

While you're at the campground, be sure to check out the nearby Obsidian Dome. This impressive mound was formed by lava that escaped from a crack in the earth's surface thousands of years ago. The rugged surface of the dome is sprinkled with large chunks of obsidian, and it looks more like some surreal moonscape than a typical Sierra scene. Reach Obsidian Dome via Glass Flow Road, 2.3 miles north of the Glass Creek Campground turnoff.

Glass Creek Campground is open May to November. No reservations. No fee.

June Lake Campground *(Hike 61, Glass Creek Meadow; Hike 62, Fern Lake; Hike 63, Parker Lake; Hike 64, Lower Sardine Lake)* The pleasant June Lake Campground boasts more than 20 roomy sites for tents or motorhomes. Many of the sites are quite close to the shoreline of June Lake, and all offer picnic tables, fireplaces, flush toilets, and drinking water.

June Lake Campground is very popular on weekends. Come early or make your reservations through the Forest Service's 280-CAMP number if you want to be assured of a site. To find the campground, turn off Highway 395 at the more southerly of the two June Lake junctions. Drive the paved road 2.5 miles to the sign for June Lake Campground, and go right.

June Lake Campground is open May to November. Reservations accepted. Moderate fee.

• •

50 CONVICT LAKE

Distance: 2.8 miles round trip
Difficulty: Easy
Starting point: 7,640 feet
High point: 7,670 feet
Map: USGS Convict Lake 7.5'

The trailhead at Convict Lake offers access to some ruggedly beautiful Sierra backcountry, including lovely Mildred Lake in the John Muir Wilderness. Unfortunately, the length and difficulty of the trail rule out a day hike for all but the most able hikers. An easy, family-style jaunt around the lakeshore seems more in order here, considering the popularity of Convict Lake and its campground with visitors of all ages and abilities.

This pleasant excursion along the shore of Convict Lake provides some stunning mountain vistas and a host of opportunities for fishing, picnicking, exploring, and getting happily sidetracked. The hike is especially nice for people staying at Convict Lake Campground, as there's no need to climb into a vehicle to reach the trailhead.

To find the Convict Lake trail, turn west off Highway 395 at the sign for Convict Lake (4.5 miles south of Mammoth Junction). Drive the paved road 2.3 miles, and angle left for "Day use parking." Find an open slot, and abandon your vehicle. Toilets are available at the parking area.

Leave the day-use parking area and descend to the paved lakeside path. Your first good look at Convict Lake will steal your heart immediately. It's really lovely—a deep blue saucer rimmed by the bulk of handsome Laurel Mountain. Linger long enough to read the information plaques along the lakeshore. They detail the history, geology, and botany of the area.

Convict Lake is named for a group of prison escapees who fled to the spot in 1871. They headed up Convict Canyon (at the upper end of the lake), with a pursuing posse hot behind them. The resulting gun battle left the posse leader dead (Mount Morrison is named for him). Several of the convicts were killed or captured. The few who eluded the law still haunt these mountains.

Begin your lakeside stroll in a counterclockwise direction, and cross Convict Lake's outlet stream on a sturdy bridge (walking along the shoulder of the auto road). Bob through the marina parking lot, and gain a gravel path that angles to the right from the far end of the lot.

You'll pick up a view of towering Mount Morrison on your left, looming above the surface of the lake. At 0.2 mile, an access trail joins

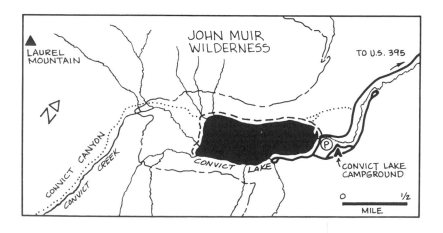

Soft-barked quaking aspens bear the defacing signatures of thoughtless visitors.

from the right. Continue on the level lakeside path, accompanied by sage and willows, fragrant wood rose, and whispering Fremont cottonwoods.

One more trail feeds in at the 0.3-mile point. Then an undulating route rolls onward, with expanding views of 12,275-foot Mount Morrison. You'll see a stringerful of anglers spaced out along the shoreline, probing the clear blue waters of Convict Lake for hungry trout.

Pass a lone Jeffrey pine at 0.8 mile, its butterscotch-scented bark clinging like a rough hide to the stout trunk. Reach the upper end of Convict Lake and a fork in the trail at the 1.2-mile mark. The route to the right leads on toward Mildred Lake, but it soon develops into a punishing climb on an exceedingly rugged path. (A series of washouts ravaged the trail in August 1989, necessitating extensive repair work.)

If you have the time and don't mind lengthening your day a bit, it's well worth the effort to explore onward an additional 0.9 mile from the junction. Climb steadily with the trail leaving to the right, and earn a view up into the legendary Convict Canyon. Snow-flecked Red Slate Mountain sits astride the headwall of the canyon, and the trail yields a fine view eastward to the haze-softened White Mountains.

To continue your lakeshore prowl, angle left from the junction, and hike in the company of Sierra junipers, mountain mahogany, Fremont cottonwoods, and quaking aspens. Reach the banks of Convict Creek at 1.4 miles. The water trickles into Convict Lake in a host of rivulets, and a grove of much-initialled quaking aspens lend their shade.

Wander over to the lakeshore to spread your picnic, wiggle your toes, or unreel your fishing line. If you're visiting Convict Lake with a boat in tow, it's possible to make "ferry" connections from this spot (as long as you don't mind a little wading).

Those exploring this hike with children will do best to backtrack to their starting point from here, but a very rough use trail does continue around Convict Lake, if you choose to brave it. Be prepared for a lot of bushwhacking, however. The route is difficult at best, and scratches, tumbles, and yellowjacket stings can make the southside scramble more exciting than you'd wish.

· ·

51 VALENTINE LAKE

Distance: 12.0 miles round trip
Difficulty: Strenuous
Starting point: 7,870 feet
High point: 9,710 feet
Map: USGS Bloody Mountain 7.5'

Although the 12-mile round-trip distance for this trek may be somewhat daunting, Valentine Lake really isn't an unreasonable day-hike destination, even for walkers of moderate ability. The trail is well graded throughout—with a final uphill push before the lake—and good footing and pleasant surroundings make the miles pass quite easily.

If the length of the trek does get to be too much for some, the little Sherwin lakes lie less than 3 miles in, offering an early stopping point for the weary.

To find the trailhead for Valentine Lake, turn off Highway 395 at Mammoth Junction. Follow Road 203 through the town of Mammoth Lakes, and go south on Old Mammoth Road. Drive 0.8 mile and veer left onto Sherwin Creek Road. You'll lose the pavement 0.2 mile later.

Continue an additional 1.1 miles on gravel and turn right at the sign for the Sherwin Lakes trailhead. Reach the unpaved trailhead parking

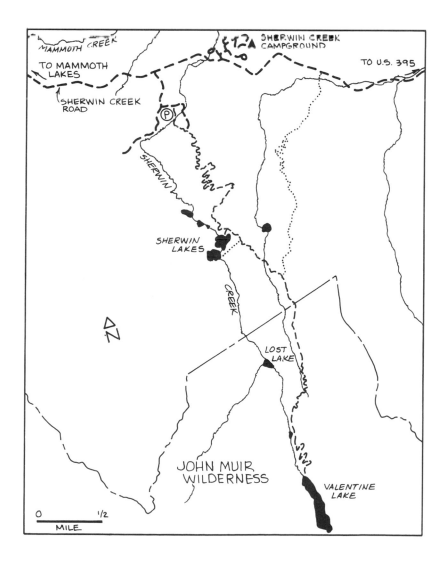

area after 0.4 mile. Non-flush toilets are available here.

Begin walking at the sign for Sherwin Lakes, setting off on a sage-lined trail where mule ears cavort in the dry soil. Scattered white firs and Jeffrey pines lend spots of shade to a sometimes stifling start. This trail seems to get the bulk of its visitors from a boys' camp situated near the trailhead, and the jubilant voices of young campers may drift your way as you begin.

Descend to cross Sherwin Creek at 0.2 mile, and then climb gently, easing into a series of long switchbacks that will last the next 30 minutes. The mellow grade intensifies at 0.9 mile, and you'll pick up views to Mammoth Lakes and its sprawling development.

Reach the crest of the switchback-scribbled hill at 2.1 miles. Then delight in a stretch of downhill and level walking, with a vista of 11,053-foot Mammoth Mountain on the right. Abandon the main trail at 2.5 miles, angling right to arrive at the first of the Sherwin lakes.

Small and rocky, the lake is certainly not spectacular, but it's nice enough to invite a rest break for the weary. When you're ready to push on, return to the main trail and wind onward through the trees. Arrive at a signed junction at 2.7 miles. A spur trail to the right leads the short distance to another of the Sherwin lakes.

Keep to the left for Valentine Lake, and pace an undulating trail through a dry landscape dotted with ancient-looking Sierra junipers. Cross a small creek at 3.1 miles, and climb steadily for a few minutes. The route flattens out to lead to yet another trail junction at the 3.3-mile point.

Shun the side trail joining in from the left (this comes from a secondary trailhead), and continue straight for Valentine Lake. Enjoy a short stretch of easy walking through junipers and pines, and then resume climbing to reach an entry sign for the John Muir Wilderness.

A gentle climb beside an aspen-lined creek will take you to a marshy wildflower wonderland at 4.2 miles. Look for tall ranger buttons, diminutive pink monkeyflower, ethereal angelica, and elusive Sierra rein orchid as you tiptoe past. You'll stride into another bout of climbing as you leave the marsh, fueled by the flowers' loveliness.

Cross a small creek at 4.6 miles, and continue your ascent with a view down to Lost Lake on the right. Droopy mountain hemlocks edge the path as you walk onward, and things begin to open up soon after. Enjoy fine views of the surrounding peaks as you work your way into the rugged canyon ruled by Valentine Lake.

Pass a grass-lined pond at 5.1 miles, and pick up the murmur of Sherwin Creek soon after. Ferns and wildflowers wiggle their toes in the creek's cavorting waters, and you'll zigzag steadily uphill while Sherwin Creek dives downward through a boulder-strewn ravine. If you find yourself groaning at the hill, console your aching muscles with the knowledge that this incline ends at Valentine Lake.

A handful of tiring switchbacks cease at 6.0 miles, and you'll

It's love at first sight for visitors to pretty Valentine Lake.

emerge on the lower lip of long and lovely Valentine Lake with trembling legs and a pounding heart. Perhaps it's love that evokes these symptoms; then again, it may just be the hill. Whatever—Valentine Lake will win your affections immediately. It's a beautiful corner of the Sierra.

Surrounding mountains wrap around the lake's blue water, encircling it like a beau's strong arms. And Valentine Lake snuggles happily into its boulder-strewn shores, clinging to the adoring peaks even as its outlet stream tumbles headlong toward the distant valley floor.

Pick a shady spot along the lakeshore, and settle in for a picnic or an afternoon of fishing. You won't tire of the view for hours. Be sure to scramble up the small bluff on the north side of the lake's outlet stream, once you've regained your energy. The brief climb yields a wonderful vista of the valley far below.

· ·

52 McLEOD LAKE

Distance: 1.2 miles round trip
Difficulty: Easy
Starting point: 8,990 feet
High point: 9,320 feet
Map: USGS Crystal Crag 7.5'

This short jaunt to McLeod Lake makes a super family outing, especially for those with junior hikers in their ranks. Although the climb to the lake is steep, it's mercifully brief, and youngsters can be lured along with promises of picnic goodies and rock skipping at the lake. Please be forewarned that McLeod Lake is closed to swimming, as it's part of the Mammoth Lakes watershed.

As with all hikes in the Mammoth Lakes area, the trek to McLeod Lake is painfully overpopulated. Please avoid weekend visits whenever possible, and lessen your impact on this trampled corner of the wilderness by using trailhead toilets and carrying out every scrap of litter.

To find the trailhead for McLeod Lake, turn off Highway 395 at Mammoth Junction, and drive Road 203 through the town of Mammoth Lakes. Reach the signed Lake Mary Road after 3.7 miles. Continue straight onto this paved thoroughfare, and proceed 5.0 miles to road's end and a large parking area beside Horseshoe Lake. (This lake offers the only swimming in the area.)

Begin walking at a sign for the Mammoth Pass Trail. Climb immediately, ascending through a forest of lodgepole pines and scattered moun-

Little McLeod Lake waits at the end of a wonderfully brief walk.

tain hemlocks. The hillside is scribbled with a dozen faint use trails, a testimony to the scores of people that make this trek every summer day. Continue up to reach a signed junction at 0.1 mile, and keep to the left for McLeod Lake.

The grade eases slightly as you press on through a sampling of western white and whitebark pines and rough-barked red firs. Savor views of the cliffy Mammoth Crest to the left as you continue up the hill, and watch for the beefy bulge of Mammoth Mountain on the right. Pant through a very steep, final uphill push to gain a second trail junction at 0.6 mile.

The trail to the right leads on to Mammoth Pass and the Devil's

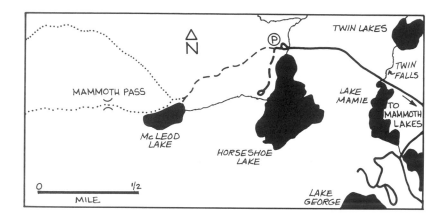

Postpile area on the west side of the Sierra crest. The largely vistaless Mammoth Pass is the lowest gap between east and west in the entire central portion of the Sierra Nevada. Rainfall on the west side of the pass ends up in San Francisco Bay, while drops that hit the east side end up in the Owens River Valley and the Los Angeles Aqueduct.

Take the trail angling left from the junction, and reach the shore of McLeod Lake soon after. This pretty, midsize lake boasts a sandy shoreline and a lakeside path sure to tempt children with excess energy. Picnic spots abound, and fishing is permissible on a catch-and-release basis. The handsome form of Mammoth Crest rules the skyline above the lake's far shore.

· ·

53 TJ LAKE AND LAKE BARRETT

Distance: 1.7 miles (loop)
Difficulty: Easy
Starting point: 9,020 feet
High point: 9,350 feet
Map: USGS Crystal Crag 7.5'

Like the preceding hike to McLeod Lake (Hike 52), this brief jaunt to TJ Lake and Lake Barrett is an ideal family outing. Those staying at the Lake George Campground will find the trek especially delightful, as they won't even need to fire up the family auto to reach the trailhead. As with all hikes in the Mammoth Lakes area, weekday visits are highly recommended.

To find the trailhead for TJ Lake and Lake Barrett, please refer to the driving directions for Lake George Campground at the beginning of this chapter. Leave your vehicle in the day-use parking area beside the campground, and begin walking at the sign for "TJ–Barrett Lakes" (near the campground information board).

Set out on a wide trail along the shore of Lake George, admiring the picturesque knob, known as Crystal Crag, that rules the ridge above the lake. Mammoth Crest is just beyond. Although it's often overwhelmed by anglers, Lake George is large and scenic. One thing's certain: its fish are certainly well fed.

The wide path narrows to a trail at the 0.2-mile point. Cross Lake George's outlet stream on a footbridge amid a leafy hedge of willows and alders, and arrive at a trail sign soon after. Abandon the lakeside trail at 0.3 mile, going left for Lake Barrett.

Climb steeply on a rocky trail, ascending beside Lake George's inlet stream. The hillside is brightened with fireweed and angelica, and stout western white pines compete with bushy whitebark pines for foot-

Crystal Crag rules the placid waters of TJ Lake.

holds in the sloping ground. The incline eases slightly at 0.4 mile. Enjoy the break—it won't last long.

Abandon your creekside prowl and climb steeply once again, sweating in the welcome shade of shaggy mountain hemlocks. At 0.6 mile, the trail branches and flattens out. Keep to the right to find tiny Lake Barrett soon after.

If you're hiking with children, they'll surely want to stop and explore this little lake, but it's really not much to look at. Take a brief breather, and then push on for TJ Lake.

Follow the gently climbing trail along the right-hand shore of Lake Barrett. A confusing mix of use trails mars the landscape here, the handiwork of irresponsible hikers. Leave Lake Barrett and ascend a short distance to gain sight of TJ Lake ahead. A quick descent leads to the lakeshore at 0.8 mile.

TJ Lake is truly beautiful, overhung by the enchanting Crystal Crag and boasting a shoreline lush with Labrador tea and mountain heather. This is a great spot for a picnic or a bit of solitary fishing (unless you prefer the elbow-to-elbow crowds down at Lake George). TJ Lake is off limits for swimming, however.

To continue your loop hike toward the parking lot, take the unmarked trail that leads downhill beside TJ Lake's outlet stream. Stay close to the water when the trail branches not long after. You'll gain a view down to Lake George and out toward Mammoth Mountain at the 1.0-mile point.

The descent picks up steam rapidly as you continue down beside the creek. The footing is tricky at times, so young children may need

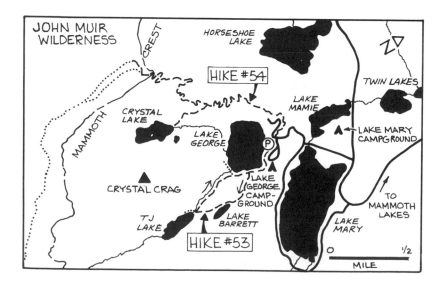

assistance. Give your braking thighs a rest with frequent stops to admire the ranger buttons, arrowleaf groundsel, and California corn lily along the stream banks.

Reach the shore of Lake George at 1.2 miles, and go right on the lakeside trail. You'll hit the junction for Lake Barrett after 0.2 mile. Continue along the shore of Lake George, retracing your steps to regain your starting point after 1.7 miles.

• •

54 CRYSTAL LAKE AND MAMMOTH CREST

Distance: 5.0 miles round trip
Difficulty: Moderate
Starting point: 9,020 feet
High point: 10,450 feet
Map: USGS Crystal Crag 7.5'

This hike shares its starting point at Lake George Campground with the preceding hike, TJ Lake and Lake Barrett. A greater distance and elevation gain make this trek the tougher of the two, but the rewards are much increased as well. One word of warning: the exposed finish atop Mammoth Crest warrants carrying a windbreaker and keeping one eye on the weather. Please don't attempt this hike when thunderclouds are present.

To find the trailhead for Crystal Lake and Mammoth Crest, please refer to the driving directions for Lake George Campground at the beginning of this chapter. Leave your vehicle in the day-use parking area beside the campground, and look for the trail's beginning directly opposite the parking-area entrance.

Start out beside a sign for "Crystal Lake–Mammoth Crest," and climb on a sandy trail shaded by an assortment of pines, firs, and hemlocks. Pinemat manzanita spreads its moisture-seeking fingers beneath the trees. You'll soon gain views down to Lake George and out toward Duck Pass, Mammoth Crest, and Crystal Crag.

A challenging ascent eases briefly at 0.4 mile. Wind onward through the trees, and climb steadily to reach a superb viewpoint above Lake George at the 0.7-mile point. Look for nearby Lake Mary, too. Continue uphill in shaded switchbacks, and arrive at a trail junction at 1.0 mile.

Angle left to make the short side trip to Crystal Lake. (If your time or energy is limited, or if you prefer to save the cool waters of Crystal Lake for your return trip, keep right at the junction to press on for Mammoth Crest.) The climb toward Crystal Lake ends at 1.1 miles, and a refreshing

Families love the excursion to Crystal Lake.

descent will bring you to the lakeshore 0.2 mile later.

Midsize Crystal Lake is a real beauty, nestled into the protecting bulk of the Mammoth Crest. Crystal Crag rules the scene, ensuring panoramic picnics for those who choose to make the lake their hiking destination.

Retrace your steps to the junction, groaning at the extra climb your detour provided. Then press on (and up) for Mammoth Crest. You'll lose the majority of traffic on the trail once past the Crystal Lake cutoff.

Endure a steady climb on a well-graded path. Stubby whitebark pines and mountain hemlocks dot the hillside, contributing very little shade to the sun-baked soil.

A particularly steep section will have you gasping just before you hit 2.0 miles, but you'll be rewarded with an excellent view of Mammoth Lakes and Mammoth Mountain not long afterward. Those familiar with the area (or familiar with an area map) can identify Horseshoe Lake, Twin Lakes, and lakes Mamie, Mary, and George sparkling in the Mammoth Lakes basin just below.

There's a fine vista to the northwest from just off the trail, encompassing the Minarets, Mount Ritter, and Banner Peak. Once you've drunk your fill, continue ascending steadily. Crystal Lake comes into view at 2.4 miles, and a handful of switchbacks leads to an entry sign for the John Muir Wilderness 0.1 mile later.

Continue up across a barren landscape of reddish volcanic stone.

You'll top a rise at 2.6 miles and start downhill with the main crest trail. Watch for an unsigned use trail exiting to the right just after the descent begins, and take this little footpath to angle uphill toward the summit of the red-hued knoll ahead.

A very steep scramble ends atop this mound of volcanic leftovers at 2.8 miles. (The use trail continues along the ridge from here, rejoining the main trail after a time.) Unless you're in the market for a longer day of hiking (refer to a topographic map for options), your Mammoth Crest ramble will end atop the knoll.

You'll have your feet planted on the Sierra Divide as you settle in to absorb a magnificent 360-degree vista. If two raindrops were to hit you on opposite shoulders while you stood here, one might end up in San Francisco Bay, while the other would probably make its way to the Owens River and the Los Angeles Aqueduct.

If you're fortunate enough to be hiking on a hazeless day, you'll be amazed by the extensive view. Look for the Minarets, Mount Ritter, and Banner Peak to the northwest. The ragged line of Mammoth Crest runs away to the southeast. To the east, the White Mountains and Nevada fade into the blue-gray distance, and an eagle's vista of the Mammoth Lakes basin completes the scene.

When you're out of sandwiches, film, or time, retrace your footsteps down the mound to regain the main crest trail. Then make the long downhill backtrack to your starting point.

55 EMERALD LAKE AND SKY MEADOWS

Distance: 4.0 miles round trip
Difficulty: Moderate
Starting point: 9,080 feet
High point: 10,050 feet
Map: USGS Bloody Mountain 7.5'

Common monkeyflowers join a host of wildflowers on the walk to Sky Meadows.

Although it involves a hefty climb, this hike to Emerald Lake and Sky Meadows is quite pleasant—and not too punishing. Time the trek for the height of the wildflower season (July or August, depending on the snow level), and you'll find a blossoming bonanza in Sky Meadows.

The trail beyond Emerald Lake may not be of much interest to youngsters in your hiking entourage; however, most children will be delighted with a supervised stop at Emerald Lake. Leave the kids with an adult while the rest of the party presses onward for Sky Meadows.

To find the trailhead, turn off Highway 395 at Mammoth Junction, and drive Road 203 through the town of Mammoth Lakes. Reach the signed Lake Mary Road after 3.7 miles. Continue straight onto this paved thoroughfare, and proceed 3.9 miles before veering left onto Road 4S09 (signed for Lake Mary and Lake George campgrounds).

Drive Road 4S09 another 3.6 miles, and go left for Coldwater Campground. Keep to the right as you pass the large campground sprawled beside Coldwater Creek. You'll see a sign for Emerald Lake parking after 0.7 mile. Toilets and drinking water are available here.

Begin at the trailhead sign for "Emerald Lake–Sky Meadows." (*Note:* This parking area holds the trailhead for Duck Pass as well. Please be sure your trail is signed for Sky Meadows.) A gently ascending path leads through a lodgepole pine forest, lively with the rhythms of Coldwater Creek.

Reach a junction with a horse trail at 0.1 mile. Keep to the right to stay with the hikers' route, and then climb steadily, savoring the enchanting selection of wildflowers beside the water. Look for arrowleaf groundsel, ranger buttons, common monkeyflower, fireweed, and purple-blossomed lupine. The incline eases at 0.5 mile, but the delights of the creek continue.

Angle left with the water at 0.6 mile, and reach a trail sign for Emerald Lake soon after. Abandon the creek to climb once more. You'll merge with the horse trail at 0.7 mile and then enjoy a gentle uphill route across a lodgepole-sprinkled hillside. Views to the right reveal the jagged Mammoth Crest.

Gain the shore of tiny Emerald Lake at 0.9 mile. The handsome shape of Blue Crag looms above the glasslike water, making this a particularly scenic stopping point for those in the mood for an easy hiking day. Picnicking and fishing opportunities abound at Emerald Lake; however, no swimming is allowed.

To press on toward Sky Meadows, angle to the left around the lake. You'll have to sift through a confusing profusion of use trails (people, people everywhere...) as you climb to a signed junction just above Emerald Lake. Go right here for "Gentian Meadow–Sky Meadows," and skirt along the hillside above the lake.

A steep climb kicks in soon afterward. Ascend beside Emerald Lake's tumbling inlet creek. Swamp onion paints the air with its pungent purple flowers, and common monkeyflower frolics on the streambanks. Cross the little waterway at 1.1 miles, and continue up more gently on the opposite shore.

The grade intensifies again as you approach the pocket-size Gentian Meadow at 1.2 miles. Angle right with the trail to push on toward your goal. A fine view of Blue Crag will lighten your footsteps for a while, and then you'll wind upward on a hemlock-shaded path. Descend briefly

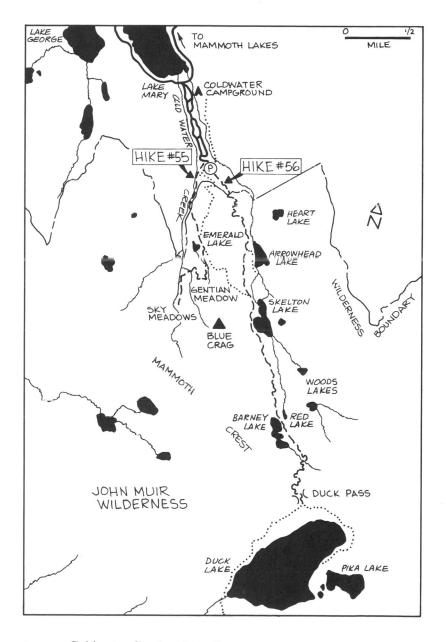

to cross Coldwater Creek at 1.5 miles.

More steep climbing follows. Link up with another arm of Coldwater Creek at 1.7 miles. Follow the creekside trail ever upward, and
arrive at a delightful waterfall soon after. What a lovely spot this is!

Cascading white water splashes in bright contrast to the cool, dark stones that catch it, and reckless yellow monkeyflowers leap among the rocks, heedless of their slippery footholds.

Leave the waterfall to face a final, wearying ascent. You'll reach the edge of Sky Meadows with 2.0 miles behind you. Break out a sandwich and a wildflower book, and settle in beneath the friendly shoulders of Mammoth Crest. The meadow's little creek is clear and icy cool, a treat for toasty toes. And the meadow flowers are magnificent.

Picnic in the presence of hikers gentian and Lemmon's paintbrush, little elephant heads, yampah, California corn lily, and willows. After you've rested your weary legs awhile, you can search the grasses and the pages of your wildflower guide for all the treasures of Sky Meadows.

Please do be careful as you explore the meadow. The popularity of this trail has taken its toll on the delicate alpine terrain. Stay on established trails, don't discard your trash, and never pick the flowers. Unfortunately, you'll probably see evidence that these guidelines have been broken here too many times.

56 DUCK PASS

Distance: 8.2 miles round trip
Difficulty: Strenuous
Starting point: 9,140 feet
High point: 10,800 feet
Map: USGS Bloody Mountain 7.5'

The Duck Pass hike is tough—no doubt about it. But this trek is worth every drop of sweat you'll shed on an often rocky, steeply climbing trail. Your legs may hate you for this hike, but your eyes will adore you for it. Be sure to bring extra water, extra film, and extra clothing for the exposed finish on Duck Pass.

To find the Duck Pass trailhead, please refer to the driving directions for the preceding hike, Emerald Lake and Sky Meadows. Proceed to the far end of the trailhead parking lot near Coldwater Campground, and begin walking at a sign for the Duck Pass Trail.

Veer left at another sign for Duck Pass shortly after. You'll climb gently to an entry sign for the John Muir Wilderness at 0.1 mile. Angle to the right to merge with the horse trail arriving from the pack station. You'll have plenty of equine company from here on out, as this route is very popular with horse-packers.

The climb to Duck Pass is tough but beautiful.

Ascend steadily through a varied forest of lodgepole and western white pines and mountain hemlocks, stealing peeks down to Lake Mary through the tree trunks. Pick up the murmur of Mammoth Creek at 0.9 mile, and then enjoy easier walking as you press on to a junction with the trail for Arrowhead Lake (to the left).

Continue straight on the main trail, and gain glimpses of sprawling Arrowhead Lake on your left. A moderate grade will take you to a rocky ridge at 1.3 miles. The trail degenerates a bit through here, and you'll have to watch your step as you pick your way uphill.

Enjoy easier walking through a meadowy basin fed by Mammoth Creek, and then pass the first of a handful of unmarked cutoff trails for Skelton Lake at the 1.6-mile point. Stay with the main trail, shunning the turnoffs to the left. You'll get a good view of Skelton Lake shortly afterward.

This attractive lake boasts a cliffy shoreline and sparkling water. It's a fine destination for those in quest of a shorter hiking day, as picnic and fishing spots are plentiful.

Resume climbing as you abandon Skelton Lake. The steady grade eases after 0.3 mile. Head into a grassy basin brightened with a wealth of wildflowers. Hikers gentian, yampah, ranger buttons, and little elephant heads line the way.

The ascent picks up much too quickly as you leave the meadow. Climb on a rugged trail with views of bulky Mammoth Mountain across the way. Begin the short descent to Barney Lake at 2.6 miles.

You'll be reminded of the increasing elevation as you gaze at Barney Lake. This lake is more barren than its lower neighbors. It boasts a rocky shoreline where willows, mountain hemlocks, and whitebark pines search for bits of nourishment. Many backpackers choose Barney Lake as their first-day destination, and the lakeshore is sprinkled with campsites.

Continue with the trail to cross Barney Lake's outlet stream. A glance to the left reveals Red Lake. You'll spot Duck Pass ahead as you hike onward (look for a notch in the ridgeline). The ascent to the pass hits full stride at 3.0 miles. Downshift and begin to climb.

Wind upward through an amazing landscape of stones and scrubby whitebark pines. This is pure High Sierra—bleak and rugged and beautiful. You'll find a whole new breed of flowers hiding among the rocks at this high elevation. Coville's columbine, mountain sorrel, alpine gentian, and brightly colored rockfringe thrive above 10,000 feet.

Struggle up through a series of well-graded switchbacks, sucking air with every footstep. The rocks seem infinite, the switchbacks never ending. You'll be glad for an excuse to stop and rest as you pause to let one of the Duck Pass Trail's frequent groups of horse-packers pass. It's unnerving to watch the froth-flecked animals slip and stumble on the granite trail.

The views continue to unfold as you gain elevation. Barney and Red lakes are just below, and Skelton Lake nestles among green pines. Look for lofty Mammoth Mountain towering above its treasures. Mount Ritter and Banner Peak pop into view as you near the crest of your ascent.

Reach Duck Pass at 4.0 miles, gasping with delight as a saw blade of jagged peaks slices through the sky ahead. Duck Lake waddles just below the pass, one of the plumpest, bluest alpine lakes you'll ever hope to see. And lovely Pika Lake is just beyond, beckoning pack-laden hikers to its secluded shores.

Press on with the trail 0.1 mile beyond the pass to gain the best view of Duck Lake. But pause before the descent to the lake begins. To the southwest, the peaks of the rugged Silver Divide glitter in the thin Sierra atmosphere. Choose your favorite vista and a comfy picnic spot, and rest awhile before beginning the long downhill backtrack to your starting point.

An experienced hiker equipped with map, compass, and cross-country skills can turn this Duck Pass hike into a loop trip by continuing along the trailless Mammoth Crest. The route descends via the Crystal Lake trail to Lake George Campground (see Hike 54, Crystal Lake and Mammoth Crest). However, this is a very long day hike, requiring superior routefinding and scrambling skills. You'll need an auto shuttle back to Coldwater Campground, too.

• •

57   SAN JOAQUIN RIDGE

Distance: 4.8 miles round trip
Difficulty: Moderate
Starting point: 9,265 feet
High point: 10,255 feet
Map: USGS Mammoth Mountain 7.5'

Warning! Check your sensory circuit breaker before you attempt this hike—the trek along the San Joaquin Ridge is sure to overload your visual fuse box.

Nearly every footstep of this hike is steeped in spectacular mountain scenery. Bring an extra roll of film and a topographic map for the peaks. Carry drinking water for the shadeless ascent to the pass. And tuck away a jacket for the sometimes chilly breeze along the ridgetop.

This challenging day hike begins at the 9,265-foot Minaret Vista and boasts a beginning view that many hikes can't match with their finales. The vistas just get better and better along the way. Even those who don't climb the entire distance to the little knob above Deadman Pass will declare this hike a winner. It's packed with thrilling scenery from start to finish.

To find the trailhead for the San Joaquin Ridge, turn off Highway 395 at Mammoth Junction, and drive Road 203 through the town of Mammoth Lakes. Reach a junction signed for Lake Mary Road and Mammoth Mountain–Devil's Postpile after 3.7 miles.

Angle right for the Devil's Postpile, and continue 5.5 miles to a sign for the Minaret Vista. The vista's paved entry road exits to the right, just before the Devil's Postpile entrance station. Drive the vista entry road 0.3 mile to reach an often busy parking area. The view will blow you away before you climb out of your vehicle!

Pause at the vista point's information plaque to familiarize yourself with Mount Ritter, Banner Peak, the Minarets, and the other mountains that will be your hiking partners for the day. Then depart from the far end of the parking area, walking past a small toilet building to descend to an unpaved four-wheel-drive road.

The challenging hike along the San Joaquin Ridge is worth every ounce of effort.

Join the four-wheel-drive road, and continue to the left. This road does have infrequent vehicle traffic, but with any luck, you won't see any of it. (One word of caution—it's easy to miss the vista parking lot on your way back, so make a special note of the point where you join the four-wheel-drive road.)

Climb on a rough roadway lined with scattered whitebark and lodgepole pines, mountain hemlocks, and red firs. The ground beneath the trees glows white with bits of pumice stone, remnants of the area's hot volcanic past. Ascend to an unsigned fork at 0.3 mile. Keep to the right, and continue up the ridgeline.

You'll be tightrope-walking on the Sierra Divide throughout this hike. This ridge is the watershed between east and west. Not much rain falls here, however, and the tiny alpine flowers that nestle among the rocks are witnesses to the fact. Look for miniature lupine, sulfur flower, and penstemon. The much larger mule ears seem to thrive in this dry climate, too.

Awesome views of the peaks to the north and northwest unfold as you press upward, and Mammoth Mountain fills the skyline at your back. A challenging ascent eases briefly at 0.5 mile, but the climb resumes with vigor less than 0.5 mile later. Just lift your gaze from the punishing incline. The unbelievable vistas will fuel your legs with renewed vigor.

Another somewhat level stretch will cheer you at the 1.1-mile point. From here, the view to the south and east encompasses Lake Crowley and the White Mountains. Start up another knob in the ridgeline, and put your aching legs in four-wheel drive. (If a jeep appears at this point in your trek, you may be tempted to take that literally.)

Struggle upward past clumps of weather-twisted whitebark pines and lovely patches of mat lupine. The steepest pitches will have you grumbling. Fortunately, the soaring melodies of the surrounding mountains drown out all complaints. Keep to the left when the road branches

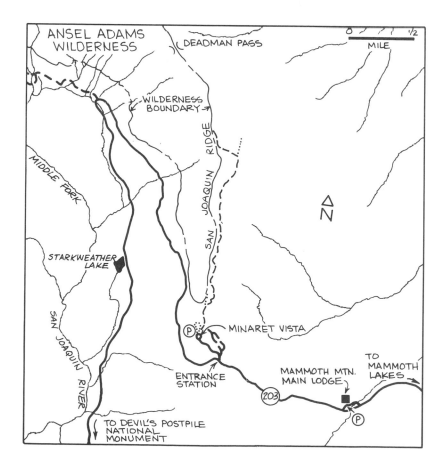

at 1.6 miles. You'll see a gruesome pitch awaiting just ahead.

Start into the steepest section of the hike at 1.7 miles. The punishment will end—not a moment too soon—at the 1.9-mile point. Rejoice in easier walking as you pick up an expanding view to the north. On a hazeless day, the vista extends to Yosemite National Park's lofty Mount Lyell.

There's one last climb ahead. Your legs will probably hate you for it. Start into the final incline at 2.1 miles, and stand atop a 10,255-foot knob in the San Joaquin Ridge with 2.4 miles beneath your weary wheels. Wow!

From here, a footpath descends to Deadman Pass, a sandy saddle in the ridgeline. But why go on?—the view doesn't get any better than this. Savor a fantastic 360-degree panorama while your trembling muscles rest. Words can't do justice to the magnificence of the High Sierra. Reverence and wonder are the emotions this spot evokes (and perhaps a rush of gratitude because the climb is over).

58 SAN JOAQUIN TRAIL TO DEVIL'S POSTPILE NATIONAL MONUMENT

Distance: 7.4 miles one way
Difficulty: Moderate
Starting point: 8,330 feet
High point: 8,330 feet
Maps: USGS Mammoth Mountain 7.5' and USGS Crystal Crag 7.5'

The San Joaquin Trail offers an ideal family outing for those camping in or visiting the Devil's Postpile area. The frequent intravalley shuttle makes one-way hiking easy and convenient, and you can tailor your walk's length to the abilities, energies, and time restrictions of your individual hiking party.

This trek along a portion of the Pacific Crest Trail follows the San Joaquin River gently downhill for 6.0 miles to enter the Devil's Postpile National Monument. Next, it cruises past the impressive Devil's Postpile. Finally, it returns to the main road at the Red's Meadow Campground shuttle stop. Pack a lunch, a camera, and a swimming suit, and plan to make a day of it!

To find the trailhead for this hike, turn off Highway 395 at Mammoth Junction, and drive Road 203 through the town of Mammoth Lakes. Reach a junction signed for Lake Mary Road and Mammoth Mountain–Devil's Postpile after 3.7 miles. Angle right for the Devil's Postpile, and continue 5.6 miles to the Devil's Postpile entrance station.

(*Note:* If you're not camping in the Devil's Postpile area, you'll

The Devil's Postpile National Monument attracts a steady stream of visitors.

need to leave your vehicle at the Mammoth Mountain ski resort before the entrance station. Take the intravalley shuttle to the stop at Agnew Meadows Campground, and follow the campground entry road 0.3 mile to the trailhead. Please see this chapter's introduction for additional information on the intravalley shuttle.)

From the entrance station, drive 2.7 miles on the paved road toward the Devil's Postpile National Monument. Then turn off the pavement at the sign for Agnew Meadows Campground. You'll find a trailhead parking lot beside the campground entry road after 0.3 mile. Drinking water and toilets are available at the lot.

From the parking area, take the trail signed for Shadow Lake, and proceed 0.1 mile to a second parking lot beside the fenced Agnew Meadows. (This trek's mileage count starts here, so add 0.4 mile to your total if you begin walking at the shuttle stop.)

Find another trailhead sign at the second lot, and walk to the rear of the sign to locate the trail proper. Cross a small creek, and angle right with the path to pace beside the heavily grazed Agnew Meadows. An

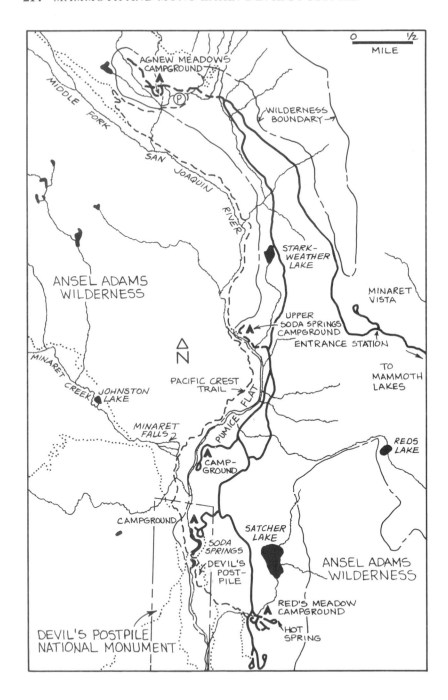

interesting assortment of Sierra trees offer their shade as you begin. Look for mountain hemlocks, lodgepole pines, red firs, Jeffrey pines, and scattered Sierra junipers. Recross the creek at 0.3 mile, and continue on a shaded path. Reach a trail junction after 0.8 mile. Go left here for Red's Meadow, and begin a gentle descent toward the San Joaquin River. Coast downhill in several well-graded switchbacks, crossing an open hillside sprinkled with sage and manzanita. Look for vistas of 11,053-foot Mammoth Mountain to the southeast as you descend. A second junction awaits at the 1.5-mile point. Continue straight for Red's Meadow, and regain the trees as you walk onward. Cross an aspen- and alder-choked creek, and enjoy more level walking with a view of Mammoth Mountain straight ahead.

You'll spot the waters of the San Joaquin River below, with 1.9 miles behind you. Follow an undulating trail on the hillside above the river, staying just out of reach of the San Joaquin's cool embrace as you press on. Reach the river level briefly at 2.6 miles, and continue in the company of red firs and lodgepole pines.

A wildflower-edged inlet stream may require some rock hopping at the 3.0-mile point. You'll be treated to glimpses of the San Joaquin River's many tempting pools and rivulets as you hike onward. This is one of the nicest sections of the river this trek has to offer, so don't be surprised if the San Joaquin's sun-warmed granite shores and sparkling pools lure you off the trail for an early picnic.

Savor easy downhill walking to a sturdy bridge across the river at 4.0 miles. (A use trail continues straight toward Upper Soda Springs Campground and a shuttle stop.) Cross the San Joaquin, and continue on through trees, climbing gently for a time. Views to the left encompass the San Joaquin Ridge and Deadman Pass (see Hike 57).

Your descent resumes through a red fir forest as you lose the river's company, and you'll spy the glowing white of Pumice Flat to the left of the trail at 4.8 miles. This outburst of volcanic rock is a reminder of the explosive history of the Mammoth area.

Rejoin the San Joaquin soon after, and continue on an undulating trail to come abreast of Minaret Falls at 5.5 miles. Cross the stream below the falls, and take the short spur trail to its base. If you're looking for a picnic spot, you might pause here to enjoy the picture painted by the falls: icy water tumbling down a rocky ladder, with bright yellow patches of Sierra arnica clinging to every dripping foothold.

Return to the main trail, and hike uphill through lodgepole pines. The forlorn appearance of the trees is due to an infestation of destructive pine beetles. A sign at 6.0 miles announces the boundary of the Devil's Postpile National Monument. Arrive at a trail junction soon after. The Pacific Crest Trail continues straight from here, but you'll abandon that route and go left to descend toward the river.

Reach another junction at 6.4 miles, and continue straight for the Devil's Postpile. Look for a reddish splash of soil on the San Joaquin shoreline, just to the left of the trail. Soda springs come bubbling to the surface here. Keep to the right with the trail, and cross the river on a sturdy footbridge.

A brief climb leads to yet another junction. Go right here for the Devil's Postpile. If your riverside trek has been peaceful and solitary to this point, it will be neither as you continue. Join the monument's tourist crowds, and reach your goal at 6.6 miles. Despite the clamor of clicking shutters and excited conversation, you'll be impressed by this lovely spot.

An informative display board beside the trail explains the geologic phenomenon of the area. Pause to let the printed words interpret the Devil's Postpile for your mind, and then allow your eyes to discover the wonders of the spot anew.

The Devil's Postpile is enchanting symmetry in stone, softened by the touch of bright green lichen. Broken columns are crumpled at the bases of their upright companions, looking like the pieces of a Roman ruin. Yet Rome was vibrant only yesterday when compared with the timelessness of these ancient stones.

When you're ready to move on, stay with the main trail, and climb away from the Devil's Postpile and the river. Sneak a view of the "backside" of the Devil's Postpile as your ascent eases at 6.8 miles. A brief descent leads on past fragrant Jeffrey pines. Leave the boundary of the national monument as the trail levels out once more.

Reach a junction at 7.0 miles, and go left for Red's Meadow. Cross a small stream and arrive at another junction not long after. Keep to the left for Red's Meadow and the campground, and reach the main road at 7.3 miles. Follow the main road to the left to arrive at the shuttle stop beside Red's Meadow Campground, with 7.4 miles behind you.

You can use the intravalley shuttle to close your loop to Agnew Meadows Campground, the Mammoth Mountain ski area, or wherever you began your hiking day.

· ·

59 SHADOW LAKE

Distance: 7.2 miles round trip
Difficulty: Moderate
Starting point: 8,330 feet
High point: 8,750 feet
Total climb: 1,020 feet
Maps: USGS Mammoth Mountain 7.5' and USGS Mount Ritter 7.5'

Majestic Mount Ritter rules the scene at Shadow Lake.

The enchanting trek to Shadow Lake shares its trailhead with Hike 58, the San Joaquin Trail, but it is Shadow Lake and the beautiful backcountry beyond it that are responsible for the throngs that come this way every summer weekend. Visit Shadow Lake on a weekday, if at all possible, and you'll avoid some of the backpackers that make this trail so busy.

Although the trip to Shadow Lake involves a bit of climbing, the trail is suitable for hikers with a wide range of abilities. And the destination is so lovely, any grumblers in your group will forget their aching muscles upon arrival. Pack along a picnic lunch and a fishing pole, and invest an afternoon in Shadow Lake's spectacular surroundings.

Please refer to the beginning of Hike 58 to start you on your way to Shadow Lake. From the junction at the 0.8-mile point, keep to the right for Shadow Lake, and continue a gentle descent with views of the San Joaquin River.

Traverse an open hillside sporting manzanita, canyon live oaks, sage, and brilliant California fuchsia. A peek behind will reveal 11,053-foot Mammoth Mountain peering over your sun-warmed shoulders.

The descent becomes an easy uphill at 1.4 miles. Continue on with the path of the San Joaquin, pacing a sandy trail lined with Sierra junipers and lodgepole pines. Turn away from the river shortly after, and climb to the shore of Olaine Lake at 2.0 miles. Midsize Olaine Lake, hemmed in by a forested shoreline and marshy shallows, is homely by Sierra standards.

Push onward through cool lodgepole shade, ascending gently to a junction at the 2.3-mile point. The riverside trail continues to the right from here, but you'll go left for Shadow Lake.

Cross the San Joaquin on a sturdy footbridge at 2.5 miles. Now the climb to Shadow Lake begins in earnest. Draw a deep breath, and throw yourself into the shadeless, rocky ascent of the canyon wall.

The trail climbs in a score of challenging switchbacks. Enjoy fine views of distant Mammoth Mountain as you labor upward. Look for chinquapin and manzanita beside the trail. Twisted old Sierra junipers contribute to the harsh and beautiful landscape.

Vistas expand as the elevation increases, and you'll spot the aptly (if coarsely) named Two Tits atop the barren ridgeline just across the San Joaquin River. Gain your first look at the lovely waterfall tumbling out of Shadow Lake's basin at the 3.3-mile point in your trek.

Push on toward the falls on a steadily climbing trail. If your legs begin to falter, tell your groaning muscles that Shadow Lake is just beyond. The wearying ascent eases at 3.5 miles. Continue beside Shadow Lake's rushing outlet steam, enjoying the company of a host of creekside wildflowers.

Arrive at serene and satisfying Shadow Lake with 3.6 miles behind you. Not only is this large, deep Sierra lake a treasure, but its setting magnifies its loveliness a dozen times. Gaze across the lake's clear blue water to find a mountain-filled canvas hung right from the sky.

The Minaret Crest, Mount Ritter, and Banner Peak tower above Shadow Lake, reaching more than 13,000 feet into the heavens. Claim a seat on a shoreline softened by Labrador tea and mountain heather, and settle in to savor the beauty of this lofty corner of the Sierra.

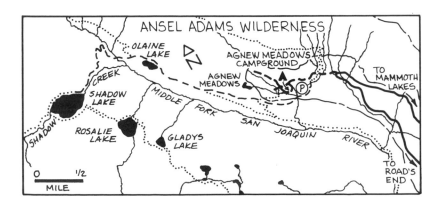

Views of distant Mammoth Mountain enhance the hike to Shadow Lake.

You may find a pot of tourists at the base of Rainbow Falls.

60 RAINBOW FALLS

Distance: 2.6 miles round trip
Difficulty: Easy
Starting point: 7,660 feet
High point: 7,660 feet
Total climb: 300 feet
Map: USGS Crystal Crag 7.5'

Although there isn't a pot of gold at the end of the trail to Rainbow Falls, this exceedingly popular hike does have several things going for it. It's short and it's easy, and it leads to an exquisitely beautiful waterfall.

Families will adore the trek to Rainbow Falls, where the Middle Fork of the San Joaquin River plummets 101 feet in a frenzy of froth and mist-shrouded rainbows. There's plenty of space for picnicking near the base of the waterfall. With all those positives listed, however, it's only fair to mention the major drawback of this outing: it's woefully overcrowded. In fact, anyone in the mood for solitude should avoid this hike like the plague. Much-adored Rainbow Falls certainly won't miss your visit, and you won't miss rubbing shoulders with the hordes that hike here on every summer day.

To reach the trailhead for Rainbow Falls, please refer to the beginning of Hike 58, San Joaquin Trail to Devil's Postpile National Monument. From the Devil's Postpile entrance station, drive 8.0 miles on the paved and winding road, and veer right at a sign for Rainbow Falls. A short gravel spur road leads to the trailhead parking area. (There's an intravalley shuttle stop nearby.)

Set out beside a sign for the Fish Creek Trail, and descend gently on the wide, sandy thoroughfare. This trek is unique by Sierra standards, as you'll hike downhill to reach your destination. Just remember that you'll have 300 feet to climb on the way back out, and allot your time and energy accordingly.

Reach a junction with the John Muir Trail at 0.1 mile, and continue straight for Rainbow Falls. You'll be joined by a trail from the Red's Meadow resort at 0.4 mile. Then enjoy more downhill hiking in the shade of white firs and lodgepole and Jeffrey pines.

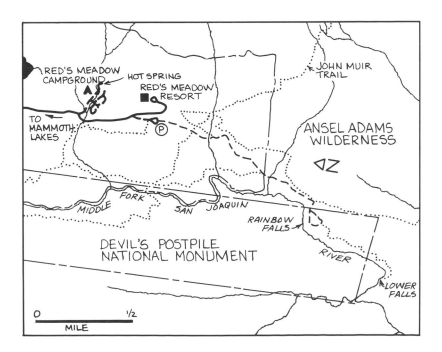

Yet another feeder trail joins from the right at the 0.7-mile point. This route arrives from the Devil's Postpile National Monument (please refer to Hike 58 for a possible linkup if you're looking for a longer trek).

The steady descent finally eases at 0.8 mile. Continue walking to a junction at 1.0 mile. Angle right for Rainbow Falls, and gain the first viewpoint of the waterfall shortly afterward.

Even if you're standing elbow to elbow with a score of camera-clicking visitors, you'll be dazzled by the beauty of the spot. Watch with amazement as the Middle Fork of the San Joaquin River leaps off a lava shelf, throwing its watery arms out wide to catch the midday sun. The resulting spray transforms the sunlight into a thousand rainbow-colored parachutes, and they drop the river noisily back into its banks, 101 feet below.

Walk on to a second viewpoint at 1.2 miles. If you're searching for a place to frolic or spread a picnic, a long stairway leads down to the river level at 1.3 miles. Children will love the setting here, and the break will provide a welcome rest before the climb back to the trailhead.

Please be careful if you visit the base of Rainbow Falls, as the rocks around the water are slippery and unstable. A teen-age youth was seriously injured in August 1989 when he fell while attempting to climb the cliff face. Please enjoy your sandwich—and the scenery—at a sensible distance.

61 GLASS CREEK MEADOW

Distance: 4.0 miles round trip
Difficulty: Moderate
Starting point: 8,170 feet
High point: 8,850 feet
Map: USGS Mammoth Mountain 7.5'

This walk to Glass Creek Meadow wanders through a wonderland of wildflowers. There are some steep sections, but much of the hike is easy going. Walkers with a wide range of abilities should enjoy the variations in both scenery and terrain.

This is one Sierra trek where high-topped shoes are particularly appropriate, as long sections of the trail are covered with deep sand. Sunglasses are a necessity for this hike as well. The glare reflected by the harsh volcanic landscape can be blinding when the sun is out.

To reach the trailhead for Glass Creek Meadow, turn off Highway 395 onto Glass Flow Road, 3.7 miles south of the more southerly June

Lake junction. Drive this unpaved thoroughfare 2.7 miles, staying left at the first junction (signed for Obsidian Dome) and then keeping to the main road as you continue.

The road branches into three separate routes as you near the trail-head. Stay to the right (don't cross the creek), and reach a small parking area soon after. The trail for Glass Creek Meadow takes off beside glittering Glass Creek.

Climb gently as you begin, struggling for footing in loose sand studded with chunks of pumice and obsidian. Nude buckwheat and scraggly broadleaf lupine grow beside the trail, and lodgepole and white-bark pines lend their shade to your endeavors.

The grade increases as you labor upward. Ascend through a cascade-filled canyon, clamorous with the rush of Glass Creek's head-over-heels tumble down the hill. The trail is sandy and very steep through here, and the difficult footing is frustrating at best. Perky pink monkeyflower and regal tower larkspur make the creekside walking lovely, though.

After about a quarter mile of punishing walking, the grade mellows noticeably. Gain a friendlier trail through sage-dotted terrain. Alpine buckwheat, sulfur flower, and ranger buttons line the way.

You may have difficulty following this section of the trail, as the path is often indistinct in the rocky soil. For the easiest walking, keep Glass Creek on your left and stay up on the hillside a short distance from the water. You'll see lots of faint footpaths through the pumice-studded sand, but don't worry—as long as you follow the creek's course upward, you'll end up at Glass Creek Meadow.

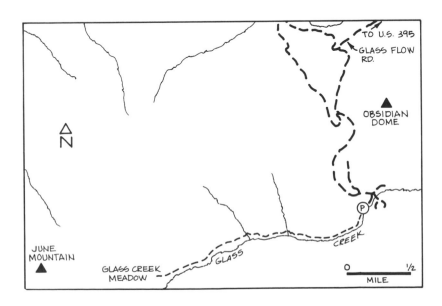

Glass Creek Meadow is abundant with wildflowers in July and early August.

Pause for views of Obsidian Dome behind you as you ascend through a desolate wasteland of glaring sand. Gain the crest of a low ridge at 1.6 miles. A vista of surprisingly green Glass Creek Meadow awaits you here. Behind the meadow, lofty San Joaquin Mountain (11,600 feet) dominates the skyline.

Press on past patches of brilliant-hued Layne's monkeyflower as you pace through salt-and-pepper expanses of pumice and obsidian. Arrive at tree-ringed Glass Creek Meadow at 2.0 miles. This lovely mountain garden spot owes its existence to the scores of small streams that filter in from higher ground, making the soil here a marshy haven for a host of wildflowers.

Those with sharp eyes and a bit of flower familiarity or a good Sierra wildflower guide will find yarrow, yampah, common monkeyflower, hikers gentian, meadow penstemon, and Brewer's lupine here. Besides the lure of the meadow flowers, the backdrop of the distant mountains makes the setting of Glass Creek Meadow spectacular.

Wander away the afternoon, or simply sit and stare at the surrounding loveliness. One word of caution: when you do decide to turn for home, be sure to stay within hailing distance of the creek to help you keep your bearings. The trail splits into a handful of confusing branches about a mile below the meadow, so you may have difficulty retracing your exact route.

62 FERN LAKE

Distance: 3.4 miles round trip
Difficulty: Moderate
Starting point: 7,330 feet
High point: 9,030 feet
Maps: USGS June Lake 7.5' and USGS Mammoth Mountain 7.5'

At 1.7 miles, the hike to Fern Lake isn't very long, but it makes up for its brevity with a punishingly steep climb. Even so, it's a pleasant walk, rich in wildflowers and vistas. And petite Fern Lake is a treat for swimmers, picnickers, and anglers alike. Sections of the trail are quite narrow, and the hillside is extremely steep in places, so families with small children may want to choose another trek.

To reach the trailhead for Fern Lake, drive Highway 395 north of Mammoth Lakes, and take the more southerly of the two June Lake

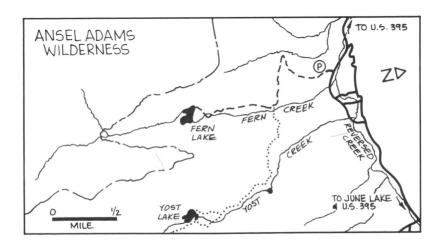

A tree-lined trail leads toward Fern Lake.

turnoffs. Drive west on the paved Road 158 for 5.3 miles, passing the town
of June Lake and the June Mountain ski resort.

Leave Road 158 at a sign for the Yost Creek Trail, and drive the short
distance to the trailhead on an unpaved road. Keep left at a metal gate,
and then stay to the right to reach the small trailhead parking area shortly
after.

A day-hikers' register and a sign for Fern and Yost lakes mark the
trail's beginning. Start climbing immediately, pacing a dusty path lined

with quaking aspens. Broadleaf lupine, scarlet gilia, and mountain penny-royal add color to the arid soil.

The grade increases much too soon, and aspens give way to white firs as your lungs begin to labor. Heavy breathing will bring you the peculiar scent of trailside sage as well as extra oxygen for your straining muscles. Earn an expanding view of the boat-dotted Silver Lake as you gain elevation, and continue climbing beneath Sierra junipers and Jeffrey pines. Angle left along the hillside to begin a long, steep switchback. The view just keeps improving. Don't let the broadening vista distract you too much, though—the narrow trail is like a tightrope walker's path across the precipitous hillside.

Struggle upward with Sierra junipers, Indian paintbrush, and yellow-blossomed mule ears for company. Look for views of distant June Lake and Gull Lake as you climb. You'll begin to hear the whisper of Fern Creek's little waterfall just before you spot it through the trees ahead. Reach a junction at 1.0 mile, and go right for Fern Lake. The trail that continues straight for Yost Lake is much mellower, but Yost Lake isn't nearly so inviting as Fern Lake. Keep telling yourself that as you endure a gruesome pitch for the next 0.25 mile. *Steep* will gain new meaning as you scramble straight uphill toward Fern Lake.

Labor steadily up past thick-trunked junipers and scattered mountain hemlocks, gasping for breath in their snatches of cool shade. Arrive at a lovely meadow with the bulk of your ascent behind you. Then endure a final steep uphill push to gain the shoreline of Fern Lake.

Reach your goal at 1.7 miles. Pretty and petite, Fern Lake is a gem. Rocky slopes surround the water, cradling the lake in a lofty bed of granite. Despite the horrendous hill, Fern Lake is worth the effort. Peel off your shoes, pull out your picnic, and enjoy!

• •

63 PARKER LAKE

Distance: 3.8 miles round trip
Difficulty: Moderate
Starting point: 7,770 feet
High point: 8,350 feet
Map: USGS Koip Peak 7.5'

The pleasant hike to Parker Lake offers fine views of Mono Lake and plenty of easy creekside walking laced with wildflowers. This is an excellent family excursion. Pack in towels, fishing poles, and sandwiches, and plan to spend the entire afternoon.

Snow-flecked mountains rise from Parker Lake.

To reach the trailhead for Parker Lake, drive Highway 395 north of Mammoth Lakes, and take the more northerly of the two June Lake turnoffs. Drive the paved road 1.5 miles to a junction signed for "Parker Lake–Walker Lake." Turn onto the unpaved road for Parker and Walker lakes, and then veer left at the junction immediately afterward.

Continue straight from here, following signs for Parker Lake at the subsequent junctions. Arrive at the trailhead 2.3 miles from Highway 395. A small parking area and a day-hikers' register await.

Set out on a sandy trail, climbing steadily past aromatic sage, dusty mule ears, and yellow sulfur flower. Reach an entry sign for the Ansel Adams Wilderness soon after, and pause for a look behind toward shimmering Mono Lake. Continue climbing, with the voice of Parker Creek humming a harmony for your footsteps.

The grade increases as you ascend past Jeffrey pines and mountain mahogany, and the views back to Mono Lake broaden with the increasing elevation. Soothe your laboring muscles with looks at lovely Parker Creek, its banks overhung with moisture-loving quaking aspens. The soft trunks of the trees have been initialled by countless pocketknife-wielding hikers across the years.

Gain a break from the steady climb at 0.4 mile, and wind on through aspens and sage with brief ascents interrupting more-level walking. Lodgepole and Jeffrey pines add their shadows to those tossed on the trail by white-trunked aspen trees.

Reach a junction and a sign for Silver Lake, and continue straight beside Parker Creek, savoring the bright blossoms of tower larkspur, California corn lily, and yarrow. Arrive at Parker Lake with 1.9 miles behind you.

Set into a curve of rugged hills, this midsize lake paints a lovely picture for trail-weary eyes. Look for a glacial waterfall in the distance, tumbling down from the icy slopes of 13,002-foot Kuna Peak. The trail

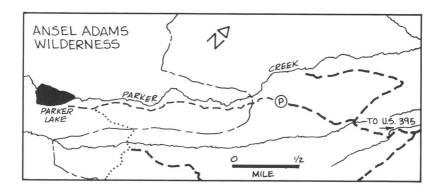

continues to the left along the shore of Parker Lake. You'll get an even better view of Kuna Peak if you walk a little farther.

If you prefer to cool your toes rather than exercise them any more, be forewarned: Parker Lake has shallow edges, but it drops off very quickly. And the water is very cold!

64 LOWER SARDINE LAKE

Distance: 7.0 miles round trip
Difficulty: Strenuous
Starting point: 8,200 feet
High point: 9,890 feet
Total climb: 2,770 feet
Map: USGS Koip Peak 7.5'

This is a challenging hike with steep inclines, but the destination is well worth the effort. Lower Sardine Lake is a petite blue beauty, snuggled into the rugged Sierra granite like a baby in a freshly laundered blanket.

To find the trailhead for Lower Sardine Lake, drive Highway 395 north of Mammoth Lakes, and take the more northerly of the two June Lake turnoffs. Follow the paved road 1.5 miles to a junction signed "Parker Lake–Walker Lake." Turn onto the unpaved road for Parker and Walker lakes, and veer left at the junction immediately afterward.

Drive 0.4 mile, and go right for Walker Lake. Continue following signs for Walker Lake to reach the trailhead 4.9 miles from Highway 395 (3.4 miles on unpaved road). There's a small parking area with an outhouse at the trailhead.

One word of warning: if you have bug repellent in your car, don't leave it behind. This trail is tormented by zillions of mosquitoes in July.

Begin at a sign for "Walker Lake–Sardine Lakes–Mono Pass." Walker Lake is exceedingly popular with anglers. If you meet any other hikers on this trail, they'll probably be carrying tackle boxes.

You may wish you had someone to reel you in as you start on a steeply climbing trail beneath stately Jeffrey pines. There's definitely no warm-up for this hike—you'll be gasping before you've covered 100 yards.

After 0.3 mile of heavy breathing, gain the crest of a small ridge. If you're interested in Sierra geology, you might note that this is actually the top of a glacial moraine, a pile of rubble left behind by a passing behemoth of ice.

A delightful vista flavors the challenging climb to Lower Sardine Lake.

Descend to the shallow gully in the middle of the ridgeline, and then climb briefly once again. Gain a view down onto sprawling Walker Lake from the far side of the ridge. You won't like what the trail does next.

Heave a sigh and dive downhill on a rough, steep path, muttering bleakly about the uphill this guarantees for your return trek. Loose stones and sand make the footing treacherous, but sage and sulfur flower squat beside the trail, doing their best to cheer you up.

Reach a junction at 0.5 mile. Although the trail sign here claims that Sardine Lake is still 3.5 miles ahead, don't be discouraged—it's really only 3 more miles to your goal. Go left for Sardine Lake, and angle along the hillside, descending gradually in the shade of tall white firs.

Walker Lake boasts a shoreline crowded with quaking aspens and bloodied by a host of airborne mosquitoes. The drone of these thirsty squadrons will keep you hustling as you cross Walker Creek. Then rush onward through a meadow colorful with broadleaf lupine, Indian paintbrush, and tower larkspur. Arrive at another junction, and keep to the left.

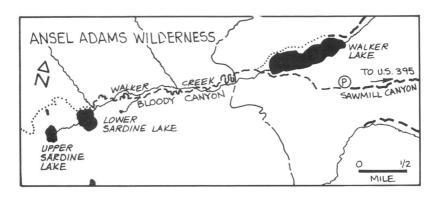

Reach an entry sign for the Ansel Adams Wilderness at 1.2 miles, and resume climbing soon after. The song of Walker Creek will keep you company as you ascend through a score of steep switchbacks. Turn back for a fine view down to Walker Lake whenever you pause to catch your breath. Mono Lake shimmers in the distant flatlands.

Continue climbing beside the creek. The hillside is riotous with wildflowers. Scarlet gilia, nude buckwheat, ranger buttons, crimson columbine, and pink monkeyflower are all well represented. Recross Walker Creek on a narrow log bridge, and then ascend steadily across a rocky slope.

The grade increases as the trail traces switchbacks up toward Lower Sardine Lake. Enjoy a brief respite as you wind into a high box canyon, imprisoned within walls of unyielding stone. The break is short but sweet. Climb in steep switchbacks once again.

Just when you're sure you can't go up another step, you'll reach the crest of a small ridge ruled by scruffy mountain mahogany. Savor easier walking for a time, and then cross the creek and climb once more. Look for a lovely alpine waterfall ahead, overhung by massive slabs of rock. Lower Sardine Lake is just above the falls.

A final brief ascent leads to the edge of 9,890-foot Lower Sardine Lake, 3.5 miles from your start. Nestled into a cranny overhung by barren cliffs, this beautiful alpine lake is deep and very cold. Lower Sardine Lake's shoreline and its tiny outlet creek are awash in brilliant wildflowers, but the view out toward Mono Lake is the real attraction on a hazeless day.

If you have the energy for a bit more climbing, the trail continues uphill to Upper Sardine Lake and Mono Pass. If you've had enough heavy breathing for the day, simply pull out a sandwich, fire up your camera, and enjoy.

Further Reading

VEGETATION

Horn, Elizabeth. *Wildflowers 3, the Sierra Nevada.* Beaverton, Oregon: Touchstone Press, 1976.

Little, Elbert L. *The Audubon Society Field Guide to North American Trees (Western Region).* New York: Alfred A. Knopf, 1980.

Niehaus, Theodore. *Sierra Wildflowers, Mount Lassen to Kern Canyon.* Berkeley: University of California Press, 1974.

Spellenberg, Richard. *The Audubon Society Field Guide to North American Wildflowers.* New York: Alfred A. Knopf, 1979.

CAMPING

Stienstra, Tom. *California Camping, the Complete Guide to California's Recreation Areas.* San Francisco: Foghorn Press, 1987.

SIERRA HISTORY

Browning, Peter. *Place Names of the Sierra Nevada.* Berkeley: Wilderness Press, 1986.

Farquhar, Francis P. *History of the Sierra Nevada.* Berkeley: University of California Press, 1965.

Index

Bold face indicates photo

KAREN AND TERRY WHITEHILL live in Portland, Oregon. Avid outdoorspeople, they have cycled all over Europe and walked 4,000 miles from Paris to Jerusalem. They are the authors of three other guidebooks for The Mountaineers: *Europe by Bike, A Pedestrian's Portland,* and the first volume in the Sierra series, *Best Short Hikes in California's Northern Sierra.* The Whitehills have spent several summers in the Sierra Nevada doing the field work for this book, and even packed their baby daughter, Sierra Jo, to the top of Mount Whitney during their research.

Look for these other books from The Mountaineers:

Best Short Hikes in California's Northern Sierra: A Guide to Day Hikes Near Campgrounds
Whitehill. $12.95. 74 hikes between the San Joaquin/Mammoth area and Donner Pass). Hikes start from featured campgrounds, include information on campgrounds and their facilities, hike distance, difficulty, trip descriptions, more.

Hiking the Southwest's Canyon Country
Hinchman. $14.95. Six two- to three-week-long itineraries of day-hikes, backpacks, and scenic drives in Colorado, Utah, New Mexico, and Arizona.

Animal Tracks of Southern California
Stall. $5.95. Tracks and information on 40-50 animals common to Southern California. A handy, pocket-size track identification guide.

Walking San Diego
Hewitt, Moore. $14.95. More than 100 fully detailed walks to natural and historical places in and around coastal wonderland San Diego.

100 Hikes in Northern California
J. Soares, M. Soares. $12.95. Covers Northern Sierra Nevada, Lake Tahoe Region, Lassen National Park, Trinity Alps Wilderness, San Francisco Bay Area, and North Coast.

High Sierra: Peaks, Passes, and Trails.
Secor. $22.95. Most complete guide to the high Sierra available. Covers all known routes to approximately 570 peaks.

Best Short Hikes In and Around the North Sacramento Valley
Soares. $12.95. Includes over 75 day hikes for children, seniors, and weekend explorers.

Lake Tahoe: A Family Guide
Evans. $12.95. A guide to 53 short hikes and bike rides through state parks, national forests, and wilderness areas within driving distance of Lake Tahoe.

Best Hikes with Children series
McMillon. Guides to day hikes and overnighters for families. Give tips on hiking with kids, safety, and fostering a wilderness ethic.
Best Hikes with Children: San Francisco's North Bay. $14.95.
Best Hikes with Children: San Francisco's South Bay. $12.95.
Best Hikes with Children Around Sacramento. $12.95.

Mac's Field Guides
MacGowan, Sauskojus. $4.95 each. Two-sided plastic laminated cards developed by a teacher of marine science. Color drawings, common and scientific names.
California Coastal Birds
North America/Birds of Prey
North America/Freshwater Fish
North America/Land Mammals
North America/Reptiles
North America/ Salmon & Trout
North California Park/Backyard Birds
North California Wildflowers
South California Park/Backyard Birds
South California Wildflowers

Exploring Oregon's Wild Areas: A Guide for Hikers, Backpackers, XC Skiers, and Paddlers
Sullivan. $14.95. Detail-stuffed guidebook to Oregon's 65 wilderness areas, wildlife refuges, nature preserves, and state parks.

Ask for these at your local book or outdoor store, or phone order toll-free at 1-800-553-HIKE with VISA/Mastercard. Mail order by sending check or money order (add $2.00 per order for shipping and handling) to:

The Mountaineers Books
1001 SW Klickitat Way, Suite 201
Seattle, WA 98134

Ask for a free catalog.

THE MOUNTAINEERS, founded in 1906, is a non-profit outdoor activity and conservation club, whose mission is "to explore, study, preserve and enjoy the natural beauty of the outdoors..." Based in Seattle, Washington, the club is now the third largest such organization in the United States, with 15,000 members and five branches throughout Washington State.

The Mountaineers sponsors both classes and year-round outdoor activities in the Pacific Northwest, which include hiking, mountain climbing, ski-touring, snowshoeing, bicycling, camping, kayaking and canoeing, nature study, sailing, and adventure travel. The club's conservation division supports environmental causes through educational activities, sponsoring legislation, and presenting informational programs. All club activities are led by skilled, experienced volunteers, who are dedicated to promoting safe and responsible enjoyment and preservation of the outdoors.

The Mountaineers Books, an active, non-profit publishing program of the club, produces guidebooks, instructional texts, historical works, natu-ral history guides, and works on environmental conservation. All books produced by the Mountaineers are aimed at fulfilling the club's mission.

If you would like to participate in these organized outdoor activities or the club's programs, consider a membership in The Mountaineers. For information and an application, write or call The Mountaineers, Club Headquarters, 300 Third Avenue West, Seattle, Washington 98119; (206) 284-6310.